CW01082371

Anticlerical legacies

Manchester University Press

Politics, culture and society in early modern Britain

General Editors

Alastair Bellany, Alexandra Gajda, Peter Lake,

Anthony Milton, Jason Peacey, Abigail Swingen

This important series publishes volumes that take a fresh and challenging look
at the interactions between politics, culture and society in early modern Britain
and beyond. It seeks to counteract the fragmentation of current historiography
by encouraging a variety of methodological and critical approaches to this period
of dramatic conflict and change that fundamentally shaped the modern world.
The series welcomes volumes covering all aspects of sixteenth, seventeenth, and
eighteenth century history, including the history of Britain's growing imperial
ambitions and global reach.

To buy or to find out more about the books currently available in this series, please
go to: https://manchesteruniversitypress.co.uk/series/politics-culture-and-society-in-
early-modern-britain

Anticlerical legacies

The deistic reception of Thomas Hobbes, *c.* 1670–1740

Elad Carmel

MANCHESTER UNIVERSITY PRESS

The right of Elad Carmel to be identified as the author of this work has been asserted by them in accordance with the Copyright, Designs and Patents Act 1988.

Published by Manchester University Press
Oxford Road, Manchester M13 9PL

www.manchesteruniversitypress.co.uk

British Library Cataloguing-in-Publication Data
A catalogue record for this book is available from the British Library

ISBN 978 1 5261 6882 5 hardback

First published 2024

The publisher has no responsibility for the persistence or accuracy of URLs for any external or third-party internet websites referred to in this book, and does not guarantee that any content on such websites is, or will remain, accurate or appropriate.

Typeset by Newgen

It must be extreme hard to find out the opinions and meanings of those men that are gone from us long ago, and have left us no other signification thereof but their books; which cannot possibly be understood without history enough to discover those aforementioned circumstances, and also without great prudence to observe them.

Thomas Hobbes, *The Elements of Law*, Part I

Contents

Acknowledgements

Writing this book has been a life-changing journey, in which many friends, colleagues, and mentors played an essential role.

Mark Philp and Jon Parkin introduced me to the worlds of Politics and History at Oxford and remained supervisors long after I completed my DPhil. I am grateful beyond words for their endless kindness and patience and for their strikingly complementary guidance and advice. Mark has been a model teacher who, despite the amazing scope of his knowledge, has always gently directed me to find the answers to my own questions. Jon taught me everything I know about the kind of study I ended up doing. His own work on Hobbes's reception has set a standard that I could only aspire to meet. That *Anticlerical Legacies* may be considered a successor to his *Taming the Leviathan* is the best compliment I might receive.

My work on this book has benefited immensely from several research fellowships and residences, including at the John W. Kluge Center at the Library of Congress, the Folger Shakespeare Library, the Lady Davis Trust at the Hebrew University of Jerusalem, and the Humphrey Institute at Ben-Gurion University of the Negev. I would particularly like to thank Aya Elyada, Raz Chen-Morris, and the History Department at the Hebrew University. It is hard to overstate the significance of this kind of support, both materially and mentally, especially in today's academic world. Independence is not always a bliss in this profession, but being able to write large parts of this book in sunny Spain or snowy New England truly was. I am grateful for the wonderful friends and colleagues I have acquired in each of these places and institutes. The breadth of their interests and expertise has been inspirational.

Many kind scholars made me think harder about the issues that I explore here, sending this book in multiple new directions. My mentors at Tel Aviv University, Tamar Meisels and Golan Lahat, were the first to encourage me to pursue this project. David Armitage, Noel Malcolm, Quentin Skinner, Patricia Springborg, and other members of the European Hobbes Society offered vital insights along the way. Mark Knights generously shared his important findings with me. Robin Mills and Maeve Mckeown were especially helpful readers. Robin Douglass consistently provided detailed feedback that was both exceptionally valuable and impossibly quick. Justin Champion was one of the most knowledgeable historians I have ever met, and I am grateful for having had the opportunity to learn from him. His work on English anticlericalism was ground-breaking and I hope that this book helps to honour his legacy.

An overview of this book's main argument has been published as 'Hobbes and Early English Deism', in Laurens van Apeldoorn and Robin Douglass (eds), *Hobbes on Politics and Religion* (Oxford, 2018), pp. 202–18. Part of Chapter 3 has appeared as 'The History and Philosophy of English Freethinking', in Anna Tomaszewska and Hasse Hämäläinen (eds), *The Sources of Secularism: Enlightenment and Beyond* (Cham, 2017), pp. 121–37. Additionally, this book draws on articles published in *Intellectual History Review* (2019) and *History of European Ideas* (2022) (copyright Taylor & Francis), available online: doi: 10.1080/17496977.2018.1523570, 10.1080/01916599.2022.2040044.

I am very grateful to Manchester University Press, especially to the Series Editors of Politics, Culture and Society in Early Modern Britain, to Meredith Carroll, and to the generous reviewers for the pleasant, productive, and uncompromising review process. My final vision for the book is indebted to them.

The friends who accompanied me on this decade-long journey had to learn more about Hobbes and deism than they probably ever wished, as Shai Hertz, Kfir Ifrah, and Sharon Shemesh can attest. Yuna Han, Dana Landau, Shiru Lim and many others have always been there to listen and advise. Dear old and new friends from around the world shared the small and big moments, celebrating the achievements or complaining about the setbacks. They are the ones who made it all worthwhile, and I am grateful for having them in my life.

My family made this book possible in countless ways. My research has often taken me far from them—further than I ever imagined I would get—yet we have only grown closer throughout these years through new adventures, travels, and cocktails. My English family, with whom I was fortunate to connect thanks to this research, immediately created a home for me. This book is dedicated to Raphi, Daphna, Shai, Amit, Lior, Rotem, Ora, and Kathryn as well as to the memory of Merlin and Dina.

Lastly, my partner, Yoel Castillo Botello, entered my life at a crucial stage of this process, and from the very first moment believed in me much more consistently than I did. His unconditional love and support throughout the last six years make this book his as much as it is mine.

Introduction

The Ecclesiastiques are Spirituall men, and Ghostly Fathers. The Fairies are
Spirits, and Ghosts. Fairies and Ghosts inhabite Darknesse, Solitudes, and
Graves. The Ecclesiastiques walke in Obscurity of Doctrine, in Monasteries,
Churches, and Church-yards.

Leviathan, 1651

Natural Religion, easie first and Plain;
Tales made it Mystery, Offerings made it gain;
Sacrifices and Feasts were at length prepar'd.
The Priests eat roast Meat, and the People star'd.

'The Deists' Plea', 1692

In 1748, the Irish clergyman Philip Skelton travelled to London to publish a work that appeared in 1749 as *Ophiomaches: Or, Deism Revealed*.
This work of fiction consists of eight conversations between a Christian and
three other individuals who are persuaded by deism to different degrees.
It was published by Andrew Millar, who, according to Skelton, consulted
none other than 'Hume the infidel' whether to print it. Skelton was treated
as a celebrity, and the work was praised by Thomas Sherlock, bishop
of London. The second edition appeared in 1751 under a more telling
title: *Deism Revealed. Or, the Attack on Christianity Candidly Reviewed in
Its Real Merits, As They Stand in the Celebrated Writings of Lord Herbert,
Lord Shaftesbury, Hobbes, Toland, Tindal, Collins, Mandeville, Dodwell,
Woolston, Morgan, Chubb, and Others.*[1]

The purpose of the work was to refute the views of the deists who challenged Christianity. Deism, for Skelton, was the conviction that one's reason
is a sufficient guide for morality and religion. Throughout *Deism Revealed*,
deism is almost synonymous with libertinism, defined as '*Self-sufficiency*',
that is, 'a self-instructing, a self-governing, and a self-pleasing Spirit'.[2] The
libertine is his own guide: 'The knowledge of religion and morality he bor-
rows from none' and 'hence his pretensions to unbounded liberty of thought

and action'.[3] The deists, Skelton explained, feared censorship and punishment and consequently they did not develop their arguments in full, pretending to be more Christian than they actually were.[4] His goal, therefore, was to expose the real deism and disprove it once and for all: 'if you are a Deist ... and if, from what is said in this work, reason, without higher assistance, should appear an insufficient guide ... then be just to your own reason, and bid Deism a final farewell'.[5]

In one of the dialogues, Shepherd the Christian explains to Templeton, his interlocutor, that '[t]he first who distinguished himself in *England* as a successful adversary to religion, and a leader in *Self-sufficiency*, was Hobbes'.[6] According to Shepherd, Hobbes did not hesitate 'to mould Christianity to a system of his own, directly repugnant to the nature and end of all religion; for he labours to establish it as a fundamental point, that the subjects of every community ought to conform, in all religious matters, to the commands of the civil magistrate'.[7] Hobbes was so arrogant as to invent an entirely new system, one which was particularly blasphemous because it granted the civil sovereign absolute supremacy, including in religious matters, and thus rendered God and revelation redundant. There was another problem with Hobbes: he was 'much read, much admired, and followed by all that sort of men who are ever glad to see religion struck at with any kind of weapon, and who, in those days, were furnished with no other, or no better'.[8] Hobbes's texts, written about a hundred years earlier, proffered the most powerful explosives for the war on Christianity in England.

The most effective weapon in this war was the questioning and ridiculing of fundamental Christian tenets. Templeton tells Shepherd how he was taught to be a libertine and a deist by mocking Christianity: 'We were often merry on almost every historical passage in the Bible ... We had a thousand sneers about Heaven and Hell'.[9] Yet, he adds, these principles were taught with some sophistication:

> You know all the Libertine writers pretend to be of our religion, and profess only an intention to recommend a truer idea of it, than that which is vulgarly entertained. This enabled my Tutor to teach me Christianity out of *Hobbes*, *Shaftesbury*, *Collins*, *Toland*, and *Tindal*; insomuch that, I assure you, I was a Libertine, almost a Deist, before I had any notion I had ceased to be a Christian.[10]

In another dialogue, Shepherd clarifies the common thread uniting this group, naming '*Hobbes*, *Shaftesbury*, *Toland*, *Tindal*, and the authors of the *Independent Whig*, who, with an infinite degree of spleen and malice, laboured to represent the Clergy as the worst of men, and then employed the hideous picture ... as if it were an argument against Christianity'.[11] In other words, this group's anticlericalism turned into anti-Christianity, and what is more, it had serious political implications: some of these writers, 'altho' they set out with fine compliments to the Clerical order, yet afterwards endeavour to prove, there is no such order among us, distinct from, and independent, of the State'.[12] In this position, Shepherd finds both the influence of Hobbes and the seeds of modern infidelity:

> When, in pursuit of *Hobbes*'s scheme, they insist, that the Clergy ought always to be the creatures of the civil power, they serve no other cause than that of Deism, or rather Atheism; for as often as the civil power is lodged in the hands of a Pagan, there can be no Ministry to preach Christianity, nor to administer its sacraments, unless we can suppose, that a Pagan Emperor or King will be at the trouble of constituting and ordaining a Ministry for the destruction of Paganism.[13]

On this view, Hobbes paved the way for a dangerous yet sophisticated kind of anticlericalism, and the Hobbesian idea of subordinating the church to the civil sovereign—what is often called Erastianism—paved the way for modern deism.[14] In sum, 'Libertinism had no considerable footing in *England* before *Cromwell*'s time', and '[d]uring this dark and stormy night of troubled dreams, *Hobbes* set up a standard for Deism, or rather Atheism; to which in a little time resorted all such as were willing to think there was nothing more in religion than hypocrisy or fanaticism'.[15] Among Hobbes's followers, then, were the names of Matthew Tindal (1657–1733), John Toland (1670–1722), Anthony Collins (1676–1729), the third earl of Shaftesbury (1671–1713), Thomas Morgan (1671/2–1743), Thomas Chubb (1679–1747), and the authors of the *Independent Whig*, John Trenchard (1668/9–1723) and Thomas Gordon (*c*. 1691–1750).

Albeit a parody, Skelton's work is one of the most comprehensive accounts of the origins and ideas of English deism as it was perceived in the mid-eighteenth century. Only a few years later, in 1754, the Presbyterian minister John Leland published *A View of the Principal Deistical Writers That Have Appeared in England in the Last and Present Century*. Leland was determined to provide a thorough account of the authors he considered to be the prominent English deists, their writings, and the controversies in which they were involved. The deists, according to Leland, 'reject all revealed religion, and discard all pretences to it as owing to imposture or enthusiasm'.[16] Their aim, therefore, is 'to set aside revelation, and to substitute mere natural religion, or ... no religion at all, in its room'.[17]

The philosopher Edward, Lord Herbert of Cherbury (1582–1648) was, according to Leland, 'the first remarkable Deist in order of time'.[18] The second figure on Leland's list of deists is Hobbes, because there 'have been few persons, whose writings have had a more pernicious influence in spreading irreligion and infidelity than his'.[19] Leland's attack on Hobbes's theory touched on a range of issues, such as the authority of the scripture being dependent on the authority of the sovereign, the questioning of aspects of the old and new testaments, the denial of our ability to know any more about God than that He exists, and so on. Hobbes took the scripture as the word and the law of God on the one hand but ridiculed inspiration and revelation on the other, and he sometimes saw inspiration as a supernatural gift but also described any pretence to it as a sign of madness.[20] Thus, '*Hobbes*'s scheme strikes at the foundation of all religion, both natural and revealed' and 'it tendeth not only to subvert the authority of the scripture, but to destroy God's moral administration'.[21] Leland concluded:

> the manifold absurdities and inconsistence of his scheme, and the pernicious consequences of it to religion, morality and the civil government, have been so well exposed, and set in a clear light, that there are not many of our modern Deists that would be thought openly to espouse his system in its full extent. And yet it cannot be denied, that there are not a few things in their writings borrowed from his; and that some of them have chosen rather to follow him than Lord *Herbert* in several of his principles; and particularly in asserting the materiality and mortality of the human soul, and denying man's free agency.[22]

Even though Leland identified Herbert as the first deist, he argued that the deists borrowed more from Hobbes. They did so, however, without always declaring they were adopting Hobbes, due to the dubious reputation of the 'Monster of Malmesbury'.[23] Particularly in his materialism and determinism, Leland argued, Hobbes had gone further than Herbert and had subsequently been followed by the deists. The deists that Leland identified are almost identical to those found in *Deism Revealed*, with the important addition of Charles Blount (1654–1693), the only deist who was active already during Hobbes's lifetime.

Leland was right to acknowledge the complexity of Hobbes's position, holding that 'none of his treatises are directly level'd against revealed religion'.[24] But was Leland also right in recognising that Hobbes was in fact one of the fathers of English deism?

Where scholars have taken Hobbes, and especially his unique anticlericalism, to be somewhat influential for the English deists, the precise nature and extent of the relationship between them remains an unsolved puzzle, partly because Hobbes's eighteenth-century reception is largely understudied.[25] Furthermore, while contemporary critics such as Skelton and Leland were quick to recognise the connections between Hobbes and the deists, to modern eyes this connection might seem surprising. One reason for this is that current scholarly debates on Hobbes's theology focus on elements which are not precisely deistic or natural, emphasising instead its sceptic, voluntarist, conventionalist, or even eschatological nature.[26] Another reason is that, as champions of liberty, those who are considered deists or freethinkers and often Whigs or republicans seem much more likely to have relied on thinkers such as Milton, Harrington, Locke, and Spinoza, from whom they could more comfortably take arguments for liberty of expression and worship and for civil religion. Moreover, scholars often separate Hobbes from subsequent radicals due to his alleged pessimism regarding human nature and his infamous absolutism, according to which the sovereign determines the nature of public worship and enjoys a right to censor doctrines that are harmful to civil peace.[27] Most famously, Jonathan Israel claims that it was Spinoza, and not Hobbes, who was the main influence for the 'Radical Enlightenment', including the English deists and freethinkers. Israel disqualifies Hobbes from serving 'as the philosophical underpinning of a broad-based philosophical radicalism opposed to all existing structures of authority and tradition, ecclesiastical power, and the existing social hierarchy, as well as divine-right monarchy, precisely because of his anti-libertarian politics, High Church sympathies, and support for rigorous political and intellectual censorship'.[28] Nevertheless, Hobbes's reception tells a strikingly different story.

The main argument of this book is that the relationship between Hobbes and the English deists was much closer than has ever been appreciated, or, in other words, that the deists were much more Hobbesian than is usually assumed. Offering the first study of Hobbes's deistic reception in England until 1740, the book aims to demonstrate the overwhelming presence of Hobbes in the works of Blount, Toland, Tindal, Collins, Trenchard, Gordon, Morgan, and others, including lesser-known writers. It examines the complex ways in which they utilised Hobbes's ideas for their own purposes and shows that they referred to Hobbes approvingly and acknowledged his novelty at a time when doing so was highly discouraged. It is evident that the deists were happy to pick and choose what they took from Hobbes and so they borrowed the aspects in his writings that they found most compelling while jettisoning ideas that did not fit with their outlook. But this relationship was richer still, it will be suggested, because even politics was not always a point of contention between Hobbes and the subsequent deists; rather, politics had a crucial role in identifying and solving the problem of out-of-control religion.

The significance of Hobbes's deistic reception is twofold. First, it offers new perspectives on Hobbes's reception into the eighteenth century and demonstrates the great degree to which Hobbes informed anticlerical thinking in particular in the decades following his death. The task of tracing the deists' Hobbes, as it were, reveals in large part what constituted the positive and sympathetic readings of Hobbes in the seventeenth and eighteenth centuries, when different aspects of his work were regularly and simultaneously challenged, and thus places Hobbes in a new intellectual context. Second, an in-depth analysis of the deists' debts to Hobbes recovers them as valuable theorists in their own right. Where the uniformity of deist thought is rightly questioned, these writers developed a sophisticated and multi-layered range of anticlerical positions and tools—more than they are often credited with—which were influential for the early Enlightenment and made an impact even beyond their own century. Their engagement with Hobbes was thoughtful and complex precisely because they were not simply radicals but serious and versatile actors in the political and religious landscape of their time. These thinkers were the initiators and transmitters of ideas which formed anticlerical legacies—and it is impossible to understand these legacies fully without studying the Hobbesian legacies that they themselves adopted.

The textual evidence in this book shows how deeply these writers were indebted to Hobbes. Each writer studied here acknowledged Hobbes in one way or another. In most cases, there is even enough evidence to suggest exactly which of his writings they read and found most helpful. The approach of the book is to examine their *engagement* with Hobbes and the *range* of ways in which they were drawing upon Hobbes's texts, both as readers and as users.[29] The primary focus is on cases where there is definite textual evidence of these writers having engaged with Hobbes directly, that is, where Hobbes's name and ideas are mentioned explicitly. In doing so, this book follows the method that Jon Parkin set out in his groundbreaking research on Hobbes's reception in seventeenth-century England, *Taming the Leviathan*, where he focused on cases in which there is an 'explicit acknowledgement of a debt or clear evidence that the ideas are in fact Hobbesian'.[30] Thus, *Anticlerical Legacies* examines the deists' references and allusions to Hobbes in their published works as well as in more private writings—manuscripts, commonplace books, or letters—where they might have preferred to acknowledge Hobbes, given his explosive reputation and the censorship that threatened them, especially prior to the lapse of the licensing act in 1695. Additionally, it explores cases where there are unacknowledged borrowings from Hobbes's texts or particularly strong resemblances between the deists' ideas and Hobbes's, as long as there is good reason to believe that the deists had Hobbes in mind—for example, if they invoked Hobbes's authority on a similar point elsewhere.

Politics of anticlericalism

The book focuses on a group of radically anticlerical writers who posed a distinctive challenge to the existing order in England, and especially to the established church and to revealed religion, and who engaged with Hobbes significantly and consistently in their writings. In light of the heterogeneous character of this group, Hobbes was more influential on some of them than others, and the nature of the influence on each was not exactly the same either.[31] Yet for all of them, without exception, he was a primary resource and ally in the historic battle against priestcraft: the corrupt tactics of the power-hungry clergy which, they believed, were designed to keep the laity ignorant and blindly obedient to the church and thus threatened the peace and stability of society.[32]

The anticlericalism of these figures was not merely hatred of priests—although their critics certainly wanted to portray them this way—but it constituted a range of historical, theological, and philosophical positions. Anticlericalism, put another way, was a cause which had to be fought for on multiple fronts and using multiple strategies. These writers produced, for example, comparative accounts of different religions, thorough analyses of competing histories of the church, erudite historical and philological studies of the scripture, and inquiries into the nature of matter and the soul.[33] They promoted a spectrum of ideas of natural and civil religion and intervened in debates on sacred and ecclesiastical history, albeit for their own subversive ends. Even if the private beliefs of these writers were heterodox, as some maintain, they nevertheless realised how powerful religion was and indeed how effective it was.[34] What is more, in their eyes, religion could be reformed precisely because it was man-made. Their campaign was not necessarily aimed against religion as such but against the misuses and abuses of religion by manipulative priests: 'To overthrow priestcraft was to purify both religion and society'.[35]

Even though Hobbes perhaps 'durst not write so boldly' as Spinoza did, he naturalised religion in a way that undermined, explicitly or implicitly, traditional faith in miracles and prophecies.[36] Hobbes cast serious doubt on the belief in revelation: anyone who claims to have had a revelation might be lying, and people *would* lie as it serves their interests.[37] Subsequent anticlerical writers continued this line of thought and radicalised it. The very fact of present revelation became questionable. For some, revelation could only confirm what natural reason already tells us; if there is a contradiction, reason should always take priority. This argument was much more explicitly heterodox than Hobbes's. The motive, however, was the same. The fairy tales of revelation were part of priestcraft and as such they were used by the clergy who endlessly sought to gain and maintain independent power. The war against priestcraft was Hobbes's war against the kingdom of darkness taken one step further.

This war was central to the most pressing political and religious debates of the period: it was a twofold war over truth—true religion in particular—and over who held the truth or who held the authority to interpret it.[38]

Anticlericalism, therefore, was inherently political.[39] The anticlerical legacies that this book explores had a clear political goal, namely, to bring about
lasting civil peace and to assure that the recent wars of religion would never
recur. The questions with which the anticlerical writers grappled were dramatic: how could the interaction between politics and religion be reshaped
entirely, and how could religion be transformed from a prime source of
instability to the basis for social and cultural stability? In this sense, the
radicals took an active part in a larger project alongside many contemporary divines who, despite their obvious differences, were equally concerned
about 'the problem of civil peace and human betterment' and who often
advocated their own versions of civil religion as a remedy for sectarianism
and conflict.[40]

The writers on which this book focuses are often considered deists or
freethinkers. Both deism and freethinking have always been contested
terms.[41] They were used originally as insults, and so their definitions were
usually given by anxious clerical critics rather than by self-proclaimed
deists or freethinkers. They were employed to signify and discredit various
kinds of heterodoxies, including a rejection of revealed religion in favour
of natural religion, a denial of Christ's divinity, and more.[42] However, it
will be shown, these labels were subsequently reclaimed and reappropri-
ated in a subtle process by the enemies of the orthodoxy, who at times
went so far as to embrace deism and freethinking as their intellectual and
social identities.[43] As a result, 'deist' and 'freethinker' were used 'simultaneously as terms of description and of abuse' as were numerous other
labels in seventeenth- and eighteenth-century England, including 'latitudin-
arian', 'papist', and 'Puritan'.[44] Indeed, as Peter Lake has shown, the latter had particularly complex history and historiography as 'both name and
thing, movement and polemically inflected construct, ascribed and internalised identity'.[45] The case of deism and freethinking followed a similar pattern. These categories have been flexible from the outset and their various
meanings depended to a large extent on who was using them and to what
purpose. To understand them better, therefore, is to think of them as a continuum of ideas that share a family resemblance, or to think of a plurality or
diversity of deisms for different writers.[46]

Most importantly, these labels are valuable when studied in relation to
the orthodoxy and in light of deliberate attempts of contemporaries to create and maintain binaries: especially the attempt of the Anglican establishment to label the threatening—and hence unifying—'other'.[47] This book
suggests that deistic views were formulated in a continual, even dialectical
process of dialogue—more or less civil—with fierce but thorough orthodox critics. Deisms could take different forms in different iterations, but
they always responded to questions that the orthodoxy generated and at the

same time they were defined and defamed by the orthodoxy.[48] Freethinking, too, was denounced even by religious writers who at the same time did not necessarily object to the basic principles of freedom of thought and intellectual inquiry.[49] Investigating these discourses in the context of the dialogue between the church and its enemies can therefore shed new light on the competing sets of political and religious values in this period. In order to do so, this book focuses on when and how 'deism' or 'freethinking' were employed, whether favourably or not, what polemical purposes they served, and what values they were meant to represent.

This process was of course also a function of changing circumstances. The threat of censorship and persecution, which loomed especially until the lapse of the licensing act in 1695 but even after, meant that it was difficult to develop and espouse such dissenting positions publicly. This book starts with writers including Charles Blount and James Boevey, who supported deism in the 1680s and the 1690s mainly in private, and it ends with writers such as Thomas Morgan and Alberto Radicati who self-identified openly as Christian deists and freethinkers in the 1730s. In between, figures such as Anthony Collins and Matthew Tindal did much to defend these labels—and more importantly their critical ideas and their right to voice them—in their battle against the Anglican mainstream.

The story is complicated further by the issue of Hobbism. Both Hobbes and Hobbism were understood and portrayed by contemporaries in various and sometimes contradictory ways, not least because they often deliberately mischaracterised Hobbes's ideas for polemical reasons. Anthony Collins, it will be shown, recognised that: 'They knew not how to answer him but by first misrepresenting him'.[50] Consequently, Hobbism and Hobbesian ideas played a strikingly complex part in the political and religious discourse of the late seventeenth century. Both Tories and Whigs attacked one another with the charge of Hobbism and at the same time reproduced some Hobbesian arguments. Connectedly, some writers whose views were relatively close to Hobbes's sometimes exaggerated the differences between them to distance themselves from the charge of Hobbism; and more than once, Hobbes's critics were those who found themselves accused of Hobbism eventually.[51]

Hobbism received various meanings with time, which of course were not necessarily identical to Hobbes's positions, but rather a caricatured or reduced version of them, ranging from atheism and libertinism to immorality and human natural unsociability.[52] Additionally, Hobbism signified some concrete doctrines, for example, regarding political obligation, namely, the idea that self-preservation is one's primary motive and that it justifies obedience to any power that offers protection.[53] In fact, Hobbism and deism were often used in similar ways: an interesting commonality between them was their perceived irreligiosity and thus their perceived denial of the divine as the basis of the moral. Indeed, the deists were once called the '*Hobbists* of the Times'.[54] Clearly, these descriptions were generally the result of the efforts of persistent Anglicans, and yet they proved influential for centuries later.

These observations highlight the need to study the use of Hobbism in addition to the use of Hobbes's ideas.[55] As with deism, this book examines how Hobbism was employed in the texts of the anticlerical writers and their critics and how it served them—for example, to advance their own ideas, sharpen their authorial identity, or discredit their enemies. In this sense, the use of such labels can be seen as a speech act, an act that constitutes an intervention in ongoing debates in particular social and political contexts, following the Skinnerian approach.[56] Put differently, these labels are themselves a part of a complex story of reception. Their frequent appearances meant that it was difficult to remain indifferent to 'Hobbism' or 'deism' in seventeenth- and eighteenth-century England: the ways in which these terms were utilised by writers with different agendas are key to deciphering what they and their contemporaries thought that they were doing.

Hobbes's art of pulling down the churches

The debate on Hobbes's religious convictions is as old as his works. His contemporaries often attempted to discredit him with the accusation of atheism, which became synonymous with Hobbism, to which Hobbes famously replied with typical shrewdness: 'Do you think I can be an atheist and not know it? Or knowing it, durst have offered my atheism to the press?'[57] Yet his complex religious views have left commentators debating to this day whether he was indeed an atheist, even if a covert one, or alternatively a more or less traditional Christian.[58] Recent scholarship has started to move away from this debate, and rightly so. Instead of searching for hints of Hobbes's so-called true beliefs, scholars have become increasingly interested in what Hobbes was doing when he wrote about religion.[59] Why, for example, did he engage with sacred and ecclesiastical history so thoroughly only to question major parts of it at the same time? One convincing answer is that Hobbes attempted to meet his readers on their own ground, which would have been sufficient reason for him to take religion seriously, even if his beliefs were more heterodox than those of his contemporaries. He might have had to use different arguments for different audiences or to write on different levels for different readers, to bring all of them to the desired conclusions.[60] Most fundamentally, Hobbes had to engage with religion to win the attention of his readers but also to reconstruct it so that it would be conducive (rather than destructive) to self-preservation and civil peace.[61]

The poet Edmund Waller said when he was asked by John Aubrey to write a eulogy for Hobbes: 'what was chiefly to be taken notice of in his elogie was that he, being but *one*, and a private person pulled downe all the churches, dispelled the mists of ignorance, and layd-open their priest-craft'.[62] Indeed, it is no exaggeration to argue that anticlericalism was one of the most significant motives behind Hobbes's work. Hobbes's anticlericalism brought him close to being a 'Christian atheist' or advocating 'de-clericalized Anglicanism'.[63] Throughout his oeuvre, Hobbes made unusually harsh accusations against the clergy for attempting to gain independent political power, and he developed a historical account of the church and of priestcraft alongside a thorough investigation into the notion of heresy. These themes featured in many of Hobbes's writings and were especially dominant in some of his later works from the late 1660s, a period in which Hobbes himself was in danger from his clerical opponents and a main target of the discussions on the atheism bill and heresy proceedings.[64] These works include, for example, *Behemoth*, *Historia Ecclesiastica*, and *An Historical Narration Concerning Heresie*, which were in scribal circulation in the mid-1670s—hence available to radical audiences in London—and published after Hobbes's death.[65] In this period, Hobbes reconstructed his public personae, as Jon Parkin has shown, and seemed on occasion to 'stage the discussion of his work as a dramatic confrontation between the forces of light and the forces of the Kingdom of Darkness', while presenting himself to his opponents as 'a sensible and law-abiding English layman whose views promoted political quietism'.[66]

Hobbes's anticlericalism was especially clear already in *Leviathan* (1651)—certainly the work that received most attention from contemporaries in Britain—perhaps because it was composed during the brief moment when there was no sovereign power in England, which enabled Hobbes to be more explicit about his opposition to any kind of clerical authority.[67] As Noel Malcolm has suggested, at the very core of *Leviathan* was Hobbes's 'Thing', namely, an all-encompassing theme with which he was obsessed: 'a complex mass of errors and absurdities, embracing false metaphysics, primitive delusions, popular superstitions, bogus clerical pretensions, and seditious political theories—all in some way connected, and all tending directly or indirectly towards the destruction of civil government'.[68] Hobbes's contempt for the 'unpleasing Priests' was evident throughout *Leviathan*.[69] Most strikingly, he blamed the priests, Catholics and Presbyterians, for being the authors of darkness, and argued that the ecclesiastics, just like the fairies, deprived people of their natural reason:

> The *Ecclesiastiques* take from young men, the use of Reason, by certain Charms compounded of Metaphysiques, and Miracles, and Traditions, and

> Abused Scripture, whereby they are good for nothing else, but to execute what
> they command them. The *Fairies* likewise are said to take young Children out
> of their Cradles, and to change them into Naturall Fools, which Common
> people do therefore call *Elves*, and are apt to mischief.[70]

The church, stated Hobbes, deliberately maintained erroneous doctrines in
order to gain political power, the worst of which was that the kingdom of
God is the present church. However, the kingdom of God that started with
Moses had ended and would be restored only with Jesus' second coming,
and hence the earthly church is certainly not the promised kingdom of God.
The authors of darkness, the ecclesiastics, used relics of demonology and
'Vain Philosophy' of 'Schoole Divinity'—the 'Aristotelity' that dominated
the universities—to keep such errors from being detected and thereby sup-
press reason and true philosophy.[71]

   This was Hobbes's art of pulling down the churches: he sought to correct
the deep-rooted errors and disprove the dangerous doctrines of the scho-
lastics and the self-interested clergy, while preserving Christianity as a civil
religion that is crucial for social harmony. Religion, in any case, was not
going to disappear. Hobbes's urgent task, then, was to change the way in
which people were thinking of religion and to eradicate the irrational and
superstitious beliefs that possessed the people and caused them to confuse
the church with the lawful power: a programme of cultural transformation,
as it has been famously called.[72] The goal of assuring unity and eliminating
any claim for competing political authority necessitated different and often
controversial kinds of interventions: his materialism, which rejected nonsensical categories such as incorporeal substances and thus led to the notion
of the corporal God; his doctrinal minimalism and biblical criticism, which
were meant to disarm false prophecies and more importantly false prophets;
and even his absolutism, which sought to deny power to the clergy and to
take away their ability to spread their vicious doctrines, hence the sovereign's infamous right of censorship.[73] Finally, Hobbes believed that his own
political theory marked the very beginning of true civil and moral philosophy, which under the right circumstances could lead almost to a utopia.[74]

   Hobbes's radicalism has been widely debated in the literature in the past
decades, and consequently his plausible support of certain models of religious toleration, Independency, or Congregationalism seems fairly established.[75] Yet there is one final point to make about Hobbes's work, which
is especially important for the present discussion of his radical reception,
namely, that his theory, and his treatment of religion in particular, was
open-ended in the sense that it allowed various readers to use it in their
own ways. This might explain the fact that different aspects of his thought
were employed to support different ideological causes.[76] Hobbes did not

necessarily commit to a specific ecclesiological model but instead chose to provide tools that could be applied according to the readers' changing circumstances. In fact, he provided such a wide range of religious criticisms that they could be picked up by different readers who had different kinds of clerical opponents. Therefore, as Jon Parkin suggests, we need to consider the possibility that 'Hobbes was leaving space for his readers to work out what his positions *could* mean', and more specifically, that Hobbes may well have expected his like-minded readers, who were interested in promoting a reformed and stable version of Christianity, to do so 'in a Hobbesian manner'.[77] By deconstructing orthodoxy in line with his materialism, for instance, Hobbes exercised freedom of thought or philosophy that could be compatible with the sovereign's directives and thus set a good example for his future readers.[78] Indeed, the deists might have been precisely the kind of audience that Hobbes had hoped for.

Hobbes's anticlericalism led him to develop methods and reach conclusions that were often unconventional and that appealed to subsequent radicals who were similarly concerned about the danger that priestly ambition and greed posed to society. The deists and freethinkers certainly shared Hobbes's strong anticlerical sentiment as well as his desire for civil peace, and indeed, they often approached the problems that they witnessed in a typically Hobbesian manner. Which Hobbesian ideas and tools in particular were resourceful for them, and what *they* did with them, is the central question of this book.

Anticlerical Legacies is organised chronologically to reach a comprehensive account of this particular processes of reception in a way that traces the developments both of Hobbes's ideas and reputation and of the family of deisms in the period between 1670 and 1740.[79] Chapter 1, which covers the period between 1670–1695, looks at early debates on human reason, natural religion, and religious toleration, in which Hobbes's political and religious ideas were strikingly present. It discusses Blount's extensive debts to Hobbes in manuscript and in print, alongside lesser-known writers such as Martin Clifford, Albertus Warren, and James Boevey. Chapter 2, which moves to the deist controversy and its aftermath between 1696–1710, assesses the substantial engagement of prominent writers such as Toland, Tindal, and Collins with a variety of aspects of Hobbes's theory, including his anticlericalism, biblical criticism, materialism, determinism, and so-called Erastianism, as well as the ways in which these connections were brought out and even overplayed by the critics, especially in the Boyle Lectures. Chapter 3 demonstrates how Shaftesbury, Collins, and Toland engaged with Hobbes between 1711–1723, a period that witnessed a significant preoccupation with freethinking. It then explores the presence of Hobbesian ideas in the *Independent Whig* and *Cato's Letters*, the journals that popularised anticlericalism and freethought. Chapter 4 reviews Hobbes's impact upon the later deistic debates between 1724–1740, including Tindal's and Collins's final works. It then examines the writings of Alberto Radicati and Thomas Morgan, the self-identified Christian freethinker and Christian deist respectively, and the response of their prominent critics, which concluded the heyday of English deism. Finally, the Conclusion suggests that these anticlerical legacies had an intriguing afterlife, especially in America, where deism continued to be coupled with Hobbes, and then once again in nineteenth-century England. Taken together, these different cases provide us with a full picture of the multifaceted yet consistent deistic reception of Hobbes and an original reading of Hobbes through the eyes of one of his most diligent and immediate groups of students.

Notes

1 E. Mossner, *The Life of David Hume*, 2nd edn (Oxford, 2001), p. 232; N. Garnham, 'Skelton, Philip (1707–1787), Church of Ireland Clergyman and Religious Controversialist', *Oxford Dictionary of National Biography* (2004), www.oxforddnb.com/view/10.1093/ref:odnb/9780198614128.001.0001/odnb-9780198614128-e-25664 (accessed 21 July 2023) (henceforth: *ODNB*).
2 P. Skelton, *Deism Revealed*, 2nd edn, 2 vols (London, 1751), vol. 2, p. 206.
3 Ibid.
4 Ibid., vol. 1, p. xii.
5 Ibid., pp. xiii–xiv.
6 Ibid., vol. 2, p. 211.
7 Ibid.
8 Ibid., p. 212.
9 Ibid., p. 216.
10 Ibid., p. 218.
11 Ibid., p. 182.
12 Ibid., p. 312.
13 Ibid., pp. 312–13.
14 Erastianism is usually understood as the doctrine according to which the church should be entirely subordinated to and controlled by the state. In *Leviathan*, Hobbes defined the church as a 'company of men professing Christian Religion, united in the person of one Soveraign; at whose command they ought to assemble, and without whose authority they ought not to assemble'. Hobbes, *Leviathan: The English and Latin Texts*, ed. N. Malcolm (Oxford, 2012) 39, p. 732 (henceforth: Lev; references by chapter and page numbers). J. N. Figgis, 'Erastus and Erastianism', *Journal of Theological Studies*, 2 (1900), pp. 66–101, on pp. 91–92, shows that the term 'Erastianism' is often used in an overly simplified way and argues that, albeit not precisely like Erastus, Hobbes 'dragged religion under the Juggernaut car of reason of State'; but see

also J. Rose, *Godly Kingship in Restoration England: The Politics of the Royal Supremacy, 1660–1688* (Cambridge, 2011), pp. 203–28.

15 Skelton, *Deism Revealed*, vol. 2, p. 222. This kind of reception of Hobbes has earlier examples. Anon., *The Character of a Coffee-House, with the Symptomes of a Town-Wit* (London, 1673), p. 5, tells about a young libertine who 'comes to abuse *Sacred Scripture*, makes a mock of eternal Flames, Joque on the venerable Mysteries of Religion' and who 'boasts aloud that he holds his *Gospel* from the *Apostle of Malmsbury*, though it is more than probable he ne'r read, at least understood *ten* leaves of that *unlucky Author*'. See also J. Parkin, *Taming the Leviathan: The Reception of the Political and Religious Ideas of Thomas Hobbes in England, 1640–1700* (Cambridge, 2007), pp. 304–11.

16 J. Leland, *A View of the Principal Deistical Writers that Have Appeared in England in the Last and Present Century* (London, 1754), p. 3. A second volume was published in the following year.

17 Ibid., p. v.

18 Ibid., p. 4. Herbert's theory became useful to deism mostly through the work of Charles Blount, but the attribution of deism to Herbert himself, albeit common, is debatable. R. W. Serjeantson, 'Herbert of Cherbury before Deism: The Early Reception of the *De veritate*', *The Seventeenth Century*, 16:2 (2001), pp. 217–38, places Herbert's *De veritate* (1624) and its contemporary reception in the context of logical and metaphysical debates.

19 Leland, *A View of the Principal Deistical Writers*, p. 40.

20 Ibid., p. 41.

21 Ibid., p. 46.

22 Ibid., pp. 47–48.

23 T. Pierce, *A Decad of Caveats to the People of England of General Use in All Times* (London, 1679), p. 3. Parkin, *Taming the Leviathan*, p. 1, argues: 'By the end of the century Hobbes had managed to acquire an extraordinary and perhaps even unique place in the English imagination as the *bête noire* of his age'.

24 Leland, *A View of the Principal Deistical Writers*, p. 40.

25 Parkin, *Taming the Leviathan*, pp. 402–409, on p. 406, argues that 'Hobbes's critical treatment of religion could be added to a deist's conceptual toolkit'. N. Malcolm, *Aspects of Hobbes* (Oxford, 2002), esp. pp. 383–431 and J. Champion, *The Pillars of Priestcraft Shaken: The Church of England and Its Enemies 1660–1730*, 2nd edn (Cambridge, 2014), esp. pp. 133–37, illuminate significant connections between Hobbes and the English radicals. P. Springborg, 'Hobbes the Atheist and his Deist Reception', in M. Geuna and G. Gori (eds), *I filosofi e la società senza religione* (Bologna, 2011), pp. 145–63, on pp. 150–51, suggests heterodox aspects in Hobbes's work that could be received as deistic, namely, '1) his equation of God and Nature; 2) his materialist epistemology and atomist ontology; and 3) his theory of representation, in particular his doctrine of the Trinity'. For other brief and sometimes hesitant suggestions in this direction, see for example P. Gay, *Deism: An Anthology* (Princeton, 1968), pp. 22–24; C. Hill, *The World Turned Upside Down: Radical Ideas During the English Revolution* (London, 1972), p. 314; M. C. Jacob, *The*

Radical Enlightenment: Pantheists, Freemasons and Republicans (London, 1981), pp. 75–77; E. Curley, ' "I Durst Not Write So Boldly" or, How to Read Hobbes' Theological-Political Treatise', in D. Bostrenghi (ed.), *Hobbes and Spinoza: Science and Politics* (Naples, 1992), pp. 497–593, on p. 572; R. Tuck, *Hobbes: A Very Short Introduction* (Oxford, 2002), p. 91.

26 See for example J. Barnouw, 'The Separation of Reason and Faith in Bacon and Hobbes, and Leibniz's *Theodicy*', *Journal of the History of Ideas*, 42:4 (1981), pp. 607–28; J. G. A. Pocock, *Politics, Language and Time: Essays on Political Thought and History*, 2nd edn (Chicago, 1989), pp. 148–201; A. Abizadeh, 'Hobbes's Conventionalist Theology, the Trinity, and God as an Artificial Person by Fiction', *The Historical Journal*, 60:4 (2017), pp. 915–41.

27 Lev 18, pp. 270–72; Lev 31, pp. 562–64, 570.

28 J. I. Israel, *Radical Enlightenment: Philosophy and the Making of Modernity 1650–1750* (Oxford, 2001), pp. 159, 602, also argues that Hobbes 'admitted (however half-heartedly) miracles and Revelation, and temporized on the immortality of the soul'; Spinoza, on the other hand, 'emerged as the supreme philosophical bogeyman of Early Enlightenment Europe' and 'no one else during the century 1650–1750 remotely rivalled Spinoza's notoriety'. For a similar argument, see R. Colie, 'Spinoza and the Early English Deists', *Journal of the History of Ideas*, 20:1 (1959), pp. 23–46, on pp. 30–31. This argument has been contested for a number of reasons: first, because it underappreciates Hobbes's radicalism; second, because it is not all that clear that the deists were themselves radical in the sense that they were entirely 'opposed to all existing structures of authority', and third, and most importantly, because the deists could have been influenced by *some* aspects of *both* Hobbes's and Spinoza's thought. For some of these objections, see Malcolm, 'Hobbes and Spinoza' and 'Hobbes and the European Republic of Letters', in *Aspects of Hobbes*, pp. 27–52, 457–545, esp. pp. 535–37; E. Curley, 'Hobbes and the Cause of Religious Toleration', in P. Springborg (ed.), *The Cambridge Companion to Hobbes's Leviathan* (Cambridge, 2007), pp. 309–34, esp. p. 329n23; J. R. Wigelsworth, *Deism in Enlightenment England: Theology, Politics, and Newtonian Public Science* (Manchester, 2009), esp. pp. 205–208.

29 R. Douglass, *Rousseau and Hobbes: Nature, Free Will, and the Passions* (Oxford, 2015), pp. 16–17, similarly explores how 'ideas associated with Hobbes were understood and utilized by those who engaged with his works directly', aiming 'to understand better why they addressed Hobbes's ideas in a certain way'. To be sure, the intention here is not necessarily to show that Hobbes *influenced* the deists in the strict Skinnerian sense, according to which, to determine that A influenced B, we must show '(i) that B is known to have studied A's works; (ii) that B could not have found the relevant doctrines in any writer other than A; and (iii) that B could not have arrived at the relevant doctrines independently'. Although such influence can certainly be shown in the case of Blount, for example, thanks to his tendency to plagiarize, for which he gained an unfortunate reputation, the deists generally integrated sources and ideas of various thinkers to construct their own arguments. Indeed, in his own

study of the ways in which Hobbes's authority was invoked by contemporaries during the 'engagement' controversy of the early 1650s, Skinner shows that writers acknowledged Hobbes in multiple ways, including those who did 'arrive at their conclusions independently of studying Hobbes's works' but would still 'quote him not as the source of their opinions, but rather in corroboration of a number of views they already hold'. Q. Skinner, *Visions of Politics*, 3 vols (Cambridge, 2002), vol. 1, pp. 75–76; vol. 3, pp. 264–86, on p. 276. Skinner's work has uncovered how informative the relationship between Hobbes and his intellectual milieu can be. It remains open to debate, however, whether Hobbes's contemporaries were necessarily in a *better* position to understand or represent his theory compared to modern interpreters; for a different view on this question, see A. P. Martinich, *Hobbes's Political Philosophy: Interpretation and Interpretations* (Oxford, 2021), esp. pp. 103–21.

30 Parkin, *Taming the Leviathan*, p. 12. For previous significant studies of Hobbes's reception, see S. I. Mintz, *The Hunting of Leviathan: Seventeenth-Century Reactions to the Materialism and Moral Philosophy of Thomas Hobbes* (Cambridge, 1962); M. Goldie, 'The Reception of Hobbes', in J. H. Burns with M. Goldie (eds), *The Cambridge History of Political Thought 1450–1700* (Cambridge, 1991), pp. 589–615.

31 Although writers such as Toland, Tindal, and Collins did not always see themselves as a uniform group, some considerable connections between them and their works are documented. Collins, for example, knew Toland and Tindal personally: he assisted the former financially and lent him several books on their mutual interests, and it is plausible that he helped the latter with the writing of *The Rights of the Christian Church Asserted* (1706). See for example J. O'Higgins, *Anthony Collins: The Man and His Works* (The Hague, 1970), pp. 1–22; S. Lalor, *Matthew Tindal, Freethinker* (London, 2006), pp. 9–36; J. Dybikowski, 'Collins, Anthony (1676–1729), Philosopher and Freethinker', *ODNB* (2008), www.oxforddnb.com/view/10.1093/ref:odnb/9780198614128. 001.0001/odnb-9780198614128-e-5933 (accessed 21 July 2023).

32 M. Goldie, 'Priestcraft and the Birth of Whiggism', in N. Phillipson and Q. Skinner (eds), *Political Discourses in Early Modern Britain* (Cambridge, 1993), pp. 209–31, on. p. 212, observes that 'fundamental to the animus of early Whiggism, was, in Hobbes's phrase, the "unpleasing" of priests'. As Goldie explains, the term 'priestcraft' was first used by James Harrington in his *Pian Piano* (1657); Hobbes himself never used it, but 'priestcraft' did appear in the English translation of his *Historia Ecclesiastica*. Hobbes, *A True Ecclesiastical History*, trans. J. Rooke (London, 1722), pp. 77, 93, 127; J. Harrington, *The Political Works of James Harrington*, ed. J. G. A. Pocock (Cambridge, 1977), p. 372. See also J. A. T. Lancaster and A. McKenzie-McHarg, 'Priestcraft. Anatomizing the Anti-Clericalism of Early Modern Europe', *Intellectual History Review*, 28:1 (2018), pp. 7–22.

33 Champion, *Pillars of Priestcraft Shaken*, shows that the past was a particularly useful tool in the hands of the radicals who reconstructed historical accounts of the corruption of Christianity to attack the histories of the church with

counter-histories of superstition and priestcraft. For other recent accounts that help to recover the complexity of the works of these thinkers, see for example F. C. Beiser, *The Sovereignty of Reason: The Defense of Rationality in the Early English Enlightenment* (Princeton, 1996), pp. 220–65; J. A. Herrick, *The Radical Rhetoric of the English Deists: The Discourse of Skepticism, 1680–1750* (Columbia, SC, 1997); J. Champion, 'Deism', in R. H. Popkin (ed.), *The Columbia History of Western Philosophy* (New York, 1999), pp. 437–45; D. Lucci, *Scripture and Deism: The Biblical Criticism of the Eighteenth-Century British Deists* (Bern, 2008); A. Thomson, *Bodies of Thought: Science, Religion, and the Soul in the Early Enlightenment* (Oxford, 2008); W. Hudson, *The English Deists: Studies in Early Enlightenment* (London, 2009); Hudson, *Enlightenment and Modernity: The English Deists and Reform* (London, 2009); Wigelsworth, *Deism in Enlightenment England*; M. Hunter, *The Decline of Magic: Britain in the Enlightenment* (New Haven, 2020), pp. 49–66.

34 Some scholars have advocated a reading of deists and freethinkers as unbelievers who had to disguise their heterodoxies to different degrees and in different ways for fear of censorship or persecution. On this reading, the deists had to hide their real message for it to reach the learned part of their audience, and we therefore need to read them in an esoteric way which pays close attention to their use of technics such as wit and ridicule. See for example D. Berman, 'Deism, Immortality and the Art of Theological Lying', in J. A. L. Lemay (ed.), *Deism, Masonry, and the Enlightenment* (Newark, 1987), pp. 61–78; Berman, *A History of Atheism in Britain: From Hobbes to Russell* (London, 1988); Berman, 'Disclaimers as Offence Mechanisms in Charles Blount and John Toland', in M. Hunter and D. Wootton (eds), *Atheism from the Reformation to the Enlightenment* (Oxford, 1992), pp. 255–72; I. Rivers, *Reason, Grace, and Sentiment: A Study of the Language of Religion and Ethics in England, 1660–1780. Volume 2: Shaftesbury to Hume* (Cambridge, 2000), pp. 7–84.

35 Champion, *Pillars of Priestcraft Shaken*, p. 24.

36 J. Aubrey, *Brief Lives, Chiefly of Contemporaries*, ed. A. Clark, 2 vols (Oxford, 1898), vol. 1, p. 357, reported that this was Hobbes's comment when Edmund Waller sent Devonshire Spinoza's *Tractatus Theologico-Politicus* after its publication in 1670.

37 Lev 32, p. 580.

38 Champion, *Pillars of Priestcraft Shaken*, esp. p. 10; R. G. Ingram, *Reformation without End: Religion, Politics and the Past in Post-Revolutionary England* (Manchester, 2018), esp. p. 9.

39 J. Champion, *Republican Learning: John Toland and the Crisis of Christian Culture, 1696–1722* (Manchester, 2003), p. 12, demonstrates convincingly the political dimension of anticlericalism, showing that 'Toland's lifetime project was an engagement with the politics of cultural authority: his ambition was to challenge, overturn and reconstruct what he regarded as a corrupt rule of priestcraft'.

40 W. J. Bulman, 'Secular Sacerdotalism in the Anglican Enlightenment, 1660–1740', in A. M. Matytsin and D. Edelstein (eds), *Let There Be Enlightenment: The Religious and Mystical Sources of Rationalism* (Baltimore, 2018), pp. 205–26, on p. 206. See also B. W. Young, *Religion and Enlightenment in Eighteenth-Century*

England: Theological Debate from Locke to Burke (Oxford, 1998); Bulman, *Anglican Enlightenment: Orientalism, Religion and Politics in England and its Empire, 1648–1715* (Cambridge, 2015); A. Walsh, *Civil Religion and the Enlightenment in England, 1707–1800* (Woodbridge, 2020).

41 Deism, in particular, has enjoyed mixed fortunes in modern scholarship. Once considered a central force of enlightenment and secularisation, more recently it has come to be questioned and even abandoned by historians. For the former interpretation, see for example N. Torrey, *Voltaire and the English Deists* (New Haven, 1930); P. Gay, *The Enlightenment: An Interpretation. The Rise of Modern Paganism* (New York, 1966); F. Venturi, *Utopia and Reform in the Enlightenment* (Cambridge, 1971). For the latter, see for example, S. J. Barnett, *The Enlightenment and Religion: The Myths of Modernity* (Manchester, 2003); J. Robertson, *The Enlightenment: A Very Short Introduction* (Oxford, 2015), esp. p. 24. This was partly due to developments in the study of the Enlightenment itself that emphasised its nuanced and multifaceted character as well as its close relationship to sacred and ecclesiastical history. See for example J. G. A. Pocock, *Barbarism and Religion. Volume 1: The Enlightenments of Edward Gibbon, 1737–1764* (Cambridge, 1999), esp. pp. 1–10; D. Levitin, 'From Sacred History to the History of Religion: Paganism, Judaism, and Christianity in European Historiography from Reformation to "Enlightenment"', *The Historical Journal*, 55:4 (2012), pp. 1117–60.

42 See for example R. E. Sullivan, *John Toland and the Deist Controversy: A Study in Adaptions* (Cambridge, MA, 1982); R. H. Popkin, 'The Deist Challenge', in O. P. Grell, J. I. Israel, and N. Tyacke (eds), *From Persecution to Toleration: The Glorious Revolution and Religion in England* (Oxford, 1991), pp. 195–215; J. C. D. Clark, *English Society, 1660–1832: Religion, Ideology and Politics during the Ancien Regime*, 2nd edn (Cambridge, 2000), pp. 324–25; J. G. A. Pocock, *Barbarism and Religion. Volume 5: Religion: The First Triumph* (Cambridge, 2010), pp. 215–19.

43 L. Schwartz, *Infidel Feminism: Secularism, Religion and Women's Emancipation, England 1830–1914* (Manchester, 2013), presents a similar case of nineteenth-century English 'Freethinking feminists' who were eventually proud to be called 'infidels'.

44 Ingram, *Reformation without End*, pp. 13–14.

45 P. Lake, 'The Historiography of Puritanism', in J. Coffey and P. C. H. Lim (eds), *The Cambridge Companion to Puritanism* (Cambridge, 2008), pp. 346–71, on p. 364. See also Lake, 'Defining Puritanism–Again?', in F. J. Bremer (ed.), *Puritanism: Transatlantic Perspectives on a Seventeenth-Century Anglo-American Faith* (Boston, 1993), pp. 3–29; Lake, 'Anti-Puritanism: The Structure of a Prejudice', in K. Fincham and P. Lake (eds), *Religious Politics in Post-Reformation England: Essays in Honour of Nicholas Tyacke* (Woodbridge, 2006), pp. 80–97. For the problematic nature of 'latitudinarianism', see J. Spurr, '"Latitudinarianism" and the Restoration Church', *The Historical Journal*, 31:1 (1988), pp. 61–82.

46 P. Harrison, *'Religion' and the Religions in the English Enlightenment* (Cambridge, 1990), p. 62; W. Hudson, 'Atheism and Deism Demythologized',

in W. Hudson, D. Lucci, and J. R. Wigelsworth (eds), *Atheism and Deism Revalued: Heterodox Religious Identities in Britain, 1650–1800* (Farnham, 2014), pp. 13–23, on p. 19. D. R. Como, *Radical Parliamentarians and the English Civil War* (Oxford, 2018), pp. 1–20, on p. 7, emphasises the 'plasticity' of such categories.

47 See also P. Lake, 'Anti-Popery: The Structure of a Prejudice', in R. Cust and A. Hughes (eds), *Conflict in Early Stuart England: Studies in Religion and Politics, 1603–1642* (London, 1989), pp. 72–106.

48 Ingram, *Reformation without End*, p. 14, explains: 'contemporaries reckoned that *orthodoxy* entailed belief in the Nicene and Athanasian Creeds; the episcopal ecclesiology of the Church of England; and the necessity of the church's legal establishment, an establishment safeguarded by penal laws'. J. G. A. Pocock, 'Within the Margins: The Definitions of Orthodoxy', in R. D. Lund (ed.), *The Margins of Orthodoxy: Heterodox Writing and Cultural Response, 1660–1750* (Cambridge, 1995), pp. 33–53, on pp. 35, 43, makes a similar point: 'we understand history better, and are more enriched by understanding it, when we understand that orthodoxy has its own history, is in history and has history in it'; Pocock identifies the threats on the English orthodoxy as the 'three menacing figures: Giant Pope, Giant Hobbes and Giant Enthusiast'. See also Pocock, *Barbarism and Religion. Volume 5*, pp. 1–3.

49 P. N. Miller, ' "Freethinking" and "Freedom of Thought" in Eighteenth-Century Britain', *The Historical Journal*, 36:3 (1993), pp. 599–617.

50 See 'The Collins–Clarke correspondence' in Chapter 2.

51 J. Marshall, 'The Ecclesiology of the Latitude-Men 1660–1689: Stillingfleet, Tillotson and "Hobbism" ', *The Journal of Ecclesiastical History*, 36:3 (1985), pp. 407–27; Malcolm, 'Hobbes and the Royal Society', in *Aspects of Hobbes*, pp. 317–35; Parkin, *Taming the Leviathan*, esp. pp. 361–68.

52 S. P. Lamprecht, 'Hobbes and Hobbism', *The American Political Science Review*, 34:1 (1940), pp. 31–53; Martinich, *Hobbes's Political Philosophy*, pp. 122–45.

53 Skinner, *Visions of Politics*, vol. 3, esp. p. 269.

54 See 'The *Deist's Manual*' in Chapter 2.

55 Douglass, *Rousseau and Hobbes*, p. 8.

56 Skinner, *Visions of Politics*, vol. 1, pp. 103–27.

57 Hobbes, *The English Works of Thomas Hobbes of Malmesbury*, ed. W. Molesworth, 11 vols (London, 1839–1845), vol. 7, p. 350. See also P. Springborg, 'Hobbes on Religion', in T. Sorell (ed.), *The Cambridge Companion to Hobbes* (Cambridge, 1996), pp. 346–80; Parkin, *Taming the Leviathan*, pp. 133–35; J. R. Collins, 'Thomas Hobbes, "Father of Atheists"', in Hudson, Lucci, and Wigelsworth (eds), *Atheism and Deism Revalued*, pp. 25–43.

58 For the atheistic reading of Hobbes, see for example Berman, *History of Atheism*; Curley, 'I Durst Not Write So Boldly'; D. M. Jesseph, 'Hobbes's Atheism', *Midwest Studies in Philosophy*, 26 (2002), pp. 140–66; P. Springborg, 'Hobbes's Challenge to Descartes, Bramhall and Boyle: A Corporeal God', *British Journal for the History of Philosophy*, 20:5 (2012), pp. 903–34. For the

more Christian reading, see for example A. E. Taylor, 'The Ethical Doctrine of Hobbes', *Philosophy*, 13:52 (1938), pp. 406–24; H. Warrender, *The Political Philosophy of Hobbes: His Theory of Obligation* (Oxford, 1957); F. C. Hood, *The Divine Politics of Thomas Hobbes* (Oxford, 1964); W. B. Glover, 'God and Thomas Hobbes', in K. C. Brown (ed.), *Hobbes Studies* (Oxford, 1965), pp. 141–68; A. P. Martinich, *The Two Gods of Leviathan: Thomas Hobbes on Religion and Politics* (Cambridge, 1992); G. Wright, *Religion, Politics and Thomas Hobbes* (Dordrecht, 2006).

59 See for example L. van Apeldoorn and R. Douglass, 'Introduction', in van Apeldoorn and Douglass (eds), *Hobbes on Politics and Religion* (Oxford, 2018), pp. 1–9, on pp. 4–5.

60 See for example K. Hoekstra, 'The de facto Turn in Hobbes's Political Philosophy', in T. Sorell and L. Foisneau (eds), *Leviathan after 350 Years* (Oxford, 2004), pp. 33–73; Hoekstra, 'The End of Philosophy (The Case of Hobbes)', *Proceedings of the Aristotelian Society*, 106:1 (2006), pp. 25–62; A. McQueen, 'Absolving God's Laws: Thomas Hobbes's Scriptural Strategies', *Political Theory*, 50:5 (2022), pp. 754–79.

61 Rousseau famously asserted in 1762 that 'the philosopher Hobbes alone has seen the evil and how to remedy it, and has dared to propose the reunion of the two heads of the eagle, and the restoration throughout of political unity, without which no State or government will ever be rightly constituted'. J. J. Rousseau, *The Social Contract; and, Discourses*, trans. G. D. H. Cole (London, 1973), p. 302. See Douglass, *Rousseau and Hobbes*, esp. pp. 144–48; Walsh, *Civil Religion*, pp. 1–3. See also S. A. Lloyd, *Ideals as Interests in Hobbes's Leviathan: The Power of Mind over Matter* (Cambridge, 1992), pp. 271–88; R. Tuck, 'The Civil Religion of Thomas Hobbes', in Phillipson and Skinner (eds), *Political Discourses in Early Modern Britain*, pp. 120–38; J. R. Collins, *The Allegiance of Thomas Hobbes* (Oxford, 2005), pp. 11–57; R. Beiner, *Civil Religion: A Dialogue in the History of Political Philosophy* (Cambridge, 2011), pp. 46–72; W. J. Bulman, 'Hobbes's Publisher and the Political Business of Enlightenment', *The Historical Journal*, 59:2 (2016), pp. 339–64; S. Mortimer, 'Christianity and Civil Religion in Hobbes's *Leviathan*', in A. P. Martinich and K. Hoekstra (eds), *The Oxford Handbook of Hobbes* (New York, 2016), pp. 501–19; J. Champion, 'Godless Politics: Hobbes and Public Religion', in W. J. Bulman and R. G. Ingram (eds), *God in the Enlightenment* (Oxford, 2016), pp. 42–62.

62 Aubrey, *Brief Lives*, vol. 1, p. 358.

63 R. Tuck, 'The "Christian Atheism" of Thomas Hobbes', in Hunter and Wootton (eds), *Atheism from the Reformation to the Enlightenment*, pp. 111–30; A. Cromartie, 'The God of Thomas Hobbes', *The Historical Journal*, 51:4 (2008), pp. 857–79.

64 Illuminating discussions on this include P. Milton, 'Hobbes, Heresy, and Lord Arlington', *History of Political Thought*, 14:4 (1993), pp. 501–46; P. Springborg, 'Hobbes, Heresy, and the *Historia Ecclesiastica*', *Journal of the History of Ideas*, 55:4 (1994), pp. 553–71; J. Champion, 'An Historical

Narration Concerning Heresie: Thomas Hobbes, Thomas Barlow, and the Restoration Debate over "Heresy"', in D. Loewenstein and J. Marshall (eds), *Heresy, Literature and Politics in Early Modern English Culture* (Cambridge, 2006), pp. 221–53; J. Parkin, 'Baiting the Bear: The Anglican Attack on Hobbes in the Later 1660s', *History of Political Thought*, 34:3 (2013), pp. 421–58.

65 Bulman, 'Hobbes's Publisher' sheds new light on the role of William Crooke's London bookshop in publishing Hobbes and making him accessible to various audiences, including the freethinkers.

66 J. Parkin, 'Hobbes and the Reception of "Leviathan"', *Journal of the History of Ideas*, 76:2 (2015), pp. 289–300, on pp. 294–95.

67 A. K. Day, 'Hobbes's Changing Ecclesiology', *The Historical Journal*, 62:4 (2019), pp. 899–919.

68 N. Malcolm, *Leviathan: Editorial Introduction* (Oxford, 2012), p. 48.

69 Lev 12, p. 186.

70 Lev 47, p. 1120.

71 Lev 46, pp. 1074–76.

72 D. Johnston, *The Rhetoric of Leviathan: Thomas Hobbes and the Politics of Cultural Transformation* (Princeton, 1986); Malcolm, *Aspects of Hobbes*, pp. 544–45.

73 K. Hoekstra, 'Disarming the Prophets: Thomas Hobbes and Predictive Power', *Rivista di storia della filosofia*, 59:1 (2004), pp. 97–153. For Hobbes's denial of incorporeal substances, see Lev 4, p. 60. Some notable accounts that emphasise the connections between these various aspects of Hobbes's enterprise are S. Shapin and S. Schaffer, *Leviathan and the Air-Pump: Hobbes, Boyle, and the Experimental Life* (Princeton, 1985); D. M. Jesseph, *Squaring the Circle: The War between Hobbes and Wallis* (Chicago, 1999); J. Overhoff, *Hobbes's Theory of the Will: Ideological Reasons and Historical Circumstances* (Lanham, 2000).

74 Hobbes, *English Works*, vol. 1, p. ix. See Tuck, 'The Utopianism of Leviathan', in Sorell and Foisneau (eds), *Leviathan after 350 Years*, pp. 125–38. I have elaborated on these themes and their implications for our understanding of Hobbes's theory in E. Carmel, '"Philosophy, Therefore, Is within Yourself": The Rational Potential in Hobbes's Theory', *Hobbes Studies*, 31:2 (2018), pp. 166–87; Carmel, 'A Commonwealth for Galileo: Imagining a Hobbesian Utopia', *Hobbes Studies* 35:2 (2022), 176–99.

75 Prominent accounts include A. Ryan, 'Hobbes, Toleration and the Inner Life', in D. Miller and L. Siedentop (eds), *The Nature of Political Theory* (Oxford, 1983), pp. 197–218; Ryan, 'A More Tolerant Hobbes?', in S. Mendus (ed.), *Justifying Toleration: Conceptual and Historical Perspectives* (Cambridge, 1988), pp. 37–59; R. Tuck, 'Hobbes and Locke on Toleration', in M. G. Dietz (ed.), *Thomas Hobbes and Political Theory* (Lawrence, 1990), pp. 153–71; J. P. Sommerville, *Thomas Hobbes: Political Ideas in Historical Context* (Basingstoke, 1992), pp. 149–56; Tuck, *Philosophy and Government 1572–1651* (Cambridge, 1993), esp. pp. 335–45; J. Waldron, 'Hobbes and the Principle of Publicity', *Pacific Philosophical Quarterly*, 82:3–4 (2001), pp. 447–74; J. Champion, '"Private Is in Secret Free": Hobbes and Locke on the

Limits of Toleration, Atheism and Heterodoxy', in C. Y. Zarka, F. Lessay, and J. Rogers (eds), *Les fondements philosophiques de la tolerance* (Paris, 2002), pp. 221–53; Collins, *The Allegiance of Thomas Hobbes*; Curley, 'Hobbes and the Cause of Religious Toleration'; A. Abizadeh, 'Publicity, Privacy and Religious Toleration in Hobbes's *Leviathan*', *Modern Intellectual History*, 10:2 (2013), pp. 261–91; T. M. Bejan, 'Difference without Disagreement: Rethinking Hobbes on "Independency" and Toleration', *The Review of Politics*, 78:1 (2016), pp. 1–25; D. Stauffer, *Hobbes's Kingdom of Light: A Study of the Foundations of Modern Political Philosophy* (Chicago, 2018).

76 Bulman, 'Hobbes's Publisher', p. 361, notes: 'The fact that so many of the solutions that were offered in the later Stuart period were Hobbesian in orientation testified to the lasting imprint that Hobbes had made upon figures of a wide variety of ideological persuasions'. See also J. T. Peacey, 'Nibbling at "Leviathan": Politics and Theory in England in the 1650s', *Huntington Library Quarterly*, 61:2 (1998), pp. 241–57.

77 J. Parkin, 'Hobbes and the Future of Religion', in van Apeldoorn and Douglass (eds), *Hobbes on Politics and Religion*, pp. 184–201, on pp. 197–98. For relevant aspects of Hobbes's rhetoric, see also I. D. Evrigenis, *Images of Anarchy: The Rhetoric and Science in Hobbes's State of Nature* (Cambridge, 2014); J. Parkin, 'Hobbes and Paradox', in Martinich and Hoekstra (eds), *Oxford Handbook of Hobbes*, pp. 624–42.

78 J. Champion, ' "The Kingdom of Darkness": Hobbes and Heterodoxy', in S. Mortimer and J. Robertson (eds), *The Intellectual Consequences of Religious Heterodoxy 1600–1750* (Leiden, 2012), pp. 95–120; J. R. Collins, *In the Shadow of Leviathan: John Locke and the Politics of Conscience* (Cambridge, 2020), pp. 90–115.

79 Here I also follow the methodological choice explained in Parkin, *Taming the Leviathan*, pp. 8–12.

1

The early days of English deism
(*c.* 1670–1695)

This chapter shows how different aspects of Hobbes's thought were picked up by various authors in the early days of deism in England. It discusses how deistic views started to develop in the 1670s and 1680s with the controversies on natural religion, the need of revelation (or lack thereof), and the sufficiency of human reason. It examines published and unpublished works by several writers, some of whom are relatively anonymous in the literature, showing how they contributed to these debates and how they engaged with Hobbes while presenting their own views. Among these writers are Martin Clifford, Albertus Warren, Charles Blount, and James Boevey.

Deism before the 1670s

In its first appearances in the sixteenth century, deism was denounced regularly. In 1564, the Swiss Protestant minister Pierre Viret, an early leader of the Reformation in Switzerland and France, asserted: 'There are several who indeed profess to believe that there is some Deity or God, as the Turks and Jews do: but as for Jesus Christ, and all those things which the doctrine of the Evangelists and Apostles testifies concerning him, they take them for fables and dreams ... I hear that some of this band call themselves Deists, a new word in opposition to that of Atheists'.[1] This analysis suggested that deism was a kind of belief in God coupled with a rejection of the divinity of Christ and the 'fables' of Christianity, particularly its supernatural elements. Viret admitted that the deists differed from one another on various issues, such as the immortality of the soul and divine providence, mentioning that some held that God does not intervene in human affairs. He was 'struck with horror' thinking that 'there are such monsters among those who bear the name of Christians'.[2] Viret was the first of many in European circles to take this tone with deists, and it was his definition that Pierre Bayle included in his *Dictionnaire*.[3]

Similarly, in England the term 'deism' appeared sporadically in the late sixteenth and early seventeenth centuries. In 1595, the church minister

Josias Nichols published *An Order of Houshold Instruction*, dedicated to
Robert Devereux, second earl of Essex. Nichols attempted to establish an
instruction which included an easy explanation of 'the principall and chiefe
points of Christian religion'. As part of this, he described the 'errors and
heresies contrarie to the good doctrine', and among those he mentioned 'all
Atheists, Deists, Sophisters, and ignorant brablers, who frame to themselves
a God, or salvation, without faith in Christ'.[4] In 1621, Robert Burton mentioned in *The Anatomy of Melancholy* the 'great Philosophers, and Deists'
who 'attribute all to naturall causes' and 'deny God as much as the rest,
hold all religion a fiction, opposite to reason and philosophy, though for
feare of magistrates (saith *Vaninus*) they durst not publikely professe it'.[5]
These early examples share a range of notions of deists who do not necessarily deny God, at least not explicitly, but in reality reject most or all elements
of religion. It is not clear, however, that deism was a distinctive set of ideas
at the time nor that there were people who actually identified themselves as
deists.[6] This picture would start to change in England in the 1670s, a period
that witnessed a dramatic upsurge in heterodox ideas, or so at least thought
the critics.

A new religion

In 1669, the scholar Meric Casaubon wrote a letter to clergyman Peter du
Moulin commenting on some claims made by the fellow of the Royal Society
Thomas Sprat on experimental natural philosophy. Sprat had argued that
'all, or most of our Religious controversies, may be as well decided, by plain
reason, and by considerations, which may be fetch'd from the *Religion* of
mankind, the Nature of *Government*, and *humane Society*, and *Scripture*
itself'.[7] Casaubon disagreed, adding that:

> It is well known that before the late troubles, a *Noble-man* of this Realm
> wrote a book intituled *De Veritate*: the end and drift whereof was, out of
> the Religions of mankind to extract a Religion that should need no Christ ...
> Since him it is well known, that some body hath taken some pains to attem-
> perate Christianity to the laws of every Countrey, and commands of Supreme
> Powers: and this he doth ground, or endeavour to ground ... upon divers pas-
> sages of *Scripture*. What can this import, in ordinary construction, but a new
> Religion?[8]

What was the new religion that Casaubon attributed to Herbert and,
although not by name, also to Hobbes?

Since the publication of *De veritate* (1624), Edward Herbert of Cherbury
was associated with ideas of minimal and natural religion, mainly due to
his system of the five common notions of religion that are rationally and

universally true. For Herbert, the system of common notions 'has been clearly accepted at all times by every normal person' and therefore 'has never erred, nor ever will err'.[9] Many believed that the attempt to arrive at a conception of religion which would be common to all times and places resulted in a thin version of religion—too thin, for some—that made revelation, or indeed Christ, unnecessary. What this had in common with Hobbes was the charge of 'indifferentism': the approach that allowed for differences in religious beliefs and practices beyond some shared fundamentals. Indeed, this was not dissimilar to Hobbes's insistence that the 'Onely Article of Faith, which the Scripture maketh simply Necessary to Salvation, is this, that JESUS is THE CHRIST', and that beyond that, the civil sovereign in every state should determine the manner of public worship.[10] In this context, Hobbes and Herbert were coupled repeatedly, and not only by readers in England, but also on the Continent. In 1656 the German statesman Johann Christian von Boineburg referred to 'Hobbes, Herbert, and other similar teachers of self-love, licence, and religious indifference', and in 1680 the German professor Christian Kortholt identified Hobbes's theory of religion with Herbert's and linked the two with Spinoza as the 'the three great impostors'.[11] Hobbes himself described Herbert's book 'Concerning truth' as 'a high point' for him.[12]

Around the time of Casaubon's letter, the former Cromwellian politician Sir Charles Wolseley published *The Unreasonableness of Atheism Made Manifest* (1669), which he followed up with *The Reasonableness of Scripture-Belief* (1672). There he wrote that 'Irreligion, 'tis true in its practice hath been still the companion of every Age, but its open and publick defence seems the peculiar of this'.[13] This newly public irreligion looked like the new religion that Casaubon warned against:

> 'Tis but of late that the world hath been told, That the notion of a Spirit implies a contradiction; That the Bible is no where in force as a Law Divine, but where by Laws civil and municipal 'tis made so to be; That Religion is nothing else but a fear of invisible powers feign'd in the Mind, and fancyed from tales publickly allowed; These and most of the bad Principles of this Age are of no earlier a date then one very ill Book, are indeed but the spawn of the Leviathan.[14]

It was following the Leviathan effect, as it were, that Wolseley sought to establish the divine authority of the scripture on rational grounds. Wolseley's goal was to demonstrate that it was reasonable to believe that the bible is God's revealed and supernatural law according to which He governs the world. In other words, it was unreasonable to accept Christianity while dismissing the bible as a man-made document. Thus, he believed that it was possible to incorporate a rational way of thinking into revealed religion without denying the authority of its very foundation, that is, the scripture.

Among Wolseley's targets were all those who 'admit the being of *God*, of *Providence*, and *Religion*, but reject the *Christian-religion* and consequently the *Bible*, as not true'.[15] These, he identified, were not precisely atheists but '*Antiscriptural men*' who 'pay no homage at all to the *Bible*, nor yield any obedience to its Authority'.[16] This distinction recurs increasingly in the works of Christian apologists in the closing decades of the seventeenth century. It was certainly not the last time when a connection was made between Hobbes and these new antiscripturists.

Wolseley argued that some of our knowledge of religion and our religious duties, although always conforming to reason, must come from revelation, and that this knowledge is contained wholly in the bible. On the other side of this debate were those who started to call the necessity of revelation into question. One of the earliest English texts that did this openly was 'Of Natural Religion, as Opposed to Divine Revelation'. This short essay was composed by an author known only as A. W. for Charles Blount, apparently between 1672 and 1682.[17] It probably circulated first as a manuscript, as it is bound in the British Library with several other manuscripts, all of which were eventually published in Charles Blount's grand collection *The Oracles of Reason* (1693).[18] 'Natural Religion,' the author explained, 'is the Belief we have of an eternal intellectual Being, and of the Duty which we owe him, manifested to us by our Reason, without Revelation or positive Law'.[19] The argument was straightforward: natural reason is sufficient in order to understand all religious matters, and hence natural religion—the belief in an eternal deity—is sufficient for our happiness. Revelation, on the other hand, is rendered unnecessary:

> That Rule which is necessary to our future Happiness, ought to be generally made known to all men.
>
> But no Rule of Revealed Religion was, or ever could be made known to all men.
>
> Therefore no Revealed Religion is necessary to future Happiness.[20]

A. W. replied directly to Wolseley's argument on the special status of revelation. He claimed that revelation cannot show us how to expiate our sins because the means by which it was understood to do this change over time. True expiation consists merely of repentance, which is 'innate, and a part of Natural Religion'.[21] Denying the need for revealed religion entirely and questioning parts of the scripture were, of course, radical moves that alarmed even Anglicans, such as Wolseley, who did not necessarily oppose a certain version of rational religion.

Later on in the 1670s, a series of critiques of deism became increasingly frequent and more informed. In 1677, Edward Stillingfleet, then archdeacon of London and future bishop of Worcester, published *A Letter to a Deist*, that was dedicated to 'a particular Person, who owned the Being and

Providence of God, but expressed a mean Esteem of the Scriptures, and the Christian Religion'.[22] In 1682, the poet John Dryden attacked 'Deism, or the Principles of Natural Worship' for being 'onely the faint remnants or dying flames of reveal'd Religion in the Posterity of Noah'.[23] Dryden's poem was an important milestone in the attack on the new threat that was presented by deism. For Dryden, deism was a system of natural religion and natural worship. He insisted that the deist is mistaken to believe that natural reason is sufficient for his religion, because the knowledge that the deist claims to have of God cannot be merely intellectual but has to be the product of past revelation. Reason, Dryden insisted, may be necessary to recognise that the scripture is the word of God, but the content of the scripture belongs to the realm of faith, not reason. Therefore, '[t]hey who wou'd prove Religion by Reason, do but weaken the cause which they endeavour to support: 'tis to take away the Pillars from our Faith, and to prop it onely with a twig'.[24] The precise position of the deist that Dryden portrayed is especially close to the one espoused by A. W.:

> But stay: the *Deist* here will urge anew,
> No *Supernatural Worship* can be *True*:
> Because a *general Law* is that alone
> Which must to *all*, and every *where* be known.[25]

It is plausible that Dryden became familiar with deism by the early 1680s through clandestine manuscripts—as we shall see, this was an important vehicle for deistic ideas—and that one of these was the essay 'Of Natural Religion'.[26] Dryden may have responded directly to A. W.—and subsequently, Blount responded to Dryden with his own *Religio Laici* (1683), which effectively defended deism publicly for the first time in England.[27] Dryden's *Religio Laici* was therefore a central event in the formulation of early English deism, and Blount was a key figure in this process, arguably the first self-proclaimed English deist.

Growing anxieties about deism and closely related heterodoxies took hold during the 1680s. In 1681, for example, it was argued that 'this *Town* and *Kingdome* is infested with such swarms of *Deists, Socinians, Atheists*, and others, that not only violate the undoubted *Regalia*, but with treasonable Blasphemy dispute the Divine *Sovereignty* of *Jesus*'.[28] In 1683, Cambridge Platonist George Rust's *A Discourse of the Use of Reason in Matters of Religion* was published posthumously against enthusiasts as well as deists 'pleading only for a Natural Religion in opposition to any Particular Mode or Way of Divine Revelation'.[29] Echoing Stillingfleet, the deists were said to 'profess to acknowledge a God and Providence, yet have withal a mean and low esteem of the Scriptures and Christianity, as if the Christian Religion were a thing that could not well be Apologized for, nor any fair and rational

Account given of it'.[30] Similarly, in 1685, the Church of England clergyman William Assheton criticised a deist who laughed at God and suspected that the disciples of Jesus had forged the stories of his miracles to win their master's approval.[31] Such writings against deism often exposed the readers to the ideas of deism no less than the deistic writings did, and moreover, they often fuelled the debate on deism better than the deists did themselves.

The controversy on human reason

The origins of the deist controversy of the 1690s—the subjects of the next chapter—were already present in the 1670s. The idea that reason was supreme and sufficient for Christian life was the message of *A Treatise of Humane Reason* (1674), written by Martin Clifford, master of Charterhouse. Following the course of this debate will reveal to us how deistic views developed in England and how close they were to some of Hobbes's views.

Clifford was a close friend of the second duke of Buckingham and acquainted with the first earl of Shaftesbury, both associated with tolerationist and early Whiggish views. Although little discussed in the literature, the several reprints of the *Treatise* since its publication indicate that it attracted attention both in England and on the Continent, and that it made a contribution to ongoing debates on liberty of conscience and religious toleration. Giovanni Tarantino suggests that 'although his office demanded adherence to the established church, Clifford seems to have been a covert deist'.[32]

In the *Treatise*, Clifford argued that 'all the miseries which have followed the variety of opinions since the Reformation, have proceeded entirely from these two mistakes, The tying *infallibility* to whatsoever we think Truth, and *damnation* to whatsoever we think Errour'.[33] It followed that one's most trustworthy guide is one's own reason, whereas revelation should be accepted only when it is consistent with reason: 'they who say they follow Authority, or they follow Divine particular Revelation, or any thing else imaginable, do it, because that agrees with their own Reason, and will quit the Party as soon as it do's otherwise'.[34] Buckingham, who praised the *Treatise*, wished to 'make the Empire of REASON sacred, and not to be invaded by any Party'.[35] Clifford and Buckingham's emphasis on rational examination at the expense of obedience to authority was clearly anticlerical, and supported their case for unrestricted liberty of conscience.

Clifford argued that there should be diversity of forms of worship which follows from the legitimate and desirable diversity of opinions.[36] For this reason, he criticised Hobbes for arguing that the sovereign should determine the manner of God's worship for the subjects.[37] As Clifford pointed out, Hobbes's justification for this was quite odd. In the passage from *On the Citizen* to which Clifford referred, Hobbes wrote that 'no one worships God, i.e. offers external honours, unless he is offering something which others accept as honours'.[38] This, according to Clifford, was simply false. Worship does not have to be accepted by others to count as genuine, and in any case, it is up to God to judge our thoughts and see through any differences in our actions.[39]

A reply to the *Treatise* was published in 1675, titled *Plain-Dealing*. Pace Clifford, its author A. M. supported religious conformity and defended Hobbes, however sarcastically: 'not for any extraordinary opinion *I* have of the Man or his Argument, but because I believe he speaks truth in it: and therefore I think it hard that he which speaketh truth so very seldom should be run down with meer words or metaphors when he doth'.[40] According to the anonymous author, people are always inclined to think that the religious choices of others, when they differ from their own, are dishonourable or even ridiculous, which is reason enough to impose uniformity.[41]

While some thought that the ideas of Clifford and Hobbes were at odds, others believed that they were very much alike. In 1679, a treatise entitled *The Spirit of Prophecy* was published in response to both Hobbes and Clifford. The author, who identified as W. H., was the Anglican minister William Howell. In a manner similar to Wolseley and others, Howell attacked the idea of 'Mr. *Hobbs* and his Complices' that religion should be made dependent on human authority 'for, to make Religion so to truckle under Civil Sovereigns ... what is it less than to clip the wings of all true Devotion towards God, and render it unable to fly higher than the Thrones and Scepters on Earth'.[42] Clifford, too, objected to this Hobbesian point, but for Howell, there was no difference between Hobbes and Clifford: he even mentioned the '*Extraordinary Wit*' that Clifford (sarcastically) attributed to Hobbes.[43]

For someone like Howell, then, both Hobbes and Clifford undermined Christianity equally: the former by favouring the civil sovereign and the latter by favouring human reason. This point would be made consistently by those who coupled the deists and Hobbes in the decades to come, as we shall see. Howell's goal in his treatise was therefore twofold: to prove the divine authority of Christianity against Hobbes, for whom the precepts of Christianity were not obliging as commands in themselves, and to prove the insufficiency of reason against Clifford, for whom revelation became redundant.[44]

The next intervention in the debate offers an interesting synthesis of Clifford's and Hobbes's positions. In 1680, Albertus Warren published *An Apology for the Discourse of Humane Reason* in defence of Clifford and in response to *Plain-Dealing*, where he argued for the supremacy of reason and for religious toleration, and at the same time, he supported a sort of religious uniformity maintained by the civil sovereign. Not much is known about Warren, yet he is worth our attention. In the early 1650s, Warren was a lawyer who advocated moderate legal reforms.[45] He was involved in the 'engagement' controversy and adopted the Hobbesian view that there is a mutual relationship between protection and obedience.[46] In 1650, he defended the de facto power arguing that the 'duties of obedience, unto the present authority, succinctly held forth as rationall, and necessary'.[47] In 1653, he argued for the preservation of the common law by the new government and the army, 'else we should be in an hostile condition, as Mr. *Hobbs* well observeth'.[48] In the 1650s Warren was an Independent; in the late 1670s he became a Whig who moved in the circle of Shaftesbury, to whom he dedicated his *Apology*.[49] He is also a candidate to be A. W., the author of 'Of Natural Religion', which was written around the same time as the *Apology*. This seems likely, it will be suggested, considering the ideas that Warren promoted in his *Apology*, including his debts to Hobbes.

In his *Apology*, Warren defended the supremacy of human reason, often following the Hobbesian logic that he had already employed in the 1650s. Reason, he argued, 'is our Light to judge of our Self-preservation by', and can alone save us from a state of war, 'for no other tye could have oblig'd us to keep Covenant, when the Violation had appear'd more profitable'.[50] He asserted that "'tis generally safer for a man to trust to his Natural Reason, than to be guided by Books; which are the Counters of Wise men, but the Money of Fools'.[51] This quote is taken from chapter 4 of *Leviathan*, where Hobbes argued that 'words are wise mens counters … but they are the mony of fooles, that value them by the authority of an *Aristotle*, a *Cicero*, or a *Thomas*, or any other Doctor whatsoever, if but a man'.[52] Hobbes argued famously against relying on the authority of old books, stating that depending on the reputation of past authors consists of faith and not knowledge and is therefore not true philosophy.[53] Somewhat ironically, Warren relied on Hobbes's authority, and applied this view—namely, that one must rely on one's own natural reason—to the realm of religion, thus arriving at a familiar argument for natural religion:

> [W]e are commanded to offer up to God our Reasonable Service, and if *Faith* were contrary to *Reason*, no body could believe at all; nay, to speak freely, tho *Faith* may be above it, yet few men, without special and particular *Revelation*, have hitherto believ'd the truth of *Canonical Scripture*, upon any other Conviction, but *Tradition* & *Comparison*, which cannot be done without *Reason*.[54]

Here Warren certainly looks like A. W., arguing that reason, and not revelation, is a universal and hence safer guide to religion. Reason is the only guide to happiness, and 'to live virtuously is to live Rationally'.[55] So, for Warren, reason obliges us to follow natural religion, and, moreover, religion must necessarily be reasonable.[56] In stating this, he was one of the first English writers—perhaps *the* first—who advocated natural religion as completely sufficient in itself. For the contemporaries, this view constituted deism.

Warren denied that reason would lead to heresy, 'understanding nothing else by the Term Heresie, but Opinion, for how can it hurt others, what I think?'[57] Here, too, Warren was indebted to Hobbes. In *An Historical Narration Concerning Heresie* (1680), Hobbes argued that the word heresy originally 'signified no more than a private opinion, without reference to truth or falsehood'.[58] We know that Warren wrote the *Apology* two years before its publication, probably in 1678.[59] We also know that Hobbes's *Historical Narration* was in circulation around the same time, and that Blount had a copy of it.[60] Assuming that Warren and Blount moved in similar circles, and perhaps knew each other through Shaftesbury, it is plausible that Warren had access to the *Historical Narration*. By equating heresy with opinion in a Hobbesian manner, Warren effectively turned the defence of human reason into a defence of freedom of thought.

Warren argued for rational religion and for religious toleration, while emphasising the duty of all subjects, including the church, to obey the king who protects them. He added that 'Subjects have Liberty in all things, where they are not restrain'd by Laws, and in such things they have restrain'd themselves. As too furious Use of Power has endanger'd many States, so the want of Power has ruin'd others'.[61] Warren's position was therefore twofold: he was concerned both with defending the individual use of reason and with ensuring public peace. Interestingly, he followed Hobbes to support both parts of the argument, while defending Hobbes's reputation and describing him as 'a most excellent Philosopher, and Great in several other respects'.[62]

Warren explained that 'our Dissenters are to know' that the magistrate can punish any '*Indecencies* … relating to the external way of honouring God', adding: 'because Peace is the end of Government, men's opinions, when publickly vented and found inconsistent with Peace, must be regulated by the Magistrate, which is not to make men see double by being dazl'd betwixt Ecclesiastical and Temporal powers, for all Power is temporal, as Power'.[63] Not only is this idea Hobbesian in essence, but it repeats Hobbes's precise words that 'Temporall and Spirituall Government, are but two words brought into the world, to make men see double, and mistake their Lawfull Soveraign'.[64] Thus, Warren argued for Hobbesian uniformity: 'I do think, 'tis best to be of the Religion of a man's Countrey, Externally at least … and for External Worship in Religion, as to time and place, it is determinable by the Supreme Magistrate (in my opinion) not as a Christian, but as King'.[65] At the same time, Warren supported toleration, although only for Protestants. He relied on Hobbes for the rest of his argument: 'as *T. H.* saith, *Paul or Cephas,* or *Apollo may be followed, perhaps as the best way, according to a mans liking*', adding: 'The *English* are loth to venture their Salvations at Cross and Pile'.[66] These quotes are taken from chapter 47 of *Leviathan*, where Hobbes stated in a famous passage—omitted from the Latin *Leviathan*—that since the power of the Pope, the episcopacy, and the Presbyterians began to be taken away, the historical knots on Christian liberty were untied, and 'so we are reduced to the Independency of the Primitive Christians to follow Paul, or Cephas, or Apollos, every man as he liketh best: Which, if it be without contention ... is perhaps the best'.[67] Not only did Hobbes emerge here as a possible supporter of religious toleration or Independency, but he also formulated the ultimate anticlerical justification for depending on private judgment in religious matters rather than on religious authority:

> First, because there ought to be no Power over the Consciences of men, but of the Word it selfe, working Faith in every one, not always according to the purpose of them that Plant and Water, but of God himself, that giveth the Increase: and secondly, because it is unreasonable in them, who teach there is such danger in every little Errour, to require of a man endued with Reason of his own, to follow the Reason of any other man, or of the most voices of many other men; Which is little better, then to venture his Salvation at crosse and pile.[68]

Warren was not the first to employ this Hobbesian position in order to argue for religious toleration, but he was the first to do so in a deistic context, with the emphasis on human reason as the only necessary means to reach religious truths.[69] He then continued to argue that there were numerous thinkers, including Montaigne, Erasmus, Stillingfleet, Milton, and Hobbes, who 'have unanimously approv'd of Reason as the best Guide, and favour'd, or cooly advis'd, a circumscrib'd Toleration'.[70] It is certainly interesting to see Hobbes's name in such a list, which indicates how some Hobbesian ideas were used to support toleration while combined with other, perhaps more intuitive sources, such as Milton.[71]

By advocating the idea of 'circumscribed toleration' and thus maintaining that power over religious matters should lie in the hands of the civil sovereign against the constant challenge of the clergy, Warren could be described as 'a Hobbesian tolerationist'.[72] The complex position which called for religious toleration alongside a powerful civil authority or a quasi-authoritarian civil religion characterised a number of the figures that this book covers.[73] Yet Warren betrayed an even deeper sympathy to Hobbes. Towards the end of his *Apology*, he praised Hobbes, 'whose Arguments no

man ever condemn'd, who read him without Prejudice', mentioning that
Hobbes was 'pious in his Life, and dying like a true Christian Philosopher'.[74]
Warren specified Hobbes's contributions, including 'his golden Book *de
Cive*, so valu'd by all Lawyers at home and abroad', Hobbes's objections
to Descartes's *Meditations*, and his correspondence with bishop Bramhall
on liberty and necessity.[75] Hobbes's arguments against Bramhall, Warren
explained, 'are so hugely fine, and so curiously, yet naturally, cogent, that,
for the future, 'twill be judg'd mere Presumption, to superadd any thing
upon that Subject'.[76] Moreover, Warren continued to praise, 'of what great
weight, and yet hardly fathom'd consequence, those Arguments are ... the
sharpest Eyes now alive cannot penetrate'.[77] The effect of Hobbes's arguments, according to Warren, could already be seen in 'the Exposing of the
School-men, and the old mistaken Physicks, as waste Paper, and Judicial
Astrology to a Ridicule'.[78]

Therefore, for Warren, Hobbes contributed to the demystification of his
age, and he recruited Hobbes for his own pursuit of natural religion. He
also used the correspondence of Hobbes and Bramhall in the *Apology*. For
example, he denied the existence of free will, arguing that 'the Will always
following, and being acted by the last Dictate of the Understanding: so that,
it not only seemeth to be, but is necessitated, being no Faculty in it self'.[79]
Hobbes's determinism served Warren almost word for word in his thesis
on human reason, and precisely the same idea served A. W. in his essay
'Of Natural Religion', where he argued that 'all Men do Ill only for want
of right Reasoning, because the Will necessarily follows the last Dictate of
the Understanding'.[80] We now have every reason to believe that Albertus
Warren is A. W., the author of 'Of Natural Religion'.[81] If this is the case,
then Warren was both a crucial link in the emergence of English deism, as
was perceived by figures such as Dryden, and an enthusiastic admirer of
Hobbes. Moreover, Warren used Hobbesian ideas to argue for natural and
rational religion as well as for religious toleration. A remarkably similar
dynamic is found in the case of Charles Blount, who knew Warren, and to
whom the essay 'Of Natural Religion' was dedicated.

When reason is against a man, a man will be against reason

Charles Blount (1654–1693) was a political activist and pamphleteer. He
was a member of the Green Ribbon Club, a Whig club of public figures
who used to meet at the King's Head Tavern in London. From the late
1670s, Blount published a series of works that took a sceptical and critical line towards religion and betrayed a strong anticlerical and especially
anti-Catholic sentiment. Although largely neglected in the literature, and

previously dismissed as a plagiarist, Blount has been recognised as a central figure in the English deist and freethinking circles of the late seventeenth century, and as an important link in the transmission of radical ideas and circulation of clandestine materials.[82] In fact, he was one of the prominent critics of revealed religion in the years leading to the deist controversy and was perceived to have been partly responsible for it. The non-juror Charles Leslie, for example, wrote that the 'execrable' Blount was 'not fit to be heard by Christian Ears', and he worried that Blount 'set himself at the Head of Deists, and after whom they now copy'.[83]

There is some evidence that Blount drew on Hobbes from an early stage. In 1678 he sent Hobbes a copy of his publication *Anima Mundi*, in which he explored various ancient views on the human soul, seemingly admitting its immortality but only vaguely and as a result of a sceptic manoeuvre. This was Blount's first significant work, and he was assisted by his father, Sir Henry Blount; the latter had been moving in libertine and anticlerical circles and London coffeehouses already in the 1650s, and, interestingly, was acquainted with Hobbes. *Anima Mundi* was ordered to be supressed and the book was eventually burnt.[84] Accompanying this work, Blount sent Hobbes a letter, praising the manuscript of his 'Treatise of Heresie' that would eventually be published posthumously as *An Historical Narration Concerning Heresie* in 1680.[85] Blount wrote in the letter that Hobbes had provided 'a more accurate and faithful Account of the Nicene Council … than is any where else to be met with'.[86] To Blount, Hobbes was 'the great instructor of the most sensible Part of Mankind in the noble Science of Philosophy'.[87]

In his *Historical Narration*, Hobbes returned to the primitive church and the problem of the Trinity to give an account of the events that had led to the Council of Nicaea. Hobbes emphasised the role that Constantine the Great had played as the sovereign in making Christianity the public religion and settling the disputes over its creed, first and foremost the one that was provoked by Arius, who claimed that Jesus was inferior to God and in fact not divine. The Council of Nicaea decided against the Arians.

In his letter to Hobbes, Blount also went back to the primitive church. His aim was to expose the cynical political interests behind the major Christian debates. He argued that Constantine had treated the Arians as Louis XIV treated the Huguenots: he supported them as long as he needed them in order to gain power, but he turned against them to assure that their own power was restricted. Blount concluded that 'there is as little Trust to be reposed in General councils, who have been Guilty of so much Ignorance and Interest, as well as so frequently contradicting one another'.[88] Blount did not attribute this view to Hobbes, but he presumably felt that Hobbes would be sympathetic.

On one matter Blount clearly followed Hobbes's position: 'You your self have very well observed, when Reason is against a Man, a Man will be against Reason; and therefore 'tis no wonder to see, from several Interests, so many Opinions and Animosities arise'.[89] This quote appears in two versions in Hobbes's writings. In the *Elements of Law*, Hobbes wrote that 'as oft as reason is against a man, so oft will a man be against reason'.[90] In *Leviathan*, Hobbes expanded this idea and stated that men 'appeale from custome to reason, and from reason to custome, as it serves their turn; receding from custome when their interest requires it, and setting themselves against reason, as oft as reason is against them'.[91] In other words, truth might be in danger once interests are at stake. In these cases, men might turn against their reason or might be manipulated to do so by others. Hobbes worried about the suppression of truth, even in mathematical matters, as a result of political and most probably clerical interests. This Hobbesian quote was used in support for toleration in Parliament in 1668, and as we shall see, it was employed by deists and freethinkers time and again.[92] In some respects, this phrase captures the essence of Hobbes's radical anticlerical legacy, which is at the centre of this book.

Following Hobbes's approach, Blount analysed religion primarily in terms of interests, and priestly interests in particular. Most importantly, he adopted the idea that earthly interests alone dictate what would be considered heresy and what would be persecuted. This is evident already in *Anima Mundi*, the work that Blount sent to Hobbes, wherein he declared: 'the ignorant Vulgar people (whose Superstition is grounded upon the assimulating God with themselves) are apt to think that every one they Hate, are God Almighty's Enemies; and that whosoever differs from them in Opinion (though in never so trivial a matter) are Atheists, or Hereticks at least'.[93] In another letter from 1678, written to the libertine earl of Rochester, Blount stated wittily that 'in all Mutations, as well Ecclesiastical, as Civil ... a Temporal Interest was the great Machine upon which all human Actions moved; and that the common and general pretence of *Piety* and *Religion*, was but like Grace before a Meal'.[94]

The two letters to Hobbes and Rochester contain extracts from Henry Stubbe's *An Account of the Rise and Progress of Mahometanism*. This text, which was in circulation in the 1670s, offered a history of religion that emphasised its human agency, portrayed both Christ and Prophet Muhammad as political figures, and praised the latter as a prudent and tolerant legislator.[95] James Jacob has described Stubbe's approach as anticlerical, even secular, Hobbesian historicism.[96] Stubbe himself corresponded with Hobbes in the late 1650s. He might have been a Hobbesian Independent, and had he not died in 1676, according to Jacob, he would have had a place at the centre of the Green Ribbon Club alongside Blount.[97]

Blount's writings from the late 1670s revealed religious scepticism and criticism which turned with time into support for universal and natural religion, free from priestly corruption and dangerous sectarianism. Blount emphasised the disastrous and destabilising impact of quarrels between religious sects, and he shared Hobbes's views regarding the groups and interests behind such quarrels. Two additional works that he published in 1679 had some more pressing goals. The first, *An Appeal from the Country to the City*, came in the midst of the attempts to pass a bill to exclude the Catholic duke of York from the throne, a motion that Blount, the young Whig, supported strongly. In this work, Blount dramatically predicted a catastrophe of another Popish Plot in which London would be set on fire by the Jesuits, who would then be able to enforce their arbitrary government. Popery was an imminent threat to the kingdom, and a Catholic heir would have been a tool in the hands of the 'Papists' to carry out their plan. This, again, was an issue of crude earthly interests:

> nothing does more justifie the Plot, than their corrupt Principles, and present Interest; which will make them (being sure to have the succeeding King on their side) rather venture to push for it now, and run the hazard of the Peoples revenge, than suffer any longer the inconvenience of an *English* Parliament, or danger of the next Successor being a Protestant.[98]

Blount suggested the Protestant duke of Monmouth as the alternative successor, and warned his readers to remain wary: 'if ever a Popish Successor comes amongst you, let his promises of keeping your Religion and Laws, or of his Conversion, be never so plausible, credit 'em not; for if you do, you will infallibly be deceiv'd'.[99] At the end of his tract, Blount inserted some Catholic principles, which he found in Gilbert Burnet's *History of the Reformation* (1679), to demonstrate how dangerous Catholicism is to civil peace, including that civil princes are subjects of the Pope, who can override their earthly laws or overthrow them altogether.[100] This commonplace anti-Catholic critique corresponded closely to Hobbes's critique of the kingdom of darkness and especially to his warning that 'seeing double'—the simultaneous loyalty to civil and ecclesiastical sovereigns—is one of the main causes of civil conflict.[101]

In the second work from that year, *A Just Vindication of Learning*, Blount argued against the renewal of the licensing act, which lapsed then for the first time. This was a manifesto for press freedom which relied heavily on Milton's *Areopagitica* (1644).[102] It has been rightly emphasised recently that, as with many contemporary supporters of this freedom, Blount 'explicitly demanded an end to licensing, but *not* to the censuring of offensive texts'.[103] While this was a cause which Hobbes himself hardly championed, Blount's rationale was quasi-Hobbesian. Blount had 'had the Happiness to peruse' Hobbes's 'incomparable Treatise of Heresie in Manuscript' before 1679, and much in its spirit he wrote that 'Faction and Heresie were things unknown in the World, till the increase of Interest, and abatement of Christian Simplicity'.[104] Blount believed that the persecution of so-called heresies was merely a form of battle between conflicting interests: 'Why should I hate men because their Understandings have not been brought up like mine … or have not the same Interest … and therefore do not determine their School-questions to the sense of my Sect or Interest?'[105] Religion, therefore, was a political tool that could be extremely dangerous in the wrong hands.

Blount cited Milton's recollection that '*Galileo* was oppressed under the *Inquisitions* Tyranny, for thinking otherwise in Astronomy, then the *Dominican* and *Franciscan* Licensers thought'.[106] Milton, who met Galileo, believed that organised religious persecution targeted great minds and destroyed the arts and sciences in Italy. Hobbes, who also met Galileo, shared a similar impression: he protested that 'it appeareth more and more, that Years, and Dayes are determined by Motions of the Earth. Neverthelesse, men that have in their Writings but supposed such Doctrine, as an occasion to lay open the reasons for, and against it, have been punished for it by Authority Ecclesiasticall'.[107] Therefore, in a primarily anticlerical context Hobbes called it an error 'to extend the power of the Law, which is the Rule of Actions onely, to the very Thoughts, and Consciences of men, by Examination, and *Inquisition* of what they Hold, notwithstanding the Conformity of their Speech and Actions'.[108] Blount's firm opposition to licensing and to the right of censorship asserted by churchmen illuminates and develops an interesting intersection of Hobbes and Milton: for all of them, as for future freethinkers, the case of Galileo and the Inquisition in general served as a collective trauma, as it were, that showed what could happen when things went terribly wrong.[109] In a similar way to Warren, Blount drew on aspects of Milton, Hobbes, and others—but went further than all of them—to advocate religious toleration, freedom of inquiry, and freedom of expression in the face of clerical attempts to supress reason and truth. In this sense, he arrived at a position that revealed a possible freethinking and perhaps even Miltonian implication of Hobbes's theory.

Last sayings

The Last Sayings, or, Dying Legacy of Mr. Thomas Hobbs (1680) appeared in London shortly after Hobbes's death at the end of 1679 as a eulogy. It was a short collection of Hobbes's critical and radical statements on politics and religion or paraphrases thereof, and hence a good demonstration of what materials Hobbes provided for the milieu with which we are concerned here. The broadside starts with Hobbes's well-known critical assertions on religion: 'Fear of Power invisible feign'd by the mind, or imagined from Tales publickly allowed, is Religion; not allowed, is Superstition'; and 'It is with the Mysteries of Religion, as with wholesom Pills for the Sick, which swallow'd whole, have the vertue to Cure; but chew'd, are for the most part cast up again without effect'.[110] It continues with the doubts that Hobbes expressed about the probability of revelations, visions, and supernatural inspirations, followed by some more direct accusations: 'The Roman Clergy are a Confederacy of Deceivers'; and 'Priest-Craft is a sort of Legerdemain, and the Roman Priests are to the rest of mankind, as the Juglers in a Fair to the rest of the People there, and must have mony given them before they will play their Tricks'.[111] Whoever put together the *Last Sayings* portrayed Hobbes as a leading critic of the corrupt tactics of the power-hungry priests, that is, an enemy of priestcraft. Thus, this text revealed the great potential in Hobbes's theory for the launching of an unprecedented anticlerical campaign, precisely as Blount and his followers attempted to do in the following years.

The suspicious attitude towards the church was reason enough to question the idea of heresy: 'There is no Doctrine which tendeth to the advancement of the Power Ecclesiastical, or to the reverence, or profit of the Clergy, but the contradiction thereof is by the Church of Rome made Heresie, and punished with Death'. This was the main Hobbesian idea that influenced Blount, and which he found, as we have seen, in several of Hobbes's works: truth and science were in danger and had to be saved from the claws of a church who suppressed any doctrine that could threaten its position. Closely related was the idea that 'in all matters, touching which a man hath great Hope, or great Fear, he is easily deceived' and so 'the Planters of false Religions, do so industriously keep all true Science from them they intend to impose upon'. Once again, therefore, Hobbes was portrayed as an enemy of persecution, and implicitly as an advocate of searching freely for the truth, while the authors notably downplayed other aspects of his politics that perhaps fitted less well with their agendas.

The question of who edited this short collection is intriguing. It was long assumed, following Aubrey's report, that Charles Blount was the editor.[112] However, Noel Malcolm suggests that Blount was connected to the editor rather than the editor himself. Malcolm bases his hypothesis on Blount's copy-book—we will return to it later on—which contains some of the quotations that also appear in the *Last Sayings*. Blount seems to have transcribed these extractions to his copy-book, probably in 1681, a year after the publication of the *Last Sayings*, which makes him less likely to have been the original editor. Malcolm suggests that Blount was copying from a manuscript that was the source both for the *Last Sayings* and another similar work.[113] Yet it is noteworthy that one of the sayings is that 'where Reason is against a man, a man will be against Reason'. Although Hobbes expressed this position twice, this version resembles the phrasing in Blount's letter to Hobbes. Since the letter is dated to 1678, two years before the publication of the *Last Sayings*, it might serve to support the hypothesis that Blount was the editor. Another option is that the editor of the *Last Sayings* is also the author of 'Of Natural Religion', since the *Last Sayings* contained an almost identical formulation of the deistic idea that appeared in 'Of Natural Religion' (and that was later attacked by Dryden):

> That Law which is absolutely necessary to Mankind's future Happiness, ought (if the Law-giver be just) to be generally made known unto all men: No one reveal'd Law was ever made known unto all men; *Ergo*, No one reveal'd Law is absolutely necessary to Mankind's future Happiness.

Thus, the two tracts share the idea that no revealed law could be necessary to future happiness. This resemblance led David Berman to suggest that Hobbes might have been the author of 'Of Natural Religion'.[114] Nevertheless, it is much more likely that Albertus Warren was the author of 'Of Natural Religion' and hence perhaps also the editor of the *Last Sayings*. Indeed, in his *Apology*, Warren demonstrated not only an open admiration for Hobbes but also a very close knowledge of the philosopher's writings. In any case, whether compiled by Blount, Warren, or someone else in their circle who was engaged in the circulation of their then unpublished manuscripts, the *Last Sayings* is an illuminating document for two main reasons. First, it shows how Hobbesian ideas were received and circulated by the deists and freethinkers of the early 1680s. Second, it shows how the new radical ideas of natural religion were promoted under a Hobbesian cloak and with an explicit invocation of the authority of the late philosopher, which gives us a sense of the overlapping sympathies, not only of the editors, but presumably also of the expected readership.

Deism formulated

In 1680, Blount published two works that presented organised religion in a dubious light. In *Great Is Diana*, he criticised heathenish practices and especially sacrifices, tracing these to the heathen priests 'who were certainly the wickedest and craftiest of men'.[115] Blount argued that the priests had promoted the practice of sacrifices because it conduced to their own profit and because it gave them absolute control: they were the only ones who could manage the ceremony.[116] He emphasised the link between priestcraft and the invention of superstition, 'the off-spring of too much Honour, and too much Fear', as the means to delude the vulgar and thereby to gain power over them.[117] Although Blount limited himself at this point to the heathenish religions, this tract could clearly be read as a criticism of religion in general, including Christianity.

The second work that Blount published in 1680 had a similar effect. It was his translation of the *Life of Apollonius* with the addition of critical notes.[118] Blount treated the miracles that were performed by Apollonius in a way that could suggest that they were comparable to the miracles of Jesus: '*Apollonius* is by many accused of Magick, and so was *Christ* himself by *Celsus* and others'.[119] He encouraged an impartial inquiry into religion, emphasising that people do not usually see beyond their interests: 'self-love is so predominant in mankind' and so 'Most men are apt to flatter their own Party, calling that Religion in themselves which in others they term Irreligion or Superstition'.[120] This line consistently featured in Blount's work. This idea was Hobbesian, as Blount had admitted in his letter to Hobbes, insomuch as it focused on interests as the motivating force behind religious disputes and divisions. Furthermore, in his notes to the *Life of Apollonius*, Blount followed Hobbes openly in his treatment of religion, pointing particularly to its social and psychological origins. He cited passages from *Leviathan* directly. For example, Blount repeated Hobbes's saying that ignorance to distinguish dreams and fancies from vision and sense gave rise to the belief in fairies, ghosts, goblins, and witches.[121] Blount followed Hobbes's naturalisation or rather humanisation of religion in order to show that it had come to be nothing but a social convention:

> Mr. *Hobbs* tells us, that in these four things, opinion of Ghosts, ignorance of second causes, Devotion towards what men fear, and taking of things casual for Prognosticks, consisteth the natural Seed of Religion; which by reason of the different Fancies, Judgments, and Passions of several men, hath grown up into Ceremonies so different, that those which are used by one man, seem ridiculous to another.[122]

By 1680, Blount had internalised what he saw as the central tenets of Hobbes's theory of religion and adopted them for his own purposes. This is evident not only in his printed works, but also in his private notes, and this fact validates further how much Blount was indebted to the philosopher that he admired. The most telling evidence is Blount's abovementioned manuscript copy-book, found currently in the library of the Athenaeum Club in London.[123] The copy-book was compiled during the early 1680s, starting from 1681 and at least until 1684, and it contains notes by Blount alongside extracts from an impressive variety of sources of different kinds and in different themes, including Restoration plays, Parliament speeches, and historical and philosophical works, by writers such as Dryden, Bacon, and Hobbes. The contents of the copy-book match Blount's interests in his published works, and especially his support of the Exclusion as well as his deep sense of anticlericalism, where his identification with Hobbes is particularly apparent. The quotations from Hobbes that Blount included in the copy-book are taken from three writings: *Leviathan*, *Decameron physiologicum* (1678), and *Considerations upon the Reputation, &c. of Thomas Hobbes* (1680). Blount probably bought these works in the bookshop of Hobbes's publisher, William Crooke, where he also read the manuscript of *An Historical Narration Concerning Heresie*. As William Bulman has shown, Crooke's shop performed a prominent intellectual and cultural function as an Enlightenment public space where freethinkers and their opponents, motivated by a shared concern for civil peace, were drawn into a learned and polite dialogue. In Crooke's shop, print and scribal publications were sold alongside one another, and Hobbes's works were sold together with the works of Anglican apologists, sometimes even in a single volume. Among these freethinkers, Bulman argues, 'Blount used Crooke's shop to bolster his print library and support his work with illicit manuscripts'.[124]

The recurring theme in the quotations that Blount copied from Hobbes is the attack on the fraudulent priests and the credulous vulgar. For example, Blount paraphrased from Hobbes that 'yᵉ Nonconformist ministers seldome or never preach agst Hypocrisie for fear of setting all their Audience a laughing', while the people 'mistake zeal to their own ends, for zeal to Gods worship'; and Blount's annotation concluded: 'zeal mistaken. vulgar superstition. Religion fals'.[125] Blount also copied Hobbes's historical thesis on the damaging effect of the 'school divinity' and on how pretended philosophers, who were 'a sort of needy, ignorant, impudent cheating fellows', introduced unintelligible philosophy as well as multiple disputes and heresies into Christianity, at which point Blount noted: 'Priests dangerous … consciences ruled. rebellion & religion'.[126]

Thus, Blount demonstrated in his private manuscript what he demonstrated in print, namely, that he had a keen interest in Hobbes's anticlerical thought, including Hobbes's detailed theory of the origins of heresy, which rested on a thorough reading of a good number of Hobbes's writings. At the same time, two annotations in the copy-book departed slightly from this pattern, where Blount noted Hobbes's proofs for God and providence. He cited Hobbes's statement that 'nothing can begin, change, or put an end to its own Motion' and remarked: 'change, motion selfmover. God proved'.[127] Similarly, he copied an extract from *Leviathan* where Hobbes provided the argument from design and noted: 'Providence proved. God asserted. Atheism opposed. Ignorance human'.[128] This is interesting for two reasons: first, because it shows that Blount recognised the complexity in Hobbes's position, namely, that his anticlericalism did not necessarily mean atheism, and second, because this is the same complexity that some deists wished to retain—as lip service if nothing else—while their critics insisted on erasing the differences between deism and atheism.

Having established unequivocally, both in manuscript and in print, the destruction that priests had caused throughout history to religion and society, Blount aspired to suggest solutions for the problems he identified, and it is at this point that he started to formulate his deism more systematically. In 1683 he published *Religio Laici* following Dryden's *Religio Laici* from a year earlier. As we have seen, Dryden's poem was a defence of revealed religion against those who were trying to diminish it in favour of natural religion, namely, the deists. Blount's response to Dryden was, therefore, the first public declaration of deism.[129]

The aim of Blount's *Religio Laici* was 'to assert an *Universal Doctrine*, such as no ways opposeth the Religion Established among us' which would bring about 'the Reconciliation of those *Dissenters* now in *England*, who have of late so disturbed the Quiet of this Realm, and who, under the Pretence of Religion, would exclude all *Governours* but *themselves*'.[130] The problem with which Blount's *Religio Laici* starts is that various religions and sects claim to have access to the exclusive truth about salvation, and they sentence everyone but their followers to future tortures. Blount was of course sceptical about such claims, arguing, as he had done in previous works, that people simply tend to think of their own truths as right and of everyone else's as wrong. This time he suggested a solution, namely, two methods of religious inquiry.[131] The first method, a historical and comparative study of all religions, would be difficult to achieve in practice. Thus, Blount turned to the second: a rational inquiry. Blount followed Herbert of Cherbury's theory of the universal principles of religion, according to which there is one God; God should be worshipped; the best form of worship is virtue, goodness, and piety; repentance is required for our sins; and there is reward and punishment in the afterlife.[132] These common notions supplied helpful materials for Blount's rationalistic attack on organised religion, and in this sense Herbert's work contributed to deism through its appropriation by Blount.[133]

For Blount, any rational inquiry would also entail, of course, freedom of inquiry, even when faced with attempts to supress it: 'in the first place, I should demand in a Rational and Judicial way, how I could be assured, that the *Priests* had received a *Revelation*, and what was the time, place, and manner thereof? In Answer to which, I conceive the *Priests* would tell me; That *Laicks* ought not further to enquire into such *Mysteries* than becomes them'.[134] Blount accused the modern priests of turning '*Religion* into *Faction*, striving to render all others of different Perswasions (though in the least matters) odious' and for being '*Incendiaries*, and *Persecutors* of one another even unto *Death*, for *Religion* and *Conscience* sake'.[135] By advocating a minimal, rational, and moral type of religion, reduced to the practice of goodness and repentance, Blount hoped that there would be less occasion for disagreement and hence less violence between different sects.[136]

Here, too, there are loud echoes of Hobbes. Blount argued that common reason should judge the truth of doctrines, rather than single witnesses from whom 'the greatest *Miracles* in all Vulgar Superstitions are mostly derived'.[137] His sceptical argument that miracles can be pretended 'by *Confederacy*, where one helps the other to abuse the People' is essentially the same one made in *Leviathan*.[138] He also argued that true prophecies should give precise details, otherwise any prediction could be said to be fulfilled 'in some *Time*, *Place*, or *Manner*'.[139] An informed reader would know to recognise Hobbes's tone here.

Thus, at the heart of deism from its very beginning lay a distinctive Hobbesian concern about the danger of religious sectarianism and harsh condemnation of those who use religion as a tool to gain illegitimate political power. Blount's work was disturbing to many precisely because he described religion in the earthly terms of self-interest and pursuit of power. He warned his readers about the dangers that corrupted religion posed to society and hence voiced an alarming call for deep social change. Yet, it is important to note that Blount's radical observations did not necessarily translate in practice into particularly radical politics. Unlike Hobbes, he did not suggest an alternative model, ecclesiastical or political, which would be more stable or peaceful than the existing one. In fact, he explicitly stated— although the truthfulness of this kind of statements is ultimately open to debate—that his goal was not to discredit the existing order.[140]

Hobbes's influence became even clearer in the second work that Blount published in 1683, *Miracles, No Violations of the Laws of Nature*. The message of this work is that the laws of nature are themselves the decree of God and, therefore, there is no reason to believe that God would work above or contrary to them, that is, in the form of miracles. Consequently, one should not look for God's dominion or providence in supernatural phenomena, but rather in the immutable and fixed order of nature, namely, the ordinary course of causes and effects. This argument was copied from the sixth chapter of Spinoza's *Tractatus*, 'Of Miracles'.[141] To that, Blount added other passages from Hobbes, borrowing Hobbes's extreme scepticism towards the possibility of the occurrence of present miracles. For example, Blount inserted a passage from *Leviathan* wherein Hobbes argued that admiration is a function of experience, and therefore phenomena like the eclipses of the sun and the moon were considered miracles only until more knowledge became available.[142] Hence, while relying upon Herbert, Spinoza, and Hobbes, Blount structured his deism as a natural religion combined with a systematic attack on priestcraft. But what did his deism entail precisely?

The most telling answers for what deism meant for Blount in the 1680s come from two manuscripts that were then unpublished. The first, 'A Summary Account of the Deists Religion', is a manuscript that Blount sent to the physician Thomas Sydenham in 1686—it is one of the abovementioned manuscripts that are bound together in the British Library and appear also in the *Oracles of Reason*. Blount was not necessarily the author of this essay but he did sign the dedication to Sydenham, where he wrote:

> The last time I had the happiness of your Company, it was your Request that I would help you to a sight of the Deists Arguments, which I told you, I had sometimes by me, but then had lent them out, they are now return'd me again, and according to my promise I have herewith sent them to you.[143]

Blount added what should have been relatively pleasing for his critics:

> Whereby, you'l only find, that human Reason like a Pitcher with two Ears, may be taken on either side; However, undoubtedly in our Travails to the other World the common Road is the safest; and tho Deism is a good manuring of a mans Conscience, yet certainly if sowed with Christianity it will produce the most profitable Crop.[144]

Deism, therefore, did not have to be at odds with Christianity.

The 'Summary Account' stated the deist's opinion of God: 'Whatsoever is Adorable, Amiable, and Imitable by Mankind, is in one Supream infinite and perfect Being';[145] and so, 'none can accuse the Deist of Idolatry'.[146] The worship of God should not be done by an image nor by sacrifice but rather by imitating God's goodness. Blount's deism was suspicious of mediators and ceremonies, and emphasised the leading of moral lives as the main duty of religion, as well as the obligation to use one's reason constantly: 'If the *Deist* errs, he errs not like a fool but *secundum verbum*, after enquiry'.[147] With regard to the probability of the deist's salvation, the account stated that '[t]he Morality in Religion is above the mystery in it', and therefore one who is good and acts in harmony with nature, God, and one's friends, is safer than 'the credulous Christian that believes Orthodoxly, but lives ill'.[148]

The second manuscript formulates deism in a rather different manner, no less typical of the freethinking spirit: a satire. This manuscript is a ballad, dated to *c.* 1682–1686, and attributed in all likelihood to Blount.[149] The tone of this ballad is humorous and subversive; it is much less polite

than Blount's published works, at times extremely vulgar, but the anticlerical stance is familiar:

> Religion's a Politick Law,
> Devis'd by the Priggs of the Schools;
> To keep the Rabble in awe
> And amuse poor Bigotted Fools.
> ... And therefore in every Towne,
> Ther's a Pimp that wee call a Parson,
> Is order'ed to preach in a Gowne,
> And a Cushion to sett his Arse on.[150]

This militant attack on religion, which highlights its political and social
functions, and especially the dubious interests of the divines and the universities, is already very much in line with the central ideas of Hobbes and
Blount. Several different versions of this manuscript exist; in one of them
Hobbes is mentioned explicitly just after the part that mocks the parsons:

> But the ingenious will not be catch'd
> With such twattles and giggumbobes
> There stuff which is piec'd and pack'd
> Could never choak old father Hobes.[151]

So, Hobbes is cast here as the antithesis of the nonsense that is sold by the
parsons to the masses. This is precisely the historic role that Hobbes wanted
for himself: the liberator who exposed and corrected the errors of the kingdom of darkness. Then, the poem goes on to ridicule many of the biblical
stories, emphasising their sexual aspects and hence the sexual motives of
biblical figures from Adam to David and Solomon. While this outlook is
perhaps more characteristic of libertines such as Rochester, the poem concludes in a way that brings to mind the message of the 'Summary Account'
as well as Blount's *Religio Laici*:

> Let Us lead a Life honest, and Morall;
> One *God*, and one *Cesar* adore;
> And ne're be such Blockheads to quarrell,
> For *Luther*'s, or *Babylon*'s Whore.
> And therefore Sirs, 'tis not amiss
> To take my Advice, though in jest:
> Let's know, what Religion first is;
> And then let us Fight for the best.[152]

It is striking that even this heterodox manuscript, that was clearly more
appropriate for clandestine circulation than for licensed publication, promoted not only a negative criticism of corrupt religion but also a positive
idea of moral religion that could be practised without being a source of

endless bloodshed. Thus, the 'Summary Account' and the 'Satyr' were two manuscripts, in the preparation and circulation of which Blount was certainly a key figure, which addressed deism explicitly. They are especially illuminating because they demonstrate two equally inherent characteristics of English deism that were present both in published and unpublished works: a sarcastic and subversive rhetoric that mocked the very core of organised religion as well as a simple philosophical doctrine that advocated true, pure, and moral religion.

A similar iteration of these ideas can be found in a poem from 1692 by Charles Gildon, who at that point was Blount's close associate and fellow deist. The poem was entitled, tellingly enough, 'The Deist's Plea':

Natural Religion, easie first and Plain;
Tales made it Mystery, Offerings made it gain;
Sacrifices and Feasts were at length prepar'd.
The Priests eat roast Meat, and the People star'd.[153]

Gildon later converted to Anglicanism, influenced by Charles Leslie's *A Short and Easie Method with the Deists* (1698).[154] Yet his poem summarises the ideas of deism precisely as they had been known by the early 1690s: that natural reason is easy and plain, and sufficient; that mystery was added deliberately and unnecessarily to religion; and that priests were enjoying the luxuries of the good life at the expense of the laity. Much of this critique came from Blount—and his reading of Hobbes. These were the first seeds of deism: the new critical, often mocking, and ultimately natural conception of religion that would continue to cause turmoil in England in the following decades.

Blount and politics in the early 1690s

Blount's early substantial political interest was his support of the Exclusion of the Catholic heir, who nevertheless became James II. It was in the name of peace and unity that he argued for the Exclusion, as well as for toleration for Protestants, which, he believed, would serve the public interest, as opposed to private or sectarian interests. Subsequently, as a supporter of the revolution, Blount justified the right of William and Mary to the Crown and defended the conquest. Two texts from the early 1690s on this topic, a printed work and a manuscript, reveal that Blount's reasoning was indebted to Hobbes also in politics, thus demonstrating that Blount's engagement with Hobbes did not end with an admiration of his anticlericalism, and furthermore, that Hobbesian ideas could even be recruited to support Whig causes.

In *King William and Queen Mary, Conquerors* (1693), Blount established the right of William and Mary to rule by conquest. First, he argued
that William and Mary had a just cause for a war against James, whose heir,
Blount attempted to prove, was likely illegitimate. The war was necessary
to save the liberties of all subjects, which otherwise would have been at
risk under the tyrannical reign of James. Second, he argued, once the war
concluded in their favour, William and Mary conquered James and thus
acquired the right to govern. Although this time Blount did not mention
Hobbes by name, he followed the basic Hobbesian argument on the mutual
relationship between protection and obedience, as Warren did: 'It is Loyalty
enough to adhere to a Man's Prince, so long as he defends his Subjects, his
Crown and Dignity'.[155] James had lost his ability to protect the people, and
therefore obedience to him could no longer be justified. On these grounds,
Blount justified allegiance to the new sovereigns in such a case 'when the
conquered Prince is no longer able to maintain his own *Regalia*, and protect
his Subjects'.[156] Furthermore, he explained, it is against the interest of the
subjects, and hence against the good of the community, to refuse an oath
to a new sovereign when the old sovereign evidently ceases to offer protection: 'He that denieth this, makes Allegiance to Governours hold in opposition to the End of Government; and doth in effect say, that Government was
ordained for the sake of Governours, and not for the sake of Societies'.[157]
Blount supported the new sovereigns because they were in a position to
guarantee individual as well as collective safety and thus, unlike the former
sovereign, to promote properly the purpose of government.

The work received considerable attention. Edmund Bohun, the Tory
licenser of the press, who licensed this then-anonymous pamphlet for publication, was dismissed and imprisoned, and the book was condemned to be
burnt. The licensing act, which was renewed in the same year, finally lapsed
in 1695. This was possibly a trap that Blount set to his rival, but even if it
was not his intention, the scandal that followed the publication of this work
left Blount's name connected to the historic lapse of the act against which
he wrote and which was aimed at supressing heterodox works much like
his own.[158]

The second work that Blount wrote on the matter was a manuscript
poem, entitled 'A Dialogue between K.W. and the Late K.J. on the Banks
of the *Boyn*, the Day before the Battel'. The poem was included in the collection *The Miscellaneous Works of Charles Blount*, which was edited by
Charles Gildon and published in 1695, two years after Blount's death.[159]
The exact date of the manuscript is not certain. It was circulated in various
versions, either before or after its publication in the *Miscellaneous Works*,
and one of these versions is dated to 1690.[160] The poem's message is close
to the argument of *King William and Queen Mary, Conquerors* as well as

to Blount's earlier *Appeal from the Country to the City*. In this dialogue between William and James, William's lines emphasise the idea that James, who sided with the French and the priests, put the safety of the nation at risk and lost his right to the throne:

> If *Right divine* does e'r to *Crowns* belong,
> They lose that *Right*, when once the *Kings* do wrong.
> … Nor can you here a *Parent's Right* pretend,
> Since *Publick Safety* knows *no Private* Friend.[161]

In addition to James's wrongdoing, Blount repeated the argument that William became the rightful sovereign once he, and not James, could offer protection to the subjects. William's concluding lines are particularly Hobbesian, starting with the origins of the sovereign power:

> When *Free-born Men* (by Providence design'd
> Both to preserve, and propagate their Kind)
> Did first their Brutish Appetites pursue,
> And Force alone was all the *Law* they knew;
> When *Sense* was Guardian, and when *Reason* Young,
> 'Twas then the Weak submitted to the Strong.[162]

And the upshot:

> For he who cou'd *Protect*, and Conquest bring,
> Was from a Captain *ripen'd* to a *King*.[163]

To sum up, for Blount, as for Hobbes, protection legitimated sovereignty and thus justified obedience. To be sure, this idea is not solely Hobbesian—Grotius's influence, too, might come to mind—but considering Blount's thorough knowledge of Hobbes's theory, we can at least assume that he was inspired by him on this point. By using Hobbes's logic to justify the revolution and the conquest, Blount's case shows that Hobbesian ideas could even be used to defend Whig causes, in manuscript as well as in print. Furthermore, this case shows that the impact that Hobbes had on the radicals of the late seventeenth century went beyond the theological sphere, like Warren and his multi-layered appreciation of Hobbes. In this sense, if Henry Stubbe was a Hobbesian Independent, we may describe Warren and Blount as Hobbesian Whigs.[164]

The *Oracles* and the critics of deism

Blount's most significant contribution to deism, and his most significant defence of Hobbes, was undoubtedly the *Oracles of Reason,* which was published in 1693, the year of Blount's premature death. There Blount's admiration for Hobbes finally became public and explicit, as indicated by its full title, namely, *Oracles of Reason ... In Several Letters to Mr. Hobbs and Other Persons of Eminent Quality, and Learning*. The *Oracles* included the letter that Blount had sent to Hobbes in 1678, but this is not the only place where he paid respect to Hobbes. Another example is found in the first letter in this collection, which Blount wrote to Gildon in 1693. This letter is a defence of Thomas Burnet's *Archaeologiae philosophicae* (1692), long extracts from which are also included in the *Oracles*, and especially a defence of Burnet's controversial treatment of Moses. For example, Blount supported Burnet's thesis that Moses had told the story of the creation in a popular way that would be easy for most people to understand. Having touched on the topic of the Pentateuch—the first five books of the bible, supposedly authored by Moses—Blount mentioned the 'late and great Modern Philosopher of this Nation', according to whom 'It is not an Argument sufficient to prove those Books were written by *Moses*, because they are call'd the Five Books of *Moses*'.[165] Blount repeated the arguments and examples given by Hobbes in *Leviathan* to question Moses' authorship, for example, the claim that the section on Moses' sepulchre must have been written after his death.[166] Blount explained that his use of Hobbes at that point was designed to show that Burnet

> is not the first that has had scruples in this kind, and that he may well make an Enquiry into the Truth of some Passages of the History, when the very Historians themselves are so much doubted of by others; not but that we may pay a just deference to the Church, and yet at the same time raise scruples for information sake, the better to arm our selves against our Antagonists.[167]

The 'scruples' of Burnet and Hobbes served Blount's main goal, which was to free men to make inquiries on their own, even on the most fundamental and sacred topics. Furthermore, the point was that biblical stories were written as they were in order to be comprehended by ordinary people, but that the issues that they describe, such as the creation of the world, nevertheless could and should be studied in depth. It is for this reason that Blount believed, as we have seen, that although the deists might err, they would not err like fools.

Hobbes clearly inspired Blount's scepticism and anticlericalism, as well as his approach to the scripture and the way he treated it as a historical document and a human work. Hence, Blount recruited Hobbes for his cause, even if Hobbes's claims were sometimes not as explicit as Blount's. He took the issues that were raised by Hobbes and others further, developing his critical thinking through them. In some cases, Blount did not have to radicalise Hobbes but simply to follow him and Spinoza where they had already been radical enough, as with the case of the Pentateuch. In these instances,

Blount was simply a transmitter of ideas and, as his critics recognised, quite an efficient one.

The *Oracles* became the most notorious deistic tract of the early 1690s, provoking numerous responses by outraged Anglicans. The critics of the emerging deism did not miss the links to Hobbes. Sometimes they emphasised these links to discredit deism through association with Hobbes, or alternatively, to use deism to discredit Hobbes. These links were perhaps made most clearly in the Boyle Lectures that were established already in 1692 especially 'for proving the Christian Religion against notorious Infidels, viz. *Atheists, Deists, Pagans, Jews* and *Mahometans*'.[168] These lectures were established at the request of Robert Boyle in his will to address the increasing attack on Christianity, as it was perceived in the eyes of the anxious Anglican divines. The inaugural series of lectures was given by the classical scholar Richard Bentley, who was concerned with the public rise of atheism in England. Bentley's first sermon addressed 'The Folly of Atheism, and (What Is Now Called) Deism', wherein he asserted:

> There are some Infidels among us, that not only disbelieve the *Christian* Religion; but oppose the assertions of *Providence*, of the *Immorality* of the Soul, of an Universal *Judgment* to come, and of any *Incorporeal* Essence: and yet to avoid the odious name of *Atheists*, would shelter and skreen themselves under a new one of *Deists*, which is not quite so obnoxious.[169]

For Bentley, as for most critics, the modern deists were nothing short of atheists. Although the deists did acknowledge the existence of God, they did so merely for practical reasons, namely, 'to decline the publick *odium*, and resentment of the Magistrate'.[170] This was a commonplace attack, but now it came from the heart of the Anglican establishment. Hobbes, too, was regularly subjected to attacks in the Boyle Lectures. Bentley, for instance, attacked his political motivation: 'there was hope, that the Doctrine of absolute uncontroulable Power and the formidable name of *Leviathan* might flatter and bribe the Government into a *toleration of Infidelity*'.[171] Not only were Hobbes's ideas the driving force behind the spreading of the new forms of atheism and deism, but his political theory aimed to make them the rule of the nation.[172]

Many critics made the case that the deists were simply atheists who found a different name for themselves, and that Hobbes, Spinoza, and Blount belonged to the same family of modern atheists. A work that was published in 1693 under the title *The Second Spira*, for example, described the miseries of a man who fell into atheism and then to melancholy: 'Oh unhappy Time when first I imbib'd these Atheistical Principles! When first I exchanged the Christian Faith for the Creed of *Spinoza* and the *Leviathan*! When first I relinquisht all *reveal'd Religion* for the *natural one*, and the *last* for *none at all*.[173] In 1695, Charles Leslie attacked the heterodox views of John Tillotson, archbishop of Canterbury, together with Blount, Gilbert Burnet, and Robert Howard's *History of Religion* (1694), a work which belonged to the genre of priestcraft history. Over all of these writers loomed Hobbes. For Leslie, Tillotson prioritised worldly peace over religion, and his sermons were 'all the Genuine effects of *Hobbism* which loosens the Notions of Religion, takes from it all that is *Spiritual*, Ridicules whatever is called *Supernatural*; it reduces *God* to *Matter*, and *Religion* to *Nature*'.[174] This, Leslie declared, led this new school 'to call in question all *Revelation*; to turn *Genesis*, &c. into a meer *Romance*, to Ridicule the whole as *Blunt*, *Gildon*, and others of the Doctor's Disciples have done in Print'.[175] The outcome was bleak:

> They now cry there is nothing but *Natural Religion*. All that which is called *Revealed*, is at most but Gods Compliance with the *Superstition* of the vulgar, and what does that concern Men of Wit and Sense? Since Religion has no deeper a Root, what Reverence, what Veneration is due to it? All the *Ordinances* and *Constitutions* of the *Law* and *Gospel* are but *Poiticks* to secure *Government* and the threatenings even of *Hell* it self are no more, and therefore, there is no *necessity*, no *certainty* that they will be inflicted ... Thus to the *Deists* Triumph![176]

In response to Leslie and to a similar attack by Francis Atterbury, future bishop of Rochester, Robert Howard wrote a *Twofold Vindication*. Howard reacted to the charge of Hobbism, arguing that it was plainly a rhetorical tool, a ready-made inflammatory label used for political purposes: 'it may be, we shall find that all this Cry about Socinianism, Hobbism and Irreligion, is nothing but this; that they are Charges, very fit for a *Jacobite* to lay to a *Williamite*, because they are black enough'.[177] Hobbism was simply one of 'the worst Names, that we can now give' and it is for this reason—regardless of its actual meaning—that this slur was weaponised.[178] Howard defended Hobbes while leaving some distance between them: *Leviathan* was 'a very ill Book' but the Epistle Dedicatory—wherein Hobbes stated: 'I am a man that love my own opinions, and think all true I say'—was 'ingenious and honest', and not as prideful as Atterbury had argued.[179] Like Hobbes and unlike his opponents, Howard stated that he could 'indulge a peaceable good Subject to differ from him, and enjoy the present Parliamentary Liberty of Conscience, without envying or censuring him'.[180] Furthermore, whereas Atterbury had called Hobbes the 'great Leader of the Libertines of this Age', Howard corrected some wrong and heretical notions attributed to Hobbes, insisting for example that '*Hobbs* openly professes that our Saviour is both God and Man'.[181] He concluded: 'I have taken Pains to vindicate *Hobbs* [who has Faults enough to answer for, without being unjustly charg'd] from these particular unjust Charges, that the Reader may understand how convenient it is, to imitate the noble *Beraeans*, and examine carefully, whether all those things are true which are sometimes told them *è Cathedrâ*'.[182] Whoever wanted to study Hobbes truly—and freely—would find in his writings positions that were much more complex than what Hobbism commonly signified.

Howard presented a similarly hesitant yet significant defence of deism, another much abused label. While Atterbury and others made no distinction between atheism and deism, Howard insisted that there was indeed a difference: 'Is a Deist quite as bad as an Atheist? ... He that from his Heart sincerely believes there is a God, and that he is a Rewarder, cannot be a very wicked Man, tho it is to be confess'd, he cannot be so good as a true Christian'.[183] Howard exposed in a Hobbesian fashion the interests behind the labels—strikingly this included the label of Hobbism—and he accused his opponent that 'he seems to have reason to make Deism and Atheism of equal respect: So that every one is concluded an Atheist that is not of the Doctor's Opinion', especially regarding the Trinity.[184] Blount, for example, was not necessarily an atheist 'but a Deist' and his work was not without merit: 'If Mr. *Blount* meant thrô the Heathen Sacrifices, to wound those of Moses, he is to be condemn'd for it; but this thing he says well, that *the Heathen Sacrifices ought no more to be spar'd, for their Resemblance to the Sacrifice of* Moses*, than a Criminal ought to be pardon'd for wearing the same colour'd Garments as the Judg*'.[185] Howard generally agreed with Blount that sacrifice was an invention—although he thought that its corruption had been more gradual than Blount did—and more importantly, that priestcraft played a decisive role in the advancement of sacrifice and idolatry.[186] As Jeffrey Collins concludes, in the *Twofold Vindication* 'Hobbes and Howard were thus cast as advocates of "a sober Liberty of philosophizing and prophesying", and Atterbury as a rebellious inquisitor'.[187] The deists were unmistakably closer to the former than to the latter.

Some years later, Josiah King published an answer to the *Oracles*, aimed at atheism and deism in general. King identified the explicit and implicit debts to Hobbes and attacked Blount accordingly. With regard to questioning the authorship of the Pentateuch, King attributed this tradition which is 'now so much valued' first to Ibn Ezra, and then to '*Hobbs, Spinosa*, and other such Politicians in Mr. *Blount*'s Commonwealth of Learning'.[188] It was precisely this commonwealth, represented by Blount, which the Anglicans were so worried about towards the end of the seventeenth century.[189]

Therefore, many of the critics thought that most of the deists were in fact atheists who were hiding behind a more sophisticated facade. They wished to expose them, and this led to a combined attack on atheism, deism, and Hobbism. The attacks on Hobbes and deism emphasised the influence of Hobbes's work upon the emergence of deism. The complexity of both Hobbes and deism was reduced in a way that clearly served the rhetorical goals of their opponents, as Howard pointed out exceptionally. The critics seem to have been successful in dismissing Hobbes and deism together through the association with atheism. But there was one more consequence. The attacks on Hobbes and deism kept the debates on both of them going, providing them with extensive exposure.[190] Perhaps the critics even drew the attention of the radicals to the overlap with some Hobbesian ideas. Moreover, the exposure could allow a reader who wished to consider deism seriously to do so and allow the deists themselves to engage with new arguments and develop their own theories respectively. In this sense, deism developed in a dialectical way, and Hobbes had a central role in this development. The deists were forced by their critics to react to the association between them and Hobbes, which they did in various ways, one of which was simply to embrace Hobbes as one of their own.

Blount took his own life in August 1693 after he could not marry the sister of his deceased wife. Gildon, who had a central role in editing and publishing Blount's work after his death, defended the suicide and provided a telling description of Blount's views: 'he kept all profane Notions of God at a Distance, and prefer'd those writ by the finger of the Almighty Creator in the minds of all mankind, to the *Obscure, unintelligible,* and *impious* Doctrines, devis'd by men to serve some turn or particular *Faction* or *Nation*'.[191] Blount, arguably the first public deist in England and Hobbes's proudest disciple, is still extremely underappreciated in today's scholarship, but it was much thanks to his work that the 1690s was the decade of the 'deist controversy', and the numerous responses to his works reflected a growing anxiety about this new and sophisticated form of heresy. Hobbes was present in all of these debates, in the writings that generated the scandal as well as in the attacks upon them.

There are many deists in all parts of the world

In the early 1690s, English deism existed mainly in Blount's circle, or his 'scribal community', in the London coffeehouses and bookstores, and in the minds of anxious clergymen. Nevertheless, there is some evidence to suggest that by that time deism had started to emerge beyond these sites and that Hobbes was an important source for deism also in its unpublished appearances. The case of James Boevey (1622–1696) offers a rare glimpse into a different kind of site of clandestine deism. Boevey was a merchant and lawyer of Dutch descent, and as a philosopher, his writings concentrated on 'active philosophy', practical knowledge on negotiating the challenges of life. He wrote on a wide variety of issues ranged from the 'government' of friendship, enmity, and love, to the 'government' of lawsuits, reputation, and secrecy; from 'The Causes of the Diseases of the Mind' to 'The Art of Preserving Wealth'.[192] Remarkably, though, except for one work on Machiavelli, all of his writings remained unpublished. Perhaps as a result of that, he is largely unknown today, and his work has started to be recovered only recently by Mark Knights.[193] While it seems clear that Boevey aimed to have some readership, Knights suggests, his work might have been intended for manuscript circulation, which is perhaps what enabled him to express his views more freely, especially with regard to religion. Boevey was apparently not part of a particular intellectual milieu, but he was not completely disconnected from the circles that this book discusses: Aubrey, for example, read his work and appreciated him as 'ever a great lover of Naturall Philosophie', and he was similarly praised by Sir Kenelm Digby, the natural philosopher and courtier who was also Hobbes's friend.[194]

Boevey's four tracts on deism were written in 1694. The treatises are found in the papers of the Cowper family in Hertfordshire, who were known as freethinking if not libertine Whigs. The diarist Sarah Cowper, perhaps the least radical in the family, was especially fond of Clifford, whose *Treatise of Humane Reason* was an important milestone in the debate on rational religion.[195] Boevey's approach to religion can be described as rational and anticlerical, very close to Blount's, and like Stubbe, he was interested in the life of Muhammad. Furthermore, the fact that he addressed deism explicitly in these texts—one for example was entitled 'The Deists' Reflections on Religion'—makes him the second known writer in England, after Blount, who identified himself with deism, even though and perhaps precisely because it was not in print. Indeed, these tracts were at least as radical as Blount's, if not more. For example, Boevey wrote against the 'Biggottism' of the priests who exploited human fears and ignorance and used miracles and prophesies as tools to supress the reason of the multitude and increase their own power. He advocated, instead, a religion that relies on one's reason and that could be summed up in the five universal notions. He thus supported a notion of a providential God who is manifested in nature, and he believed that worship consisted in piety, virtue, and charity, indeed a very similar doctrine to what we have seen in the 'Summary Account'.[196]

Especially interesting is Boevey's manuscript on 'The Character of the Deist or Theist', where he developed some of these themes and had explicit debts to Hobbes.[197] Boevey started the tract with the interesting statement that 'There are many Deists in all Parts of the World': these are people who 'refuse to believe Priests cheats' and 'are mostly well natur'd, rational people and would not perhaps be Deists did they not find such grosse Absurdities in other sorts of Religions'. Boevey's intriguing defence of deism could indicate

that there were people, like himself, who actually started to think of themselves as deists. Boevey's deists were 'men who do good by Impulse of their
Natural religion, honesty and good conscience'. It was at this point that
Boevey quoted Hobbes's treatment of God as the spirit agitating 'mighty
matter'. The reference to Hobbes is notable due to the proximity to the
description of the good-natured deists and due to the fact that Boevey was
otherwise reluctant to admit the influence of other authors.[198] Furthermore,
this reference is striking because this was not simply a caricatured Hobbist
position but what seems to be a well-informed interpretation of Hobbes's
account of God as an all-encompassing corporeal spirit.[199]

Subsequently, Boevey discussed the laws of nature and their harmony
with the laws of morality, arguing for example that 'Do as you would be
done by' is a natural law. For Boevey, the natural law is intelligible and
rational, imprinted even 'in the most ignorant mind, that without any
instruction it may read & understand'. This view seems to be compatible
with the other areas of his philosophy, wherein he encouraged a prudential conduct in the world, assuming the sufficiency of human rationality.
It is also similar to Hobbes's idea in *Leviathan* that the natural law is
intelligible to all through the easy formula of the golden rule, although
Boevey seems to have believed that men were more naturally virtuous
than what Hobbes granted.[200] Due to this deistic emphasis on reason and
nature, miracles which did not correspond to the laws of nature and hence
to reason were to be rejected as 'ridiculous and absurd'. Thus, Boevey cast
doubt on miracles in a similar manner to *Miracles, No Violations*: 'the
doctrines attested in miracles lye in heaps & confusion, & if such things
are related for miracles, why do they not still continue'. Furthermore, he
suspected the human motives of those who claimed to have had revelation. In this context he was evidently Hobbesian. He inserted a quote
from Hobbes when he argued that 'to say that a man has had a vision,
or heard a voice, is to say that he dreamt between sleeping and waking',
and added, paraphrasing Hobbes, that 'There is no greater argument of
madness than the arrogating to a mans self inspiration'.[201] Finally, scripture itself became a tool of priestcraft: 'the bible hangs at every girdle
too near the sword, which animates to kill and persecute, contrary to the
dictates of charity, & only conforme to ambition, covetousnesse &
revenge'.

If the anti-scriptural man of the 1670s turned into the deist of the 1690s,
then Boevey was precisely it. His unpublished manuscripts, written before
the lapse of the licensing act in 1695, were probably circulated, and are
therefore a highly valuable source that shows what free writing on deism
looked like. Boevey's manuscripts, then, seem to confirm the story that also
started to emerge in print and that the critics witnessed nervously: a story

of a fundamental challenge to the politics of religion that was gathering momentum in England, and in which Hobbes was consistently acknowledged as a key character.

Notes

1 Quoted in P. Bayle, *The Dictionary Historical and Critical of Mr Peter Bayle*, 2nd edn, 5 vols (London, 1734–1738), vol. 5, p. 482.

2 Ibid.

3 See also Leland, *A View of the Principal Deistical Writers*, pp. 2–3.

4 J. Nichols, *An Order of Houshold Instruction* (London, 1595), sig. E7r.

5 R. Burton, *The Anatomy of Melancholy. Volume 3: Text*, ed. T. C. Faulkner, N. K. Kiessling, and R. L. Blair (Oxford, 1994), pp. 400–401.

6 C. J. Betts, *Early Deism in France* (The Hague, 1984), esp. pp. 6–15, 90.

7 T. Sprat, *The History of the Royal-Society of London, for the Improving of Natural Knowledge* (London, 1667), p. 22.

8 M. Casaubon, *A Letter of Meric Casaubon D.D. &c. to Peter du Moulin* (Cambridge, 1669), p. 17. See also Serjeantson, 'Herbert of Cherbury before Deism', p. 228; Malcolm, *Aspects of Hobbes*, pp. 333–34.

9 E. Herbert, *De veritate*, trans. M. H. Carré (Bristol, 1937), p. 291. Among the five common notions are that there is a God, who must be worshipped, and that there is reward and punishment after this life; see 'Deism formulated' in this chapter.

10 This article has the virtue of being relatively easy: 'For if an inward assent of the mind to all the Doctrines concerning Christian Faith now taught (whereof the greatest part are disputed,) were necessary to Salvation, there would be nothing in the world so hard, as to be a Christian'. Lev 43, pp. 938–40.

11 Malcolm, *Aspects of Hobbes*, pp. 472–84; quoted on pp. 478, 481.

12 Hobbes, *The Correspondence of Thomas Hobbes*, ed. N. Malcolm, 2 vols (Oxford, 1994), vol. 1, p. 32.

13 C. Wolseley, *The Reasonableness of Scripture-Belief. A Discourse Giving Some Account of Those Rational Grounds upon Which the Bible Is Received as the Word of God* (London, 1672), sig. A4r.

14 Ibid. See also Parkin, *Taming the Leviathan*, p. 305.

15 Wolseley, *Reasonableness of Scripture-Belief*, p. 68.

16 Ibid., p. 69.

17 P. Harth, *Contexts of Dryden's Thought* (Chicago, 1968), pp. 109–13, makes this assessment based on the fact that this text was written following Wolseley's *Reasonableness of Scripture-Belief* (1672) and probably before J. Dryden, *Religio Laici: Or, a Layman's Faith. A Poem* (London, 1682).

18 Tracts on Religion, British Library, 873.b.3; Harth, *Contexts of Dryden's Thought*, p. 84. The manuscripts include two letters from Blount to Hobbes and Rochester as well as 'A Summary Account of the Deists Religion', all of which are discussed below.

19 C. Blount, *The Oracles of Reason … In Several Letters to Mr. Hobbs and Other Persons of Eminent Quality, and Learning* (London, 1693), p. 195.

20 Ibid., p. 196.

21 Ibid., p. 198.

22 E. Stillingfleet, *A Letter to a Deist, in Answer to Several Objections Against the Truth and Authority of the Scriptures* (London, 1677), sig. A3r. The letter is dated 11 June 1675. Stillingfleet might have referred to Spinoza, whose *Tractatus* was published anonymously five years earlier in the Netherlands. See also Israel, *Radical Enlightenment*, p. 603.

23 Dryden, *Religio Laici*, sig. a1v.

24 Ibid., sig. a2r.

25 Ibid., p. 11.

26 Harth, *Context of Dryden's Thought*, esp. pp. 80–94.

27 C. Blount, *Religio Laici Written in a Letter to John Dryden, Esq.* (London, 1683).

28 T. A., *Religio Clerici* (London, 1681), p. 113.

29 G. Rust and H. Hallywell, *A Discourse of the Use of Reason in Matters of Religion: Shewing, That Christianity Contains Nothing Repugnant to Right Reason; Against Enthusiasts and Deists* (London, 1683), sig. a1r.

30 Ibid., sigs. a1r–a1v.

31 W. Assheton, *An Admonition to a Deist* (London, 1685), esp. pp. 8, 22, 38.

32 G. Tarantino, 'Clifford, Martin (c. 1624–1677), Headmaster and Author', *ODNB* (2004), available at: www.oxforddnb.com/view/10.1093/ref:odnb/9780198614128.001.0001/odnb-9780198614128-e-5656/version/0 (accessed 21 July 2023). See also Tarantino, 'Martin Clifford and His *Treatise of Humane Reason* (1674): A Europe-Wide Debate', in R. Savage (ed.), *Philosophy and Religion in Enlightenment Britain: New Case Studies* (Oxford, 2012), pp. 9–28.

33 M. Clifford, *A Treatise of Humane Reason* (London, 1674), p. 14.

34 Ibid., pp. 90–91.

35 G. Villiers, second duke of Buckingham, *The Second Volume of Miscellaneons* [sic] *Works*, ed. T. Brown (London, 1705), p. 67.

36 Clifford, *A Treatise of Humane Reason*, pp. 36–40.

37 Ibid., pp. 45–47.

38 Hobbes, *On the Citizen*, ed. and trans. R. Tuck and M. Silverthorne (Cambridge, 1998), 15.17, p. 183. Tarantino, 'Martin Clifford', p. 18n60, mentions that Clifford seems to have translated the passage from *De cive* himself.

39 Clifford, *A Treatise of Humane Reason*, pp. 49–51.

40 A. M., *Plain-Dealing, or, a Full and Particular Examination of a Late Treatise, Entituled, Humane Reason* (London, 1675), p. 73.

41 Ibid., pp. 75–76.

42 W. [Howell], *The Spirit of Prophecy* (London, 1679), sigs. A3r–A3v.

43 Ibid., p. 199. Cf. Clifford, *A Treatise of Humane Reason*, pp. 45–46. See also Bulman, 'Hobbes's Publisher', p. 358; Collins, *In the Shadow of Leviathan*, pp. 214–16.

44 [Howell], *Spirit of Prophecy*, pp. 197–204, 214–22.

45 B. Worden, *The Rump Parliament 1648–53* (Cambridge, 1974), p. 111.

46 Cf. Lev, 'A Review, and Conclusion', p. 1141. See also S. State, *Thomas Hobbes and the Debate over Natural Law and Religion* (New York, 1991), pp. 128–29; Skinner, *Visions of Politics*, vol. 3, p. 276; Parkin, *Taming the Leviathan*, pp. 128–29.
47 A. Warren, *The Royalist Reform'd* (London, 1650).
48 A. Warren, *Eight Reasons Categorical: Wherein Is Examined and Proved, That It's Probable, the Law-Common Will Stand* (London, 1653), p. 5.
49 J. R. Jacob, *Henry Stubbe: Radical Protestantism and the Early Enlightenment* (Cambridge, 1983), pp. 141–43; Tarantino, 'Martin Clifford', p. 23.
50 A. Warren, *An Apology for the Discourse of Humane Reason* (London, 1680), 'Preface' (unnumbered).
51 Ibid.
52 Lev 4., p. 58.
53 Lev 46, p. 1052.
54 Warren, *Apology*, 'Preface' (unnumbered).
55 Ibid., p. 4.
56 For example, ibid., p. 73.
57 Ibid., p. 17.
58 Hobbes, *English Works*, vol. 4, p. 387.
59 Warren, *Apology*, p. 97.
60 Blount, *Oracles of Reason*, p. 97.
61 Warren, *Apology*, p. 74.
62 Ibid., p. 83.
63 Ibid., p. 80.
64 Lev 39, pp. 732–34.
65 Warren, *Apology*, p. 84.
66 Ibid., pp. 80–81.
67 Lev 47, p. 1116.
68 Lev 47, p. 1116. See 'Hobbes's art of pulling down the churches' in the Introduction for prominent accounts on Hobbes and toleration.
69 *Leviathan* was first used to support toleration already in the early 1650s, when the lawyer John Austin inserted quotes from Hobbes selectively to make the case for toleration for Catholics in England (ironically, given Hobbes's explicit anti-Catholicism). See W. Birchley [J. Austin], *The Christian Moderator* (London, 1651), p. 12; Birchley, *The Christian Moderator. Third Part* (London, 1653), p. 21; Parkin, *Taming the Leviathan*, pp. 101–102, 129–30.
70 Warren, *Apology*, p. 142.
71 M. Dzelzainis, 'Albertus Warren on Milton and Toleration: An Unnoticed Allusion', *Notes and Queries*, 46:3 (1999), pp. 335–36.
72 Jacob, *Henry Stubbe*, p. 141.
73 Similar arguments for prudential toleration, that is, toleration for the sake of a quiet and ordered society, were made by figures such as Andrew Marvell and even Buckingham himself. See J. Parkin, 'Liberty Transpros'd: Andrew Marvell and Samuel Parker', in W. Chernaik and M. Dzelzainis (eds), *Marvell and Liberty* (Basingstoke, 1999), pp. 269–99; Parkin, *Taming the Leviathan*,

pp. 242–44, 300, but also A. Marvell, *The Prose Works*, eds M. Dzelzainis and A. M. Patterson, 2 vols (New Haven, 2003), vol. 1, pp. 212–13, arguing that Marvell actually separated himself from Hobbes. Marvell was once identified, most probably wrongly, as A. M., the author of *Plain-Dealing*. See Dzelzainis, 'Albertus Warren on Milton and Toleration', p. 335n3.

74 Warren, *Apology*, pp. 116–17.

75 Ibid., p. 117.

76 Ibid.

77 Ibid., p. 118.

78 Ibid.

79 Ibid., p. 66. In *Leviathan*, Hobbes defined: 'In Deliberation, the last Appetite, or Aversion, immediately adhaering to the action, or to the omission thereof, is that wee call the WILL'. Lev 6, p. 92. In the correspondence with Bramhall, Hobbes endorsed the idea that the will is the last dictate of the understanding, to which Bramhall objected fiercely. Hobbes clarified that the will 'followeth the last opinion of the goodness or evilness of the object, be the opinion true or false'. Hobbes, *English Works*, vol. 5, pp. 76–77, and pp. 316–17, 323.

80 Blount, *Oracles of Reason*, p. 206.

81 Further support for this hypothesis is found in Jacob, *Henry Stubbe*, p. 141; D. Wilson, 'Reading Restoration Freethought: Charles Blount's Impious Learning' (Unpublished PhD thesis, London, 2003), pp. 182–92.

82 For a common dismissal of Blount as a 'hack', see for example Mintz, *Hunting of Leviathan*, pp. 147–48, but for an apt appreciation of his work and significance, and especially of his centrality in the reading culture of freethinking circles, see for example Harth, *Contexts of Dryden's Thought*, pp. 91–92; J. A.Redwood, 'Charles Blount, Deism, and English Free Thought', *Journal of the History of Ideas*, 35:3 (1974), pp. 490–98; Wilson, 'Reading Restoration Freethought'.

83 C. Leslie, *A Short and Easie Method with the Deists* (London, 1698), pp. xii–xvi.

84 Blount, *Anima Mundi, or, an Historical Narration of the Opinions of the Ancients Concerning Man's Soul after This Life* (London, 1679). See also Hobbes, *Correspondence*, vol. 2, p. 791; D. Pfanner, 'Blount, Charles (1654–1693), Freethinker and Author', *ODNB* (2004), available at: www.oxforddnb.com/view/10.1093/ref:odnb/9780198614128.001.0001/odnb-9780198614128-e-2684 (accessed 21 July 2023).

85 Hobbes, *Correspondence*, vol. 2, p. 759. See also in Blount, *Oracles of Reason*, pp. 97–105.

86 Hobbes, *Correspondence*, vol. 2, p. 759.

87 Hobbes, *Correspondence*, vol. 2, p. 763.

88 Hobbes, *Correspondence*, vol. 2, p. 762. See also J. R. Collins, 'Thomas Hobbes's Ecclesiastical History', in Martinich and Hoekstra (eds), *Oxford Handbook of Hobbes*, pp. 520–44, esp. pp. 541–42.

89 Hobbes, *Correspondence*, vol. 2, p. 759.

90 Hobbes, *The Elements of Law: Natural and Politic*, ed. F. Tönnies (Cambridge, 1928), 'Epistle Dedicatory', p. xvii.

91 Lev 11, p. 158.

92 When Parliament discussed measures of response to dissenters in March 1668, this Hobbesian idea was quoted by MP Edward Seymour, at the time an advocate of toleration. The debate was on 'Abuses committed by several persons, in interrupting and disturbing of Ministers in their Churches, and holding Meetings of their own'. It started with the Anglican Edmund Wyndham suggesting that the solution was 'to enforce these assembling people, of all sorts and sects, to be quiet'. In a fierce response, Seymour referred to 'the strictness of the institution of the Spanish Inquisition' as 'one of the greatest causes of the decay of that Monarchy', adding: 'Mr Hobbes says, That when reason is against a man, a man is against reason—Why should we proceed in a way, that answers not our end?' Seymour continued to speak out against the persecution of dissenters in a rather Hobbesian tone: "'tis said, that they are outrageous against Churchmen; if they have offended against law, let them be punished by law'. A. Grey, *Debates of the House of Commons from the Year 1667 to the Year 1694*, 10 vols (London, 1763), vol. 1, pp. 103–104. See also Tuck, 'Hobbes and Locke on Toleration', p. 159; Parkin, *Taming the Leviathan*, p. 243; Parkin, 'Baiting the Bear', pp. 445–46.

93 Blount, *Anima Mundi*, sig. A2r.

94 Blount, *Oracles of Reason*, p. 156. On Rochester, Blount, and Hobbes, see S. Ellenzweig, *The Fringes of Belief: English Literature, Ancient Heresy, and the Politics of Freethinking, 1660–1760* (Stanford, 2008), pp. 31–51.

95 N. Matar (ed.), *Henry Stubbe and the Beginnings of Islam: The Originall & Progress of Mahometanism* (New York, 2013); J. Champion, 'Legislators, Impostors, and the Politic Origins of Religion: English Theories of "Imposture" from Stubbe to Toland', in S. Berti, F. Charles-Daubert, and R. H. Popkin (eds), *Heterodoxy, Spinozism, and Free-Thought in Early-Eighteenth-Century Europe: Studies on the Traité des Trois Imposteurs* (Dordrecht, 1996), pp. 333–56.

96 Jacob, *Henry Stubbe*, pp. 64–77.

97 Ibid., pp. 8–24, 143. See also Parkin, *Taming the Leviathan*, pp. 171–76.

98 Blount, *An Appeal from the Country to the City, for the Preservation of His Majesties Person, Liberty, Property, and the Protestant Religion* (London, 1679), p. 24.

99 Ibid., p. 4.

100 Ibid., pp. 27–28. Cf. G. Burnet, *The History of the Reformation of the Church of England. The First Part, of the Progress Made in It During the Reign of K. Henry the VIII* (London, 1679), pp. 257–64.

101 For another probable source of this work, see P. Kewes, '"The Idol of State Innovators and Republicans": Robert Persons's *A Conference About the Next Succession* (1594/5) in Stuart England', in P. Kewes and A. McRae (eds), *Stuart Succession Literature: Moments and Transformations* (Oxford, 2018), pp. 149–85, on pp. 174–75.

102 For example, he cited Milton's well-known assertion that 'You had almost as good kill a Man, as a good Book; for he that kills a Man, kills but a Reasonable Creature, Gods Image: Whereas he that destroys a good Book, kills Reason it self, which is as it were the very Eye of God'. Blount, *A Just Vindication of Learning, or, an Humble Address to the High Court of Parliament in behalf of the Liberty of the Press by Philopatris* (London, 1679), p. 3. Cf. J. Milton, *Areopagitica* (London, 1644), p. 4. See also Blount, *Reasons Humbly Offered for the Liberty of Unlicens'd Printing* (London, 1693).

103 J. Peacey, R. G. Ingram and A. W. Barber, 'Freedom of Speech in England and the Anglophone World, 1500–1850', in R. G. Ingram, J. Peacey, and A. W. Barber (eds), *Freedom of speech, 1500–1850* (Manchester, 2020), pp. 1–27, on p. 16.

104 Blount, *Oracles of Reason*, p. 97; Blount, *A Just Vindication*, p. 15.

105 Blount, *A Just Vindication*, pp. 15–16.

106 Ibid., p. 11. Cf. Milton, *Areopagitica*, p. 24.

107 Lev 46, p. 1100.

108 Lev 46, p. 1096.

109 For a recent study of the relationship between Hobbes and Galileo, see G. Baldin, *Hobbes and Galileo: Method, Matter and the Science of Motion* (Cham, 2020).

110 All quotations are from Anon., *The Last Sayings, or, Dying Legacy of Mr. Thomas Hobbs of Malmesbury Who Departed This Life on Thursday, Decemb. 4, 1679* (London, 1680) (unnumbered). Cf. Lev 6, p. 86; Lev 32, p. 578.

111 Cf. Lev 44, p. 956.

112 Aubrey, *Brief Lives*, vol. 1, p. 356.

113 Anon., *Memorable Sayings of Mr. Hobbes in His Books and at the Table* (London, 1680). See Hobbes, *Correspondence*, vol. 2, pp. 793–94; Parkin, *Taming the Leviathan*, pp. 346–50.

114 D. Berman, 'A Disputed Deistic Classic', *The Library*, s6–vii:1 (1985), pp. 58–59.

115 Blount, *Great Is Diana of the Ephesians, or, the Original of Idolatry Together with the Politick Institution of the Gentiles Sacrifices* (London, 1680), p. 45.

116 Ibid., p. 36.

117 Ibid., p. 22.

118 Blount, *The Two First Books of Philostratus, Concerning the Life of Apollonius Tyaneus: Written Originally in Greek, and Now Published in English: Together with Philological Notes upon Each Chapter* (London, 1680).

119 Ibid., p. 5.

120 Ibid., pp. 5–6.

121 Ibid., pp. 28–29. Cf. Lev 2, p. 34.

122 Blount, *Life of Apollonius*, pp. 32–33, and pp. 151–52, 212. Cf. Lev 12, p. 170. See also Redwood, 'Charles Blount', p. 493.

123 Blount's Miscellanea MS, Athenaeum, London, 100Ab (henceforth: copy-book). This manuscript is analysed in detail in Hobbes, *Correspondence*, vol. 2, pp. 793–94 and Wilson, 'Reading Restoration Freethought', pp. 96–131.

124 Bulman, 'Hobbes's Publisher', p. 344. On Blount as an integral member of a 'scribal community', in which circulation of controversial clandestine

manuscripts was key, and particularly on Blount's performance of a 'scribal network', see Wilson, 'Reading Restoration Freethought', esp. pp. 132–50, 192–203. See also H. Love, *Scribal Publication in Seventeenth-Century England* (Oxford, 1993).

125 Blount, copy-book, p. 6. Quoted in Wilson, 'Reading Restoration Freethought', p. 112. Cf. Hobbes, *English Works*, vol. 4, pp. 430–31.

126 Blount, copy-book, pp. 25–26. Quoted in Wilson, 'Reading Restoration Freethought', pp. 112–13. Cf. Hobbes, *English Works*, vol. 7, pp. 76–78.

127 Blount, copy-book, p. 27. Quoted in Hobbes, *Correspondence*, vol. 2, p. 794. Cf. Hobbes, *English Works*, vol. 7, p. 85.

128 Blount, copy-book, p. 56. Quoted in Hobbes, *Correspondence*, vol. 2, p. 794. Cf. Lev 11, p. 160: 'by the visible things of this world, and their admirable order, a man may conceive there is a cause of them, which men call God; and yet not have an Idea, or Image of him in his mind'. Hobbes expressed a similar view elsewhere: 'it is very hard to believe, that to produce male and female, and all that belongs thereto, as also the several and curious organs of sense and memory, could be the work of anything that had not understanding'. Hobbes, *English Works*, vol. 7, p. 176. For Hobbes's casual argument and the argument from design, and hence the extent to which he provided a rational and natural understanding of God, see for example K. C. Brown, 'Hobbes's Grounds for Belief in a Deity', *Philosophy*, 37:142 (1962), pp. 336–44; A. Pacchi, 'Hobbes and the Problem of God', in G. A. J. Rogers and A. Ryan (eds), *Perspectives on Thomas Hobbes* (Oxford, 1988), pp. 171–87.

129 It is plausible that Blount's *Religio Laici* was an answer to Dryden's, disguised as a sequel, or alternatively, if Dryden was aware of Blount's plans, then his own *Religio Laici*, albeit earlier, was possibly aimed against Blount. Harth, *Contexts of Dryden's Thought*, pp. 93–94; M. B. Prince, '*Religio Laici* v. *Religio Laici*: Dryden, Blount, and the Origin of English Deism', *Modern Language Quarterly*, 74:1 (2013), pp. 29–66. The title of the work is borrowed from E. Herbert, *De causis errorum: una cum tractatu de religione laici, et appendice ad sacerdotes* (London, 1645).

130 Blount, *Religio Laici*, sigs. A8v–[B1r].

131 Ibid., pp. 2–4.

132 Ibid., esp. pp. 49–50. Cf. Herbert, *De veritate*, pp. 291–307.

133 Serjeantson, 'Herbert of Cherbury before Deism'.

134 Blount, *Religio Laici*, pp. 18–19.

135 Ibid., pp. 25–26.

136 Blount, *Oracles of Reason*, pp. 88–96.

137 Blount, *Religio Laici*, p. 32.

138 Ibid., p. 36. Cf. Lev 37, p. 692.

139 Blount, *Religio Laici*, p. 38.

140 Ibid., sigs. [B2r–B2v].

141 B. de Spinoza, *Theological-Political Treatise*, ed. and trans. J. Israel and M. Silverthorne (Cambridge, 2007), pp. 81–96. This was the first text by Spinoza ever translated into English, and Blount might have been the translator of Spinoza's full *Tractatus* which appeared in English in 1689. See Popkin, 'The

Deist Challenge', pp. 206–207; Israel, *Radical Enlightenment*, pp. 604–605; M. Goldie and R. Popkin, 'Scepticism, Priestcraft, and Toleration', in M. Goldie and R. Wokler (eds), *The Cambridge History of Eighteenth-Century Political Thought* (Cambridge, 2006), pp. 79–109, on p. 85.

142 Blount, *Miracles, No Violations of the Laws of Nature* (London, 1683), pp. 2–3. Cf. Lev 37, p. 684. See also Parkin, *Taming the Leviathan*, p. 408.

143 Blount, *Oracles of Reason*, p. 87.

144 Ibid.

145 Ibid., p. 88.

146 Ibid., p. 91.

147 Ibid., p. 92.

148 Ibid., p. 91. While Blount seems to have shared Hobbes's objection to moral good and evil in nature in the *Life of Apollonius*, the 'Summary Account' disagreed with Hobbes on that. A possible explanation might be that the 'Summary' was written by someone else in Blount's circle, perhaps Charles Gildon. Blount, *Life of Apollonius*, pp. 151–52; Blount, *Oracles of Reason*, p. 93. J. Harris, *A Refutation of the Objections Against Moral Good and Evil* (London, 1698), esp. pp. 5–7, recognised this point.

149 Apparently never printed, it was published in full only recently in G. Manning, 'The Deist: A Satyr on the Parsons', *The Seventeenth Century*, 8:1 (1993), pp. 149–60.

150 Ibid., p. 155.

151 Ibid., p. 153.

152 Ibid., p. 158.

153 C. Gildon, *Miscellany Poems upon Several Occasions Consisting of Original Poems* (London, 1692), p. 27.

154 J. Sambrook, 'Gildon, Charles (c. 1665–1724), Writer', *ODNB* (2008), available at: www.oxforddnb.com/view/10.1093/ref:odnb/9780198614128.001.0001/odnb-9780198614128-e-10720 (accessed 21 July 2023).

155 Blount, *King William and Queen Mary, Conquerors, or, a Discourse Endeavouring to Prove That Their Majesties Have on Their Side, Against the Late King, the Principal Reasons That Make Conquest a Good Title* (London, 1693), p. 42.

156 Ibid.

157 Ibid.

158 Yet it has been noted that there is no evidence that the scandal with Bohun was directly related to the lapsing of the act, which, in fact, had more to do with the opposition to the privileges that the act granted to the Stationers' Company. M. Goldie, 'Charles Blount's Intention in Writing "King William and Queen Mary Conquerors" (1693)', *Notes and Queries*, 223 (1978), pp. 527–32; M. Treadwell, 'The Stationers and the Printing Acts at the End of the Seventeenth Century', in J. Barnard and D. F. McKenzie with M. Bell (eds), *The Cambridge History of the Book in Britain. Volume 4: 1557–1695* (Cambridge, 2002), pp. 755–76. See also Hobbes, *Correspondence*, vol. 2, pp. 794–95; Pfanner, 'Blount, Charles'.

159 Blount, *The Miscellaneous Works of Charles Blount, Esq.* (London, 1695), pp. 25–27 (notice that page numbering is not consistent with other parts of this collection).

160 Wilson, 'Reading Restoration Freethought', pp. 153–58.

161 Blount, *Miscellaneous Works*, p. 26.

162 Ibid, p. 27.

163 Ibid.

164 Another arguably (and still uncommon) Hobbesian Whig was William Cavendish, future duke of Devonshire, who was active as a member of the House of Commons in the debates on the proposal to exclude James, and who spoke unequivocally for the Exclusion. Cavendish, *Reasons for His Majesties Passing the Bill of Exclusion in a Letter to a Friend* (London, 1681), pp. 2–3, stated: 'according to Mr. *Hobbes*, that Monarchical Government is form'd by an Agreement of a Society of Men, to devolve all their power and interest upon one Man, and to make him Judge of all Differences that shall arise among them; 'tis plain, that this can be for no other end, than the Security and protection of those that enter into such a Contract'. Cavendish went from there to argue that 'the Succession of Princes in Hereditary Monarchies, cannot be binding, nor ought to be admitted, where it proves manifestly inconsistent with those ends'. He, too, was concerned about the unity and safety of the commonwealth, remarking that 'this very Religion, that is the Bond of Union between a Prince and his People, when both profess the same, must of necessity produce the contrary Effects, and be the seed of the most fatal Disorders, nay of the Dissolution of Governments, where they differ'. The idea that religion is a tool in the hands of the magistrate that can be used to bring people to obey the government—or alternatively, when the religious differences are too extreme, might take governments down—is clearly something that Cavendish and other Whigs took from *Leviathan*. See E. Carmel, "I Will Speake of That Subject No More": The Whig Legacy of Thomas Hobbes', *Intellectual History Review*, 29:2, pp. 243–64; but see also Hobbes, *Writings on Common Law and Hereditary Right*, ed. A. Cromartie and Q. Skinner (Oxford, 2005), pp. 175–76, where Skinner questions this Whig appropriation: 'If Hobbes had not died a year earlier, this would surely have been enough to kill him off'.

165 Blount, *Oracles of Reason*, p. 16.

166 Ibid. Cf. Lev 33, pp. 586–608, on pp. 590–92; Spinoza, *Theological-Political Treatise*, pp. 118–54. Both Hobbes and Spinoza cast doubt upon Moses' authorship of the Pentateuch, and they both suggested that the high priest Ezra composed at least some of the bible. They interpreted several scriptural passages, some of them identical, speculating about their estimated time of writing. Malcolm, 'Hobbes, Ezra, and the Bible: The History of a Subversive Idea', in *Aspects of Hobbes*, pp. 383–431, esp. pp. 411, 429, shows that it is probable that Hobbes, Spinoza, and the French Millenarian Isaac La Peyrère relied on shared sources, hence the similarities in their approaches to the scripture. Malcolm traces these theories back to Ibn Ezra and his commentators as well as to other theologians and biblical scholars such as Cornelius à Lapide (Cornelis van den Steen) and Bonfrerius (Jacques Bonfrère). Thus, while some theories on problematic passages in the bible were previously available, the three writers 'set them off in a new direction': from questioning the Mosaic authorship of those passages they went on to question the authorship of the bible as a

whole. Malcolm argues that 'on the one hand, Hobbes's and Spinoza's theories about the Pentateuch were taken up enthusiastically by free-thinkers such as Charles Blount in England and Antonie van Dale in Holland; on the other hand, there were critics who insisted on the Pentateuch's Mosaicity, dismissing even the commonly accepted proofs of interpolations as a threat to true faith', which shows that Hobbes and Spinoza were also influential in that they 'polarized opinion, pushing many people to extremes of acceptance or rejection'. See also H. G. Reventlow, *The Authority of the Bible and the Rise of the Modern World*, trans. J. Bowden (Philadelphia, 1985), pp. 194–222.

167 Blount, *Oracles of Reason*, p. 18.
168 R. Bentley, *The Folly and Unreasonableness of Atheism Demonstrated*, 4th edn (London, 1699).
169 Ibid., p. 6.
170 Ibid., p. 9.
171 Ibid., p. 31.
172 The association of atheism and deism with the long-refuted Epicurean and Hobbesian ideas was a useful strategy for Bentley in his following sermons as well, such as 'Matter and Motion Cannot Think'.
173 R. Sault, *The Second Spira: Being a Fearful Example of an Atheist, Who Had Apostatized from the Christian Religion, and Dyed in Despair at Westminster, Decemb. 8. 1692* (London, 1693), p. 30.
174 C. Leslie, *The Charge of Socinianism Against Dr. Tillotson Considered* (Edinburgh, 1695), p. 13.
175 Ibid., p. 14.
176 Ibid. Tillotson's 'Hobbesian moment' was during his sermon *The Protestant Religion Vindicated, from the Charge of Singularity and Novelty* (1680), where he was understood as advocating Hobbesian conformity that required dissenters not to offend the established religion in public. See Marshall, 'Ecclesiology of the Latitude-Men'; Parkin, *Taming the Leviathan*, pp. 358–61, 390.
177 R. Howard, *A Twofold Vindication of the Late Arch-Bishop of Canterbury, and of the Author of the History of Religion* (London, 1696), p. 37.
178 Ibid., p. 38.
179 Ibid., pp. 67–68. Cf. Lev, 'Epistle Dedicatory', p. 6; F. Atterbury, *Fourteen Sermons Preach'd on Several Occasions* (London, 1708), pp. 151–52.
180 Howard, *Twofold Vindication*, p. 68.
181 Ibid., p. 77. Cf. Atterbury, *Fourteen Sermons*, p. 160.
182 Howard, *Twofold Vindication*, p. 78.
183 Ibid., p. 184.
184 Ibid., p. 8.
185 Ibid., pp. 99, 101. Cf. Blount, *Great Is Diana*, pp. 2–3.
186 Howard, *Twofold Vindication*, pp. 134–36.
187 Collins, *In the Shadow of Leviathan*, pp. 320–23, on p. 322. Cf. Howard, *Twofold Vindication*, p. 69.
188 J. King, *Mr. Blount's Oracles of Reason, Examined and Answered* (London, 1698), p. 33.

189 See also K. Sheppard, *Anti-Atheism in Early Modern England 1580–1720* (Leiden, 2015), pp. 247–57.

190 See also Parkin, *Taming the Leviathan*, pp. 391–96, 407–409.

191 C. Gildon, 'An Account of the Life and Death of the Author', in *Miscellaneous Works*, sig. A5v.

192 M. H. Porter, 'Boevey, James (1622–1696), Merchant and Philosopher', *ODNB* (2006), available at: www.oxforddnb.com/view/10.1093/ref:odnb/9780198614128.001.0001/odnb-9780198614128-e-70859 (accessed 21 July 2023); M. Knights, 'The "Highest Roade to Happiness": The "Active Philosophy" of James Boevey (1622–1696)', in M. J. Braddick and J. Innes (eds), *Suffering and Happiness in England 1550–1850: Narratives and Representations* (Oxford, 2017), pp. 173–89.

193 M. Knights, *The Devil in Disguise: Deception, Delusion, and Fanaticism in the Early English Enlightenment* (Oxford, 2011), pp. 103–107; Knights, 'Highest Roade to Happiness'.

194 Aubrey, *Brief Lives*, vol. 1, p. 113; Knights, 'Highest Roade to Happiness', p. 176.

195 Knights, *Devil in Disguise*, pp. 100–101.

196 Bundle of Small Volumes Presumed to Belong to Dame Sarah Cowper, Hertfordshire Archives and Local Studies, DE/P/F47, 5 vols. See in Knights, *Devil in Disguise*, pp. 104–106.

197 The following quotes are from Hertfordshire Archives and Local Studies, DE/P/F47. I am enormously grateful to Mark Knights for sharing this manuscript with me. He intends to continue his research on Boevey with a book-length treatment.

198 I thank Mark Knights for drawing my attention to the last point.

199 In the third appendix to *Leviathan* that deals with 'Some Objections to *Leviathan*', A, the challenging interlocutor, asks: 'Then, near the beginning of Chapter 4 he denies that there are any incorporeal substances. What is this if not to deny that God exists or to assert that God is a body?' B unequivocally replies: 'He does indeed assert that God is a body'. In the correspondence with Bramhall, Hobbes elaborated: 'To his Lordship's question here: What I leave God to be? I answer, I leave him to be a most pure, simple, invisible spirit corporeal'. Lev, 'Appendix to *Leviathan*' 3, pp. 1228–29; Hobbes, *English Works*, vol. 4, p. 313. As Hobbes explained both in *Leviathan* and in the correspondence with Bramhall, spirit is a kind of fluid, invisible body. Hobbes, *English Works*, vol. 4, p. 309; Lev 34, p. 612.

200 Lev 15, p. 240.

201 Cf. Lev 32, p. 580; Lev 8, p. 114.

2

The deist controversy (1696–1710)

In the mid-1690s, deism ignited serious controversy and anxiety in England. In the midst of this storm was John Toland's *Christianity Not Mysterious*, published in 1696 between the lapse of the licensing act in 1695 and the new blasphemy act of 1698. Toland argued that at first there had been no mysteries in religion and that the clergy made religion mysterious and obscure only to ensure that laypeople would always depend on them for explication. Subsequently, Matthew Tindal and Anthony Collins, among others, did much to develop precisely this line of thought. They all believed that Christianity should be and indeed had been clear, simple, and intelligible to all through reason. They did not deny God—at least not explicitly—but the elements that they thought had been added to Christianity unnecessarily and maliciously. Previously, the richness of the links between them and Hobbes has been understudied. This chapter shows how these authors engaged with Hobbes and borrowed various theological and political aspects of his works, including his methods of studying the scripture and the history of religion as well as his materialism, determinism, and Erastianism. It explores how they acknowledged these debts both publicly and in private correspondence and how their critics continued to recognise and often overstate their closeness to the notorious philosopher.

Anxieties about Hobbism and deism in the mid-1690s

Texts against deism in the mid-1690s mentioned Hobbes regularly, often alongside Spinoza. Various writers seemed to agree on the role that Hobbes had played in the emergence of deism, and they continued to assert that there was no significant difference between deism, atheism, and Hobbism. In *A Conference with a Theist* (1696), written against Blount, Thomas Burnet, and others, Williams Nicholls expressed the concern that these doctrines were now overly popular: 'For *Atheism* and *Theism* are now got from the Court to the *Exchange*, they begin to talk them in *Shops* and *Stalls*, and

Spinosa and *Hobbs* are grown common, even to the very Rabble'.[1] Similarly, *A Satyr Against Atheistical Deism* (1696) gave a particularly unflattering portrait of 'The Genuine Character of a Deist', whose 'Apostle' is Hobbes and 'dearest darlings' are Hobbes, Spinoza, and Blount, and whose villainy apparently could not be overstated: 'he's a transcendental Evil … or if you will, he is a Constellation fix'd in direct opposition to all Good, composed of Malice, Hatred and Self-conceit … and is truely the greatest plague that can be inflicted on a human *Society*'.[2]

These themes were elaborated in *A Letter to the Deists* (1696) by Humphrey Prideaux, future dean of Norwich. Prideaux stated that 'the Outcry against Deists is now grown so strong, that no body can suppose it to be wholly without ground'.[3] According to him, deism originally meant a belief in the deity, but now it came to signify 'a Denial of the Grounds of Revealed Religion' while some deists seemed to 'deny the very Principles of Natural Religion also'.[4] The deists that Prideaux saw were dangerous men who 'ought so much the more carefully to be watched, by how much the more their Title and Outside is less apt to give any suspicion of their Design'.[5] His tone, too, was severe, declaring that the deists' 'several Schemes do equally lead to Irreligion; And consequently to the utter ruin of Humane Societies'.[6] Describing the irreligious deists, Prideaux argued that

> Some Men, because Mr. *Hobbs* rellished not the sound of Immaterial Substances … fear not, upon his Authority, to ridicule the Notion of Spirit. These, without trying their Skill upon particulars, resolve in general the Structure of the whole Universe, and of all the Animate Beings which replenish it, into the unexplicable Powers of Matter and Motion.[7]

This development had highly dangerous consequences. Hobbesian materialism in the hands of the deists came to mean that 'God (as they would call it) must be liable to all the changes that happen in the Universal Mass of Matter'.[8] The result was a material God, and once allowed, 'we can not avoid to acknowledge him subject to Disturbances, Diseases, Passions, and all manner of Alterations that are incident to Matter, and altogether unsuitable to the Perfections which we must of necessity attribute to the Supream Deity'.[9] The conventional perception of the critics was that there was nothing that the deist would not somehow undermine and ridicule, however sacred.

The Boyle Lectures continued to advance the case against Hobbes and the deists. In 1697, Francis Gastrell linked 'the *Hobbist*, and the *Deist*' with 'the *Epicurean*' and 'the *Sadducee*' to prove that even 'those whose other Opinions declare they have nothing at all, or very little, to hope or fear from a God' still had to acknowledge His existence.[10] In the following year, John Harris argued that these radicals contributed to the view that the notion of God 'owes its Original to the foolish Fears and Ignorance of some Men, and to the crafty Designs of others'.[11] The purpose of Blount's *Great Is Diana*, for example, was to show 'That the first Original of all Religion, was from Craft and Imposture, and that it was cultivated and carried on by the Cunning and Avarice of the Priests'.[12] Harris found further evidence in Blount's works to suggest that he reduced religion and consequently the notion of God to priestcraft and pagan corruption. Spinoza similarly associated religion with superstition and traced it back to human fear, whereas '[t]he Author of the *Leviathan*, speaks yet a little plainer as to this Point', and for him 'Religion and Superstition differ only in this, that the latter is a Lye and a Cheat standing only on the Authority of Private Men, whereas the former is supported by the Power of the Government'.[13] Thus, Harris identified a tradition that implied that the very notion of God was an invention, but he found this absurd: had there not been a God, no inventor would have been able to create such a notion.[14] Moreover, Harris added, even if it was possible for a man to invent the notion of God for political reasons, it would have been foolish of him to do so; Hobbes's sovereign would have enjoyed even greater power if he was not only the mortal God but also the only one.[15] Harris's point was that none of these writers were original and that they merely repeated each other's arguments while falsely presenting theirs as unique. Furthermore, he claimed that most of their arguments could be found in the writings of the ancient atheists, namely, Epicurus, Lucretius, and Sextus Empiricus. Yet all of them pretended to 'the Glory of first leading Men into the way of Truth, and delivering them out of the dark mazes of Vulgar Errors'.[16]

Deism was attacked so widely in the mid-1690s that even writers who were themselves rather anticlerical had to distinguish themselves from the new demon that emerged. A key example is *An Account of the Growth of Deism in England* (1696) by the Whig Anglican William Stephens. Deism, Stephens argued, was 'a denial of all reveal'd Religion', and the deists rejected the gospels, dismissing them as forgeries.[17] In his *Account*, Stephens described the opinions of some of his deist acquaintances. Some deists were simply 'Men of loose and sensual Lives', he argued, but others had arrived at deism through false reasoning.[18] One of the reasons for the spread of deism in England was that some young gentlemen travelled to countries such as Italy, Spain, and France, where they were exposed to the corruption of Catholicism and developed an anticlerical sentiment that they applied to the Church of England when they came back. While in Europe, they witnessed the '*Popery*' that 'was only a device of the *Priesthood*, to carry on a particular Interest of their own'.[19] When they returned to England, they saw the religious conflicts of the 1640s between Anglicans and Presbyterians who similarly competed over 'what Sect of the *Clergy* should make the best

Market of the *meer Lay-men*'.[20] The impression that the entire clergy was power-hungry led these gentlemen to think that the ancient clergy had been similarly corrupt and thus capable of inventing the scripture.[21] The upshot was that it was the misconduct of the clergy that led these individuals to deism, but not without some help from wicked philosophers: 'having read *Spinosa* and *Hobbes*, and been taught to laugh at the story of *Baalam*'s Ass, and *Sampson*'s Locks; they proceed to ridicule the reality of all *Miracle* and *Revelation*'.[22] In his comment on Stephens's *Account*, the clergyman Richard Willis underscored Hobbes's role in the rise of deism even further:

> Mr. *Hobbs*'s Philosophy and that of some others came much in Vogue, which brought in some loose Principles, and encouraged Men in a Sceptical Humour, and made them suspect every thing: and when once Men of ill Lives are unhinged in their Principles, they will hardly be at the pains to think deep enough to set themselves right again; especially when their Religion is so contradictory to their Lusts.[23]

The deism that emerges from these accounts was essentially anticlericalism, which in many cases was justified even in the eyes of the critics. But it was a sort of anticlericalism that went one step too far to question the divinity of the scripture and sometimes of Jesus himself, and consequently to reject all miracles and revelation. At least for critics such as Willis, it was undeniable that Hobbes's philosophy, with its unconventional outlook on religion, provided the theoretical framework for the 'unhinged' public mood and thus had a decisive effect on this process.

The fact that Hobbes and deism became so entangled also meant that some writers found themselves denying the association with both almost at the same time. The most high-profile case in the mid-1690s is John Locke. Locke was criticised heavily for his alleged Hobbism in this period, and the attacks often came precisely from those who also took issue with deism. Stillingfleet and Willis, whose views against deism we have encountered, were also two of Locke's persistent adversaries. As Jeffrey Collins shows, they 'demonstrate how charges of Hobbism could work to suggest Locke's proximity to cynical statecraft, ethical conventionalism, a reduction of conscience to arbitrary opinion, and *politique* tolerationism'.[24]

The key event was the publication of *An Essay Concerning Human Understanding* (1690), where Locke rejected innatism and was understood to have rejected the natural foundation of moral obligation, and where he implicitly espoused materialism and even allowed the idea of thinking matter.[25] He also developed in the *Essay* a conception of reason as part of the formation of knowledge, defined as the perception of agreement or disagreement of ideas; this account would serve as a starting point for Toland, Tindal, and Collins, whom Locke knew personally (with the latter he had an especially close friendship).[26] Things became worse for Locke after the publication of *The Reasonableness of Christianity* (1695), which was an important part of the polemic of the 1690s against priestcraft. In this work, Locke took upon himself 'the sole Reading of the Scripture' given the 'little Satisfaction and Consistency' he found in 'most of the Systems of Divinity'.[27] He betrayed an anticlerical sentiment when he argued that priests had 'talked of the Ghosts below, and a Life after this' in a manner that was designed 'to keep Men to their Superstitious and Idolatrous Rites', and so people 'suspected it presently of Priest-craft'.[28] Yet he refused to make reason the sole judge. For Locke, the answer to priestcraft was not unaided reason—it was, in fact, part of the problem—but Jesus and his promise to reunite the spiritual and the ethical.[29] Locke employed mainstream Anglican arguments for conformity in trying to establish a unifying church ecclesiology.[30] Thus, for Locke, when a revelation is acknowledged as divine, it must be accepted even without rational demonstration. In addition, the belief in Jesus as the Messiah was all that was required for salvation: for this position in particular, Locke was accused of Hobbism, since Hobbes also held that the only article of faith necessary for salvation was that Jesus is the Christ.[31] Now, both Hobbes and Locke, and following them the modish deists, were associated with Christian minimalism at best, which could easily be a stop on the way to complete atheism.

As a result, in the second half of the 1690s, Locke had to fight on a few fronts simultaneously, and it was then that he defended himself against both accusations of Hobbism and deism. He took a similar tactic in both cases: first he tried to ignore them, and when he could not do so any longer, he moved to deny his proximity to the heretics, and in the case of Hobbes, to deny his knowledge of his work altogether. Locke clarified eventually that his view, albeit anticlerical, was aimed against deism. In his *Second Vindication of the Reasonableness of Christianity* (1697), he explained that he had hoped that his work would be useful for those 'who thought either that there was no need of Revelation at all, or that the Revelation of our Saviour required the Belief of such Articles for Salvation, which the settled Notions and their way of reasoning in some, and want of Understanding in others, made impossible to them'.[32] Such objections, he argued, were 'made by *Deists* against *Christianity*; But against *Christianity* misunderstood'.[33]

As for the Hobbesian idea of the single article of faith, Locke argued that he had 'borrowed it only from the Writers of the Four *Gospels*, and the *Acts*; and did not know that those words he quoted out of the *Leviathan*, were there, or any thing like them'.[34] Later, he even stated that he was 'not so well read in *Hobbes* or *Spinoza*, as to be able to say, what were their Opinions' regarding the nature of the soul.[35] However, this was an odd claim that has been long doubted, given that Hobbes and Spinoza were among the best-known philosophers of the time, if only because of their volatile reception. The striking recent discovery that Locke 'almost always had the *Leviathan* by H. on his table' seems to provide the conclusion for this debate: that Locke knew Hobbes's work well enough is now evident; that his insincerity about this fact is another indication that he was, after all, quite close to some of Hobbes's views is at least plausible.[36]

Toland's early works

Only three years passed since Blount's *Oracles of Reason* when another text, similarly and radically anticlerical, caused turmoil in London. This text was *Christianity Not Mysterious* (1696), which argued in a very telling subtitle *That There Is Nothing in the Gospel Contrary to Reason, nor above It: And That No Christian Doctrine Can Be Properly Call'd a Mystery*. The message was clear: we must not believe in things we cannot conceive by our own reason. The author, Irishman John Toland (1670–1722), is perhaps the best-known figure in the literature on deism, although he never identified himself as a deist.[37] Toland was a scholar and a philosopher. He was an eclectic thinker and writer who worked with various sources, including classical, republican, and biblical materials. He communicated his ideas to various audiences, including the most senior Whig politicians of the 1700s as well as Prince Eugene of Savoy and Sophia, Electress of Hanover. As Justin Champion has shown, Toland was also a political actor, committed to the rule of reason and liberty and to the war against tyranny, both spiritual and civil.[38] His theological commitments were, therefore, complex and probably deliberately evasive. It was recognised already in his day that labels would hardly capture him:

> As for Religion, as Mr. *Toland*, like most *Free-Thinkers*, rather made it his Business to *pull down* than to *build*; rather to find out and expose the *Inconsistencies* of the present *Systems* of Religion, than to make own his known; so it is more easy to guess what he was not, than to tell what he was, 'Tis certain, he was neither Jew, nor Mahometan: But whether he was a Christian, a Deist, a Pantheist, an Hobbist, or a Spinosist, is the Question?[39]

To some extent, Toland was probably all of these things and more, but whether he built a system of his own or not is not all that definitive. He was certainly a 'Hobbist' in a number of places, in addition to often being a 'Spinosist'.[40] Hobbesian ideas featured in his political and religious criticism, thus contributing to his own deist, pantheist, or indeed (however controversial) Christian ideas. In *Christianity Not Mysterious*, Toland identified himself simply as a Christian, and he argued against 'those Gentlemen who love to call Names in Religion', because divisions to parties and sects were used to invoke accusations of heresy.[41] Then, he added an allusion to the famous passage from *Leviathan*: 'I assure them, that I am neither of *Paul*, nor of *Cephas*, nor of *Apollos*, but of the Lord Jesus Christ alone'.[42]

The main point of *Christianity Not Mysterious* was that Christianity in its original and uncorrupted form, as found in Jesus' teachings and the gospels, had been simple and plain. Mysteries were introduced later by the Jews and gentiles and were maintained by the ambition and craft of the priests, with the assistance of philosophers, or 'divinity schools'. Eventually, Christianity ceased to be intelligible and degenerated into mere paganism, consisting of ridiculous and foolish rituals and ceremonies.[43] It is texts such as *Christianity Not Mysterious* that demonstrate, as Michael Hunter has emphasised recently, that 'Deists were at the forefront in condemning magical beliefs and using the language of "priestcraft" in excoriating them and accounting for them'.[44]

Some of Toland's arguments follow Hobbes's anticlericalism closely, and there is good reason to believe that the resemblance is not coincidental. Toland believed that the clergy were motivated by their own interest to become a separate political body, thus corrupting Christianity for their own advantage. Like Hobbes, he saw the actions of the clergy as 'Usurpations upon Mankind' and believed that it was this political interest that led the clergy to retain the sole right to interpret scripture and, most importantly, to claim infallibility.[45] These actions 'did strangely affect, stupify, and amaze the Minds of the ignorant People' and earned the clergy an extremely dangerous social status: 'They seem'd almost a different and more divine Species of Creatures, distinguishing themselves from other Men in their *Garb*, in their manner of living by *Tithes* and *Donations*, in their *separate Places* at Church, and several other ways. By this means the *Clergy* were able to do any thing'.[46] Diametrically opposed to the claims of the clergy, Toland maintained that everyone could read the bible, and 'with that Equity and Attention that is due to meer Humane Works', because there is no 'different Rule to be follow'd in the Interpretation of *Scripture* from what is common to all other Books'.[47]

Furthermore, Toland warned his readers against 'the Systems of *Plato*, of *Aristotle*, of *Epicurus*, of the *Academicks*, &c. many of whose Principles are directly repugnant to common Sense and good Morals'.[48] He shared Hobbes's conviction that there was so-called philosophy, especially Aristotle's metaphysics, that had to be corrected because it could otherwise be exploited viciously:

> For as in *Philosophy* so in *Religion* every Sect has its peculiar Extravagancies, and the *INCOMPREHENSIBLE MYSTERIES* of the latter do perfectly

answer the *OCCULT QUALITIES* of the former. They were both calculated at first for the same Ends, *viz. to stop the Mouths of such as demand a Reason where none can be given, and to keep as many in Ignorance as Interest shall think convenient.*[49]

For Toland, therefore, '*Reason* is the only Foundation of all Certitude', and it should be employed to examine all things, revelation included.[50] This is where Toland was closer to Blount than to Hobbes and Locke: there could be nothing in religion contrary to reason, and there could be nothing in religion above reason. Reason was the only judge and hence all alleged mysteries were to be categorically rejected. *Christianity Not Mysterious* was hoping 'to make it appear, that the Use of Reason is not so dangerous in Religion as it is commonly represented', thus targeting those who 'mightily extol it when it seems to favour 'em, yet vouchsafe it not a hearing when it makes against them, but oppose its own Authority to it self'.[51] So, the idea was not only that true religion is always a reasonable religion, but also that we should be suspicious of the ways in which men appeal to reason, that is, whenever and however it best serves their interest. Along the same lines, the title page of *Christianity Not Mysterious* included the following quote: '*We need not desire a better Evidence that any Man is in the wrong, than to hear him declare against Reason, and thereby to acknowledg that Reason is against him*'. In other words, when men object to the use of reason, it must be because reason leads to undesirable conclusions for them. This quote is taken from Tillotson's sermon on 'The Excellency of Abraham's Faith and Obedience' (1686) and it is a paraphrase of the Hobbesian quote—and the Hobbesian idea—that had already been used by Blount: when reason is against a man, a man will be against reason.[52]

A few words on Tillotson are in order. The future archbishop belonged to the moderate wing of Anglicanism, often referred to as the latitudinarians, whose religious views pointed to rationalism and moralism and opposed puritan theology, and who, at the same time, were willing to give the civil magistrate the power to preserve the established, true religion against the dissenters' pretence to conscience. To many, this made Tillotson and his fellow 'latitude-men' seem rather Hobbesian.[53] The use of Tillotson's quote by Toland might have been an attempt to create the impression that *Christianity Not Mysterious* was not too far from the Christian mainstream—an unsuccessful one, considering the furious clerical response to this work, which was burnt in Dublin in 1697.[54]

In his sermon on 'Abraham's Faith and Obedience' Tillotson argued for the necessity of using reason in matters of faith. Divine revelation is to be judged by reason, 'for when God reveals any thing to us, he reveals it to our understanding'.[55] Reason is therefore necessary in order to distinguish between true and false claims for divine inspiration. It is necessary in order to reach true belief as well as to convince others of the truth of religion.[56] Reason, in fact, has always been a decisive criterion for religious belief: 'None are reproved in Scripture for their unbelief, but where sufficient reason and evidence was offered to them'; thus, we must not 'turn off reason here', Tillotson concluded, as limited as our reason may be.[57] At this point, he attacked those who opposed the use of reason in religion, suggesting in Hobbesian words that they do so simply because reason is not by their side. He added:

> I have often wondered that people can with patience endure to hear their teachers and guides talk against reason; and not only so, but they pay them the greater submission and veneration for it. One would think this but an odd way to gain authority over the minds of men: But some skilful and designing men have found by experience, that it is a very good way to recommend them to the ignorant; as nurses use to endear themselves to children, by perpetual noise and nonsense.[58]

This was Tillotson at his most pungent.[59] It is plausible that Tillotson paraphrased Hobbes consciously in his sermon, and it is even more plausible that Toland knew the Hobbesian connection of the quote that he included in his title page: in 1700, Toland published Harrington's edited works, in which the original Hobbesian quote appears, together with its source.[60]

If the gestures to Hobbes in *Christianity Not Mysterious* remained implicit, Toland explicitly acknowledged his debt to Hobbes's anticlericalism elsewhere. In an essay 'Concerning the Rise, Progress, and Destruction of Fables and Romances' (1695), Toland similarly investigated the historical origins of fables 'thought necessary to sweeten and allure the minds of men, naturally Superstitious and Credulous'.[61] He traced this invention back to the philosophy and mythology of 'the Eastern Nations', including the Hebrews and the Greeks. Then, '[t]he Sacred Authors themselves complied with this Humour of Parables and Fictions, the Holy Scripture being altogether Mysterious, Allegorical and Enigmatical', while the Jewish Talmud and Muslim Alcoran were no different.[62] Precisely as he did in *Christianity Not Mysterious*, Toland showed how such mysterious language was recruited to corrupt Christianity: 'From these fountains the Christian Monks drunk in the art of Lying, and composing of Legends'.[63] This time he credited Hobbes openly:

> To this *Essay* of Fables and Romances, the History of *Demonology* doth properly belong, with all the terrible troops of *Spirits* and *Witches*; but I find this Part is so Judiciously and Learnedly Treated of by our Countryman Mr. *Hobbs* in that Book of his *Leviathan*, called the *Kingdom of Darkness*.[64]

Toland also identified his biblical criticism with Hobbes's. He believed that he witnessed an age of rational religion and flourishing natural philosophy. People like Copernicus, Galileo, Mersenne, Gassendi, and Descartes 'are not esteem'd the worse Christians, because they contradict the Scriptures in Physical or Mathematical Problems'.[65] The reading of the scripture, too, had to be adjusted to reach a better, natural understanding of the world: 'the Sacred Writers spoke to a Generation of Men, who were never famous in Arts and Sciences; therefore they adapted all their sayings to the vulgar Idea's of that Time and Nation'.[66] The scripture had originally been written in order to establish a theocracy but now it could be revisited. Clearly, however, this development was still disputed: 'The Philosophick History of the Bible, is not always to be embraced; for what an outcry against Mr. Hobs! because he describ'd God Almighty as Corporeal, though Moses and the Scriptures had done so before him'.[67] In other words, Hobbes's materialist position was not only compatible with the new natural philosophy but also with the scripture. Furthermore, Toland's explanation for the attacks on Hobbes was no less interesting, in that he explained them in terms of sectarian interests: 'Things are denominated Heresie and Atheism, not by any certain Rules of Truth, or Falshood, but according to the Caprice, or Interests of Sects and Parties'.[68] As we have seen, this was the precise view of both Hobbes and Blount.

Hobbes's biblical criticism and his materialism, combined together, were therefore powerful tools for subsequent philosophers who dared to question the unquestionable. As John Harris argued in one of his Boyle Lectures from 1698, 'there must be some substantial Reason why Deists and Antiscripturists are always Corporealists'.[69] For Harris, Hobbes and Spinoza were the greatest corporealists and consequently atheists of all; deism was nothing but another manifestation of the same dangerous approach. Toland's materialism was about to be the new offspring of this very tradition.

In subsequent works, Toland developed his skills and his persona as a biblical scholar. One of the most significant products was a catalogue of apocryphal scripture that he composed, starting with works attributed to Jesus and the apostles, which aimed to determine which were authentic and which were forged. Toland started this catalogue in his *Amyntor* (1699) and expanded it gradually, until the final version was published posthumously in 1726, after being in circulation as a scribal work in the 1710s. Toland's research was thorough: for the final version he examined evidence to determine the authenticity of more than one hundred titles.[70] As Justin Champion has shown, Toland used patristic sources and commentary of erudite scholars, and thus he was 'playing a complex inter-textual game, not only by implicating the Church Fathers in his schemes, but perhaps more importantly, by engrossing the editorial labours of his orthodox contemporaries to his own purposes', namely, 'his project of compromising the canonicity of received Scripture'.[71]

Here, too, there was a striking, albeit implicit, Hobbesian connection. In *Leviathan*, Hobbes mentioned the Council of Laodicea (363–64), which issued a canon of the recognised books of the bible. Hobbes did not question the canon explicitly but provided a good reason to do so. He wrote that at the time of the Council, 'ambition had so far prevailed on the great Doctors of the Church, as no more to esteem Emperours, though Christian, for the Shepherds of the people, but for Sheep', and so these churchmen 'thought such frauds as tended to make the people the more obedient to Christian Doctrine, to be pious'; however, he added,

> I am perswaded they did not therefore falsifie the Scriptures, though the copies of the Books of the New Testament, were in the hands only of the Ecclesiasticks; because if they had had an intention so to doe, they would surely have made them more favorable to their power over Christian Princes, and Civill Soveraignty, than they are.[72]

Hobbes decided not to accuse the Council of forgery due to lack of evidence, not because this would have been implausible. Now was Toland's turn to question the Council more boldly. In the original catalogue that he composed in 1699, Toland argued that the Council of Laodicea 'could not among so great a variety of Books as were then abroad in the World, certainly determin which were the true Monuments of the Apostles' except for in one of two ways: a revelation, which we do not know that happened during the Council, or 'by crediting the Testimony of their Ancestors'.[73] Such testimony, argued Toland, could be available, in which case he would have had the same sources, or it could be fake, as a result of 'the monstrous Fables of Papists, Rabbins, Turks, and the Eastern Nations both Christians and Idolaters'.[74] An in-depth examination of the authenticity of the apocryphal books was therefore warranted due to the likely possibility that books were included in the bible, or alternatively excluded from it, simply 'for not suiting all the Opinions of the strongest Party'.[75] And so Toland did: his ambitious project, scholarly as it was subversive, derived from the suspicion that even decisions on the canonical books had been dictated by cynical interests.

Although Toland did not acknowledge Hobbes here, we have good reason to believe, based on the acknowledged and unacknowledged references in his other works, that Toland was familiar with this Hobbesian insinuation. If this is true, then this is a typical case that shows how Hobbes provided the tools for the radicals, who then took his advice to the next level: following Hobbes, and more radically than Hobbes, Toland questioned the Council of Laodicea, precisely in the same manner that Blount questioned the Council of Nicaea twenty years earlier. Furthermore, he did so as a freethinker who encouraged his readers to consider the evidence on their own, 'to judge for themselves, and to build what they please with those Materials I shall furnish 'em'.[76]

In the following years, the critics continued to point to Hobbes's influence upon the radical assault on religion. An anonymous book titled *Visits from the Shades* (1704) contained a fictional dialogue held between Hobbes and the eccentric author John Asgill, in which the latter tells Hobbes: 'had you not writ at all, I question whether the *Oracles of Reason*, or *Christianity not Mysterious*, had ever seen the Light'.[77] Hobbes is described there as admitting that his works 'have pull'd down the Christian Religion; but I am convinced', says the fictional Hobbes, 'I only lay'd the Foundation, and raised the Scaffolding; for the Structure of Heresie has gone on apace since I left the World'.[78] Then, he elaborates:

> Yes, for I invalidated the Miracles of *Moses*, and all the *Major* and *Minor* Prophets of the Old Testament: I made their Inspiration no more than common Dreams, and ordinary Visions: I lessened the stupendious Actions of our blessed Saviour; I levelled the cures of the Dumb, the Leperous and the Blind, as things incident to an ordinary Physician; nor stopp'd I at any thing, but perverted one Text by another, till I shook the Belief of them all.[79]

Hobbes's sceptical approach towards miracles and prophecies and his critical analysis of the scripture are identified here as the means through which he meant to 'overturn all Models of Religions, and Constitutions of all Churches whatsoever'.[80] It was this radical legacy that the critics could find, word for word, in the works of Blount, Toland, and their like.

Toland's active matter and Clarke's response

Toland, a supporter of the Protestant succession, was introduced to the Hanoverian court in Berlin in the early 1700s. He was acquainted with the Electress Sophia and her daughter, Sophie Charlotte, queen of Prussia. The philosopher had long conversations with the queen, who was impressed by his wit, as well as with Gottfried Leibniz, who took a great interest in Toland's work.[81] When he returned to England, he published *Letters to Serena* (1704), which was written for Sophie Charlotte. This work contained several letters. In the first three letters, Toland explored the history of the heathenish idea of the immortality of the soul as well as the origins of prejudice and idolatry. In line with his previous works, he reminded the reader 'how in very many and considerable Regions the plain Institution of Jesus Christ cou'd degenerate into the most absurd Doctrines, unintelligible

Jargon, ridiculous Practices, and inexplicable Mysteries: and how almost in every corner of the world Religion and Truth cou'd be chang'd into Superstition and Priestcraft'.[82] Again, this was a historical-anthropological thesis. The ancient Egyptians, Persians, Romans, and Hebrews, Toland argued, had a plain religion at first, but all sorts of strange, man-made inventions were added later, including various heathenish conceptions and practices of dealing with the dead. This was the beginning of idolatrous rites and worships and superstitious thinking about gods, stars, and ghosts: it is this kind of thinking that led people to paint the sun and the moon 'like a Face with Eyes, Nose, and a Mouth' and to believe 'Heaven to be over their Heads, and Hell under their Feet'.[83] Toland claimed that hope and fear were the main causes of superstition, and that not knowing the future, people would take anything for an omen, and turn both to astrologers and priests for advice, which was like a sick person preferring 'a ridiculous Charm to the most excellent Remedy'.[84] He went on to accuse the heathens, and especially the Egyptians, for having found divine attributes even in animals and plants and worshipped 'the Bird Ibis, Hawks, Cats, Dogs, Crocodiles, Sea-horses, Goats, Bulls, Cows, Onions, Garlick, and what not'.[85] This list resembles the list provided by Hobbes in *Leviathan* where he argued that 'there is almost nothing that has a name, that has not been esteemed amongst the Gentiles, in one place or another, a God, or Divell' including 'Men, Women, a Bird, a Crocodile, a Calf, a Dogge, a Snake, an Onion, a Leeke'.[86] Finally, to summarise the third letter that dealt with idolatry, Toland inserted a verse that was 'in every body's mouth': this was an almost identical variation of Charles Gildon's abovementioned 'Deist's Plea'.[87]

The main innovation of *Letters to Serena* was in the fourth and fifth letters, wherein Toland presented his idea of active matter and thereby formulated his materialism fully. He suggested that motion is essential to matter and rejected the idea that 'Matter is or ever was an inactive dead Lump in absolute Repose, a lazy and unwieldy thing'.[88] For Toland, the idea of active matter accounts for all the motion in the world and finally disproves the existence of vacuum. If motion is essential to matter, then matter is self-moving, and the implication is clear: the need for a God in such a world is reduced significantly. Yet Toland claimed to have stayed neutral on this question:

> But if I be able to prove from the nature of the thing it self, and not to favor or oppose any Cause, that *Action is essential to Matter*, that Matter cannot be rightly conceiv'd nor consequently be rightly defin'd without it ... then they may quarrel (who have a mind to it) with God or Nature, and not with me, who am but their humble Interpreter.[89]

At this point, Toland's God seems very similar indeed to Spinoza's 'God or Nature'.[90] In a number of his writings, he certainly came close to subscribing to pantheism—the view that identifies God with nature—a term which he coined himself.[91] But Toland thought that his version of 'God or Nature' was an improvement, given that Spinoza's conception lacked an explanation for motion and consequently for change in nature. Toland believed that his addition was crucial, and therefore had to be accepted regardless of one's notions of God and the creation:

> such as believe Matter created, may as well conceive that God at the beginning endu'd it with Action as well as with Extension; and those who believe it eternal, may as well believe it eternally active, as eternally divisible … My only business is to prove *Matter necessarily active as well as extended*, and thence to explain as much as I can of its Affections; but not to meddle in the Disputes which others may raise about its Original or Duration.[92]

Despite his best efforts, the critics could hardly consider Toland's idea as a humble interpretation. Toland could easily be accused of Spinozism, despite the fact that he posed a serious challenge to Spinoza's view. At the same time, there is some evidence to suggest that Toland's active matter was not strictly Spinozist, but that it was indebted also, perhaps even primarily, to Hobbes's plenist materialism. Exhibit A, presented by Stewart Duncan, is a letter sent from Leibniz to Sophie in 1702, in which Leibniz described Toland's view prior to his idea of active matter as

> Hobbes's view that there is nothing in nature but shapes and movements. This was also the view of Epicurus and Lucretius, except that they admitted the vacuum and atoms or hard particles, but Hobbes thought that everything is full and fluid, which is also my view. But I think that we ought to look for the origin of action, perception, and order underneath matter, that is, underneath that which is purely passive and indifferent to movement.[93]

Toland, according to Leibniz's interpretation, was a Hobbesian materialist and plenist, for whom 'everything is full and fluid', but by 1702 he had not been able to explain the action of matter. Two years later, Toland provided his explanation for action as being intrinsic to matter, believing that this idea supported the plenist theory. It seems, therefore, that Leibniz's criticism may have caused Toland to modify his previous view by adding an explanation for all the motion in the world. If Toland's new idea in 1704 was a response to Leibniz, then his active matter was a development of (at least what the two considered to be) a Hobbesian position.[94]

Toland also thought of his idea as an addition to Newton's system; but for the Newtonians who wanted to keep God and His providence in the picture, this was one step too far, leading Newton's laws into extremely dangerous territory.[95] Samuel Clarke, the Newtonian theologian and philosopher, responded to this idea in his Boyle Lectures of 1704–1705.[96] Clarke attacked Toland's active matter together with the materialism of Hobbes and Spinoza, as well as what he described as the deistic belief in a non-providential God. The connections that Clarke drew between these positions are striking.

Clarke started with those whom he considered to be outright atheists. His main target at this point was Spinoza, 'the most celebrated Patron of Atheism in our time'.[97] To Clarke, as to many others, Spinoza represented the modern atheist who reduced the world to mere matter and necessity. According to Clarke, the material world could not possibly have been the original, self-existing being, and this was the main question at stake with the atheists. Instead, the world and its beauty, order, and well-being had to be caused by an intelligent being with liberty and choice.[98] Not only must there be some other unchangeable cause to all the changeable things in the world, but this cause must also be independent and external. Thus, Clarke attacked Toland for his idea that motion is essential to matter, arguing that such essential motion could not be directed in a certain way unless it was determined by an external cause. If motion was essential, everything would have moved in every way at once, which is impossible.[99]

As part of his attack on the idea of necessity of matter, Clarke criticised Hobbes for explaining the operations of the mind as necessary effects of motion. He rejected the way in which Hobbes explained all sensation and consciousness as phantasms caused by the pressure of objects on organs, arguing that this could explain only how an image occurs but not how it is perceived by the brain. Clarke read Hobbes as explaining perception only in material terms and as asserting, as a necessary though absurd consequence of that, that matter itself is endowed with perception. Clarke linked Hobbes to those who 'would make Thinking to be an Affection of *Matter*', presumably referring to Locke.[100] Clarke's goal was to make the contrary point, namely, that willing and thinking are in no way qualities of matter, at least not when matter is defined only in terms of figures and motions. Rather, willing and thinking must be faculties of immaterial substances, which also means that the soul is a distinct substance from the body, and that men can act without being acted upon, hence the existence of free will.[101]

Thus, Clarke started by refuting atheism, mostly through fighting materialism and necessitarianism which he attributed to Hobbes, Spinoza, 'and their Followers', such as Toland.[102] Then, he moved on to attack other and more evasive forms of atheism, and it is at this point that his discussion of deism began. Clarke referred to those deists who believe in God as a supreme intelligent being that made the world, '[t]hough at the same time they agree with the Epicureans in this, that they fancy God does *not at all concern* himself in the *Government* of the World, nor has any regard to, or care of, what is done therein'.[103] Clarke did not reject the idea that God could theoretically order the world so that necessary causes would regularly produce effects 'without the immediate interposition of his Almighty Power upon every particular occasion', but he firmly denied the idea that God created a certain quantity of matter and motion and then left the world to be shaped by them with no clear direction.[104]

Clarke was worried about the deistic view of God's non-intervention in the same way that he was worried about the idea of active matter, because the implication was the same: Epicurean atheism, according to which the material world running by mere chance is all there is. Moreover, Clarke denied that the seventeenth century's mechanical philosophy, and Newton's in particular, had to lead to such a notion, arguing that recent discoveries showed that 'the very original Laws of Motion themselves cannot continue to take place, but by something Superior to Matter, *continually* exerting on it a certain Force or Power', which is 'entirely different from that by which Matter acts on Matter'.[105] Clarke's purpose was to reject any talk of the world only in terms of motion and matter, that is, with no continual direction by God. Against the deists, he asserted that God governs the world and that the world 'depends every Moment on some Superior Being, for the *Preservation* of its Frame'.[106] Clarke asserted that denying God's concern with the world was to deny His being omnipresent, intelligent, and all-powerful, which was to deny His existence altogether. To Clarke, although these deists confessed in words that there was a God, they denied Him in reality.

Clarke identified three other types of deists. First, those who believe in God and His providence, but naturally rather than morally, that is, they maintain that God is not concerned with good or evil actions. Second, those who do recognise the moral aspects of God's government, but do not believe in the immortality of the soul, that is, they believe that humans perish entirely at death. Third, those who have all the right notions—that God is an intelligent being, and the creator, governor, and preserver of the world; that He communicates His goodness and happiness to His creatures, and that they are obliged in turn to promote the general good of the world and the happiness of each other—but despite these beliefs, they claim that everything is discoverable by reason alone and therefore reject divine revelation. Clarke used similar arguments to show why these categories led straight to atheism, except for the last one, which represented the true deists who just had to be taught to interpret and accept Christianity properly. Adherence to the obligations of natural religion and sincere inquiry, Clarke argued, were not necessarily problematic if they were accompanied by the recognition of revelation; in fact, this form of religion had been practised by Socrates and Cicero. It was the contemporary deists, however, who were characterised by 'their trivial and vain Cavils; their mocking and ridiculing, without and before examination' and by 'their loose, vain, and frothy Discourses; and, above all, their vitious and immoral Lives'.[107]

Later on, Clarke also attacked the idea of a 'modern Author', namely, the author of the essay 'Of Natural Religion' in Blount's *Oracles of Reason*, according to which the fact that revelation is not universal shows that it cannot be a necessary part of Christianity, 'and herein all the Deniers of Revelation agree with him'.[108] Clarke's response was twofold: first, God is not obliged to make revelation equally and universally available to all; and second, if this claim were true, then natural religion, too, would have to be disregarded as unnecessary, since God has not made everyone equally and universally rational either, '[a]s these Gentlemen themselves upon some occasions are willing enough to own, when they are describing the barbarous Ignorance of some poor Indian Nations'.[109] In so arguing, Clarke replied to Blount and Warren, who had replied to Charles Wolseley; and precisely the same debate would continue when Collins and eventually Tindal reply to Clarke.

It is illuminating to see how Clarke created a continuum, starting with the outright materialist Spinoza, through Hobbes and Toland, to the deists: they all posed the same threat of describing a materialistic godless world; they just did it with different degrees of sophistication. Here, Hobbes's materialism, combined with Spinozist and even Lockean ideas, was presented as particularly influential for Toland and his fellow deists. This kind of attack on the deists formed a common ground among Anglican critics at the time, but Clarke's definition of deism and its notions was considerably more elaborate, and his respectable reputation made him particularly central to this debate. Consequently, his classification of the deists became highly influential and an important milestone in the historiography of deism.

Hobbes played an important part in this story as Clarke told it. Subsequent deists attacked Clarke, but they also accepted some of the premises that Clarke attributed to deism. As we will see, Matthew Tindal replied to Clarke in his *Christianity as Old as the Creation* (1730), mentioning that 'the Dr. got immortal Honour by that Discourse'.[110] These were the dialectics of deism: a concept whose definition was often subjective and flexible, and which was nevertheless at the centre of a deep and sincere, even if heated, dialogue between a provocative group of anticlerical writers and the rightfully alarmed orthodoxy.

The *Deist's Manual*

Some Anglicans expressed more subtle and nuanced views on the subjects of their critique. One example is the *Deist's Manual* of 1705. Its author was Charles Gildon, whom we know as the former deist and friend of Charles Blount. Gildon had a central role in the publication of Blount's works after the latter's death, but he later converted to Anglicanism. The *Manual*, Gildon explained, was written after realising the error of his ways and in order to fix the erroneous views which were spreading. Reconsidering his deistic past, Gildon stated that he aimed to defeat those '*Hobbists* of the Times', whom he considered to be speculative atheists.[111]

The chapter of the *Manual* on natural law offers a thorough discussion of Hobbes. The discourse is structured as a dialogue. Gildon's character, Christophil, is critical towards Hobbes, while another interlocutor, Pleonexus, is on the side of the deists and claims to have the books of Hobbes and Spinoza. Pleonexus clearly thinks highly of Hobbes; he wonders how the others can 'think so little of a Man, the whole *English* World so loudly applauds' and maintains that he 'can find nothing but Magnificent Expressions of the Deity in him'.[112] The image of Hobbes as represented in the *Manual* was thus multi-layered. A close look at the discourse suggests that Gildon recognised that Hobbes's account of natural law was rather complex, containing agreeable elements with others that were more difficult to swallow.

Following the mainstream Anglican criticism of Hobbes, Gildon argued that his state of nature was impossible in reality as well as in theory, and that God Himself would not have allowed such an awful state to ever exist. Second, he argued, 'Mr. *Hobbs* and his Followers, shou'd not suppose, that all Men are so fond of Fighting'.[113] Reason is given to us by God to reach happiness, so it must teach us the laws of nature, which consist of duties to ourselves, to our neighbours, and to God. These duties include self-love and self-preservation, and consequently moral virtues such as sobriety and prudence as well as justice and benevolence.[114]

Even though Gildon refuted Hobbes, his account was not substantially different. Through the words of the fictional Pleonexus, Gildon argued that it is possible that 'Mr. *Hobbs*'s System of the *State of War*, wou'd do the Business every jot as well' given that it should lead men to choose peace.[115] Gildon claimed that men could never have been irrational, but he did not reject the idea that Hobbes's account could work once they are recognised as rational. Hobbes's main problem is that it is not clear how men had at some point obtained reason.[116] Moreover, Gildon admitted that the laws of nature are discoverable 'by a more Divine, tho' equally rational and natural Rule of *Doing as you wou'd be done by*, which ev'n Mr. *Hobbs* allows to be the Test of all the Laws of Nature'.[117] Gildon recognised what others might have overlooked or intentionally misrepresented: that on Hobbes's account it is human reason that leads men to establish peace and society, and that the essence of Hobbes's natural law has moral value, represented in the formula of the Golden Rule.[118] After his conversion to Anglicanism, Gildon ostensibly opposed Hobbes and Hobbism almost entirely. Nevertheless, when read carefully, his discussion in the *Manual* reveals a more complex attitude towards Hobbes, arguably even a degree of respect where he thought that Hobbes deserved it.

It is perhaps Gildon's background that makes this example a particularly illuminating demonstration of the relationship between Hobbes and deism. The positions of Hobbes and the deists, depicted here as rather close, were complex in that they subverted religion but did not overthrow it entirely, at least not openly. Their views on reason and natural law were rather conventional; their criticism was certainly of a new radical kind, but neither Hobbes nor the deists ever denied the existence of God. Gildon was aware of these nuances. His *Manual* reflected a subtle reception of a complex set of positions. This ambivalence was not necessarily unique to Gildon. At the time, Hobbes was the admired villain, almost a symbol that must be attacked as it served the interest of the writer. The deists, it seems, were to become the next generation of villains.

Striking at the root of antichristian priestcraft

Matthew Tindal (1657–1733) became a fellow at All Souls College, Oxford, in 1678. During the 1680s he converted to Catholicism but later returned to the Church of England. His conversion was perceived as an opportunistic move aimed to secure the wardenship of All Souls under James II. In the 1690s, Tindal frequented London coffeehouses and became a strong critic of the Church of England's clergy. He was a defender of the revolution, and he gained a reputation as a lawyer loyal to the regime of William III, an allegiance that was reflected in his early political tracts. At All Souls, Tindal 'gathered around him a group of secular whig lawyers opposed to the religious requirements made of fellows by the college's statutes', and at the same time, his reputation in the college became rather dubious, and he was accused of immoral behaviour, debauchery, and 'sensual indulgence, both sexual and at the table'.[119] Tindal's most notorious work was *The Rights of the Christian Church Asserted, Against the Romish, and All Other Priests Who Claim an Independent Power Over It* (1706). This work is often mentioned alongside the *Oracles of Reason* and *Christianity Not Mysterious*, and it was described by the non-juror and Tindal's former tutor, George

Hickes, as a 'Commonplace-Book of *Atheists* and *Deists*'.[120] In order to assess this work in detail, we first need to review the positions that Tindal started to develop in the 1690s.

During the 1690s, Tindal produced a series of essays that contained a systematic political theory. He appeared as a natural law thinker influenced by Grotius, a champion of religious toleration following Locke, and an advocate of freedom of the press inspired by Milton.[121] In his *Essay Concerning the Power of the Magistrate* (1697), Tindal aspired 'to encourage impartial Liberty and mutual Toleration; which instead of ruining, is the only way to preserve both Church and State'.[122] He argued 'That Government is from the People, who had a right to invest the Magistrate with a Power in those Matters of Religion which have an Influence on Humane Societies, but not in others that are meerly Religious, or have no such Influence'.[123] The magistrate can, for example, punish a subject who denies the existence and providence of God and thus injures the whole of society, and so atheists should not be tolerated as they could be recognised even in the state of nature as enemies of mankind. But the power of the magistrate does not extend to things indifferent (*adiaphora*), such as '*Opinions* that are meerly Speculative, or Practices that are purely Ceremonial', because it is outrageous 'to suppose a Man's Rights to the enjoyment of this Life, ought to depend upon his thinking just as the Magistrate does about Things relating to the next'.[124]

Tindal justified this argument with a standard natural law theory, which followed Locke's theory of toleration as well as the Hobbesian-Lockean theory of the social contract.[125] He structured his argument as follows. Men must constitute a government by consent, in accordance with the law of self-preservation, to avoid the dangers of the state of nature. Then they give powers to the magistrate, but only those that they had originally possessed. The magistrate is thus responsible for determining right and wrong and for everything that concerns the welfare of society, which includes matters of religion insofar as they influence the life of society. The sovereign's power reaches its limit in those things that are merely religious. A man can only be punished for causing injury to another, but not when worshiping God as one sees fit, even if others think it to be wrong. In fact, the opposite is true: forcing others to join a religion in which they do not believe is indeed an injury, while the prevention of injury is one of the ends of society. Toleration is, therefore, just another form of protection of people from those who may try to invade their purely private concerns. Persecution rather than toleration is destructive of society, particularly for the happiness of the people, the preservation of which is the main aim of the magistrate.[126]

Tindal emphasised that God endowed men with reason, which should serve them as the only guide to understand His laws. Men are obliged to use their own reason to judge what is true and false in religious matters, so in matters that are merely religious the individual is equal to the magistrate.[127] Tindal derived the natural right to worship God according to one's conscience and conviction, 'which is antecedent to all Government, and can never be subject to it'.[128] Natural reason and natural law formed the basis of Tindal's political theory, just as they later served him to establish his deism in *Christianity as Old as the Creation*. This was not merely a rationalistic theory, but also an extremely anticlerical one, a dimension that is evident from Tindal's account of priestcraft. Tindal argued that it was the pride and ambitions of the priests, sometime with the help of 'persecuting Magistrates', that caused the corruption of religion, 'which being a thing so plain and easy in it self, and suted to the Capacity of the People, would never have been so much and so universally depraved, had there been an entire Liberty of Conscience'.[129] Religion must not be unintelligible nor obscure and therefore everyone must think through religious matters for themselves. Persecution, on the other hand, tends to keep people ignorant and superstitious, while serving the interests of the priests who promote doctrines that advance their power at the expense of true religion:

> And they that succeeded them, made it their Business to render Religion more and more mysterious and unintelligible, that the Laity should admire them for their profound Knowledg in things past their own understanding, and be wholly governed by them in Matters of Religion, as being above their Apprehensions ... Thus it was that Priest-craft began, and Persecution compleated the Ruin of Religion. And if this was the Method the Clergy took in the most early Times, what reason is there to suspect, that in these latter Times they are less in love with Power and Dominion?[130]

Tindal's account of the emergence of priestcraft and the corruption of religion resembles that of Hobbes in *Leviathan* as well as Toland's *Christianity Not Mysterious*. According to all these philosophers, religion was corrupted by heathen philosophers who brought absurd metaphysical notions into the church, and thereby vain philosophy intruded into Christianity. Tindal used this account to preach for liberty of conscience and, unlike Hobbes, also for the liberty of the press; indeed, he has been recently named 'the first true apostle of freedom of expression in England'.[131]

Tindal's political theory had another dimension which focused on the power of the magistrate. It is here that the link to Hobbes becomes particularly apparent. Tindal's discussion of the state of nature and the right to self-preservation in the *Essay* already had a Hobbesian-Lockean resonance, as did his main assertion that the civil magistrate should have authority in all religious matters that influence society. Tindal was more explicit about these issues in *The Rights of the Christian Church Asserted* of 1706, a work of a thorough scholarly nature. As Jeffrey Collins argues, this work was not only one of the most prominent manifestations of the Hobbesian-Lockean position in the early eighteenth century, but it also displayed a more nuanced reading of Lockean toleration through a Hobbesian lens, with a considerable anticlerical and prudential tone.[132]

The *Rights* offered an historical investigation to show that clerical conduct contradicted the original uncorrupted spirit of the church. Like previous deists, Tindal believed that the clergy had complicated and mystified religion to gain independent power in church matters; and so 'distinctly Hobbesian was Tindal's presentation of Trinitarian orthodoxy as a weapon of clerical tyranny'.[133] The church, he argued, should seek legitimacy from its members in a democratic manner; even God ruled over the Jews only after they gave their consent. It is only this kind of church that could be conducive to the happiness of human kind, that being the primary design of God. As Hobbes did, Tindal reminded the readers of John 18:36, 'My kingdom is not of this world', to show that priests did not have any actual power.[134]

Here, too, Tindal argued that people should make their own judgement in religious matters unrelated to the public interest, including the manner in which they worship God or even the religion they choose.[135] At the same time, he argued that the civil magistrate should have supreme power in all religious matters insofar as they affect the public good. Thus, he granted the civil sovereign total authority over the church, as well as the 'Right, when the Good of the Society requires it, to cut off any one, whether Lay or Clergy, from all Church Communion, by Banishment, Imprisonment, or Death', and what is more,

> by virtue of this Power he can oblige any of his Subjects to serve his Country, tho that Service confine him to Places which have no Christian Church, or none he can communicate with; nay, to fight for the Safety of his Country against Men of his own Church and Religion: which shows that the Good of the Society is the supreme Law, and that all Church Considerations, as well as everything else, must give place to it; and that no Person, on any Church pretence whatever, can be exempt from the Magistrate's Jurisdiction, and consequently that there cannot be two Independent Powers in the same Society.[136]

The *Rights* was aimed against the highly dangerous doctrine (in Tindal's eyes) that there can be two independent powers in the same society, namely, civil and ecclesiastical. Tindal sought to establish the unequivocal supremacy of the civil magistrate in all things related to the public good, including some kind of a right to censorship: according to Tindal, the magistrate should instruct the church to promote only principles conducive to the public good, and 'see that all Doctrines which make for it are to the utmost inculcated'.[137] As Alex Barber shows, this was an interesting development in Tindal's thought: having previously believed in free speech also in the pulpit, he came to see how high churchmen abused this right to preach seditious and offensive sermons and he modified his view accordingly.[138] Thus, Tindal argued, the magistrate has the right to authorise ministers to speak publicly for peaceful doctrines and to silence them when they do not do so. Finally, when 'Ministers have acquir'd greater Riches, than 'tis the Interest of the Commonwealth they should have', then the magistrate 'has a Right to rectify this Abuse'.[139]

Like Hobbes, Tindal reached an Erastian position driven by a strong anticlerical motivation. The basic message was that of Matthew 6:24, which Tindal cited on the title page of the *Rights*, and which Hobbes cited in *On the Citizen*: 'No man can serve two masters'.[140] Tindal argued fiercely against the coexistence of two independent powers in society: magisterial and ecclesiastical, precisely what Hobbes identified as the danger of 'seeing double'. Tindal was aware of the resemblance:

> What's premis'd concerning the Natural Rights of Mankind, was but necessary; lest when I show that there cannot be two Independent Powers in the same Society, and that the Magistrate has all the Power relating to Religion that Man is capable of, I might seem to give him as great a Power as *Hobbs* complemented him with; between whom and those who claim an Independent Power in Church matters, how much soever they may rail at him, there's no other difference, than that he will have the Magistrate to judge for the People as well as himself, but they wou'd have both blindly follow them.[141]

The great difference between Tindal and Hobbes, as the former perceived it, was that Hobbes relinquished some natural rights to the sovereign, namely, the right of everyone to judge for themselves and to follow their conscience, especially in the worship of God, whereas Tindal preserved these rights for the individual.[142] Certainly, this is not a negligible difference.[143] But Tindal also knew that he was likely to be attacked on the basis of his resemblance to Hobbes and this concern may well have motivated him to distinguish himself from the latter. If this is the case, then this paragraph illuminates not only the difference between Tindal and Hobbes, but also the common ground between them. Evidence for this assumption comes from previous cases of accusations of Hobbism, of which Tindal was evidently aware. One such case was Samuel Parker, bishop of Oxford. Parker was anxious about the dangers of toleration, and he attacked Hobbes for his supposedly tolerationist tendencies. Ironically, he ended up being attacked himself for arriving at a Hobbesian theory since he developed a position which effectively gave the sovereign an unrestricted power to determine all religious matters to ensure peace. We can assume that Tindal, whose own solution was not all that different, did not want to share Parker's fate. Therefore, in another work, Tindal accused Parker along similar lines for having given 'our Kings as great a Power, as ever *Hobbs* did; for he say's, in Disputes of a publick concern, private Men are not to be directed by their own judgment, but by the Commands and Determinations of the publick Conscience'.[144]

It is true that Tindal's support of toleration went a lot further than Hobbes or Parker. But just as Hobbes and Parker did, Tindal gave the sovereign full discretion in all public matters. Notably, this includes the determination of what actually counts as public. Moreover, Tindal's references show that he was extremely aware of this similarity. After all, his main goal was to show that the clergy should not have independent power in society, given the grave danger of priestcraft. In this there was absolutely no difference between him and Hobbes. This is not to say that Tindal was a Hobbist, merely that there are undeniable similarities both in the problem that they identified and in the solution that they offered.

The links between Tindal and Hobbes were also recognised by contemporaries, and Tindal did not manage to escape the association with Hobbes, despite his attempts. George Hickes made this connection particularly explicit. In the late 1680s and 1690s Hickes attacked Hobbes and Hobbism in a number of occasions: he identified Hobbes with Milton and with de facto ideas that could support the revolution, and he identified latitudinarians like Tillotson with Hobbes, as Charles Leslie did.[145] In 1707, Hickes published *Two Treatises* as a response to the publication of Tindal's *Rights*. He condemned the attack made by the *Rights* on the church and argued that its then anonymous author 'hath licked up the Venom of *Hobbes*, *Selden*, and *Marvel*, and disgorged it upon the Church'.[146] He stated harshly that 'The Deists, and Atheists of late, by this and other such writers, have *exalted their Voices against the Lord*, and his Church' and that '[i]t concerns all good Christians to distinguish themselves from them, and to resist them as they would the Devil', because 'if they can once persuade Men, that Church Government, and Discipline is nothing but Invention, and Craft of Priests, they will soon persuade them, that the Christian Doctrines are so too'.[147] According to Hickes, these men, following their 'dear Fathers', namely, Hobbes, Selden, and Spinoza, simply hated the scripture as well as the priesthood.[148] But their views were only table talks; in publishing them they took liberty that 'would not be suffered in any other Christian Countrey'.[149]

Hickes clearly associated Tindal's political theory with Hobbes's. The idea of the state of nature, which Tindal took up, was a 'wild Notion' that 'hath been so many times unanswerably confuted by the Writers against *Hobbs*' as well as Locke.[150] He claimed that Tindal's argument that the clergy had mischievously made the sovereign dependent on them in ecclesiastical matters was also modelled on Hobbes.[151] Tindal's twofold ambition of 'defending the Natural Rights of Mankind' and 'striking at the Root of Antichristian Priestcraft' would have made '*Hobbs,* and *Bl[o]unt,* and many other Sons of *Belial,* brag'.[152] Finally, doctrines that promoted the power of the civil rather than ecclesiastical government were likely to result in '*something like that of* Erastus*, or perhaps of the Super-Erastians*, Hobbes, Selden, and other such Writers, who have endeavour'd to destroy the Being, and Constitution of the Church, as a Society'.[153] This is precisely what Hickes thought Tindal was trying to do.

Hickes did not stop there: two years after the *Two Treatises* he republished another work which he discovered and stated that had he known about this work earlier he would not have published his own response to Tindal.[154] This work was *A Modest Plea for the Clergy* from 1677, written by Lancelot Addison, dean of Lichfield and archdeacon of Coventry, and the father of the Whig writer Joseph Addison, although his identity was unknown to Hickes. As William Bulman shows, the *Plea,* which was originally printed by Hobbes's publisher, Crooke, engaged with Hobbes in a sophisticated way by employing some Hobbesian methods to arrive at different conclusions.[155] For example, Addison investigated the origins of the clerical institution, admitted that part of it might have originated as a 'blind Tradition', and showed how people would have been inclined to submit to it in a scenario akin to the state of nature, all in order to defend the social function and necessity of this institution.[156] For Hickes, who was certainly less interested in a thoughtful engagement with Hobbes or the *Rights,* the *Plea* was enough to 'obviate the wicked design of that profane Piece, wherein Men of the basest Interest, and worst Principles, the Sons of *Epicurus, Hobbes,* and *Spinoza,* have said almost all that the *wicked* DAEMONS could inspire them to speak against the *Christian Priesthood*'.[157] Using the *Plea,* Hickes therefore had another opportunity to attack Tindal and his fellow deists, in whose popular books it was no wonder 'to see the Scriptures banter'd, the Priestly Office prophan'd, and laid in common to Men and Women', and the priests 'represented as Thieves'.[158]

Similarly, Charles Leslie attacked the *Rights* in 1707, disparaged Tindal who 'turn'd *Papist* … but return'd since with the Fashion', and considered Anthony Collins a co-author and 'a constant Champion for the *Deists* and *Sectarists* of the Age'.[159] Leslie believed that the *Rights* aimed to take away the special and binding status of the church for society, and the divine authority of its government, and that it reduced the church simply to a sect like all others. The defenders of the *Rights,* he argued, were 'Men who have no real value for Religion of any kind'.[160] Their message was pursued by the '*Deists, Socinians,* and all our *Libertines* who make use of their *Artillery* and wage War with the *Church* and all *Instituted Religion* upon their very *Principles*'.[161] For Leslie, these men were wolves in sheep's clothing since their denial of the divine authority of bishops and kings alike meant, in fact, that they were unfaithful church members as well as disloyal subjects.[162] These were men who insisted on making up and spreading their own rules, and so 'A *Whigg* is a State *Enthusiast*, as a *Dissenter* is an *Ecclesiastical*'.[163] It is not surprising to find in Leslie's work, too, the comparison between the authors of the *Rights* and Hobbes and Erastus, and especially the argument that the *Rights* developed the Hobbesian doctrine that made the authority of the scripture depend on the civil magistrate, from which it would follow 'that the *Parliament* may make a new *Bible* for us'.[164]

Hobbes, Tindal, and indeed Collins sought to deny power to the clergy, so the non-jurors might have been right to think that they simply hated the priests. But more than mere hatred, they shared similar ideas on the uses and abuses of religion when it met politics. Their efforts to rewrite a history of religion and of the church, to expose clerical corruption and to offer a programme of civil religion rid of priestcraft, were at the very core of the project of early Whiggism and early Enlightenment.[165] In the end, Tindal recognised that a certain degree of authoritarianism would be a useful tool in the fight against priestcraft. Even the infamous right of censorship that Hobbes granted the sovereign, Tindal gave to the magistrate in religious matters: a necessary principle of both their theories was that the civil authority had to stop priests from propagating doctrines that endangered the safety of the commonwealth—camouflaged with false mysteries and vain philosophy—and from voicing these doctrines in public. Their substantial differences notwithstanding, it would be reasonable to assume that at least on issues of ecclesiastical politics Hobbes and Tindal could have agreed.

The Collins–Clarke correspondence

Around the same time, Anthony Collins (1676–1729) engaged with the question of the nature of the soul, after the theologian Henry Dodwell published his controversial work on the topic in 1706, and Samuel Clarke published his response. Collins's intervention in this debate started as a defence of Dodwell's right to follow his reason and express his views, which anticipated his agenda of freethinking, but soon turned into a deep and long discussion, now known as the Collins–Clarke correspondence of 1707–1708.[166] Dodwell's work was alarming already from its title, *An Epistolary Discourse Proving, from the Scriptures and the First Fathers, That the Soul Is a Principle Naturally Mortal*.[167] According to Dodwell, the soul had been immortal until the fall but then became mortal, and now it can be immortalised only through baptism by bishops. Although Dodwell's intentions were not necessarily sceptical, the suggestion that the soul is presently and naturally mortal made this one of the most explosive works of the decade. In his letter to Dodwell, Clarke admitted that Dodwell might not have intended to draw impious conclusions from his thesis, but he feared that the 'imprudent Title' of his work would lead the uncareful reader to conclude that the soul perishes when the body dies, and what is more, the 'Libertines' would also conclude from this work that they could escape an eternal punishment.[168] Such libertines, who are 'Men of loose Principles and vicious Lives', seem to resemble the deists that Clarke had attacked only a year earlier, and in particular those deists to whom he attributed the belief that humans perish entirely at death.[169]

Clarke objected to the implication that the soul might be material, thus developing the arguments that he had presented in his Boyle Lectures against Hobbes, Spinoza, and Toland. He raised the issue of consciousness to disprove the materiality of the soul. The argument was that matter is divisible and consists of particles, and so its separate particles would have separate consciousnesses (if they had consciousness at all), whereas the soul has an individual consciousness, which is its power of thinking.[170] Collins picked up this argument in his letter to Dodwell, where he answered Clarke, thus reviving the debate on whether or not matter can think and developing the position previously attributed to Locke, Hobbes, and their followers.

Collins's argument was that a system of matter may have a certain kind of power even if its parts do not have this power when taken apart. Thus, the particles of the brain may not have the power to think separately in themselves, but they may well have this power once they are combined together. Here Collins came close to Toland's thesis of the active matter, arguing that this power may either flow necessarily from the particles or be superadded to them by God.[171] Subsequently, Clarke rejected Collins's objection, arguing that the 'real Qualities' of any system of matter, such as magnitude and motion, are exactly the sum of the qualities of its parts. Thus, assuming that thinking is a real quality, it cannot reside in a system of matter if it does not reside in its particles. Clarke then moved to dismiss other qualities that are mistakenly thought to reside in matter, including sensations such as tastes and smells, which are only modes of perception, or powers such as gravitation and magnetism, which are merely abstract names that signify some effects of motion.[172] As matter cannot be attributed with thinking, it cannot be attributed with inherent action either; here was the common thread between Clarke's attack on Toland and his subsequent attack on Collins. But as with these kinds of attacks, once again it only encouraged his interlocutor to take and justify the precise positions that were refuted. This was particularly clear in the case of gravity: while it was important for Clarke to assert that gravitation is 'only an *Effect* of the continual and regular Operation of some other Being upon [Matter]', Collins replied that 'it does not appear but that Matter gravitates by virtue of Powers originally placed in it by God, and is now left to itself to act by those Original Powers'.[173]

Thus, while Collins revealed his views about the possibility of matter thinking as well as moving itself, Clarke continued to insist that these must be the powers of immaterial beings, namely, the soul and God. Subsequently, Collins clarified that 'Thinking is an Action that begins not in us, till we are operated on by external material Objects, that act on us by Motion and Contact; no more than a Windmill begins to go till the Air or some other Body strikes against the Sails'.[174] Thinking is a material act that must start with sensation; even in thinking, therefore, matter in motion is all there is. As Clarke pointed out, Collins's materialism was also deterministic: every motion depends on an impulse that causes it and is therefore always necessary. For Clarke, this meant that Collins's position in this correspondence was 'utterly destructive of Religion', because his portrayal of the human mind made it analogous to the mechanism of a clock: 'Now what *Ends and Purposes of Religion* mere Clocks and Watches are capable of serving, needs no long and nice Consideration'.[175] Moreover, Clarke claimed that Collins's scepticism regarding the immateriality of the soul denied possibility to future rewards and punishments, both because it denied possibility to resurrection, and because 'by introducing such an absolute and fatal *Necessity* of all human Actions, as Mr. *Hobbes* and *Spinoza* formerly attempted to establish by the same *numerical* Argument ... it manifestly makes all future *Reward unreasonable*, and all *Punishment unjust*'.[176]

By attacking Collins, Clarke kept his former attack on Hobbes as alive as ever. When he previously argued that thinking cannot be an attribute of matter, that the soul is not material, and that the operations of the mind are not merely necessary motions, his main target was Hobbes 'and his Followers', especially Toland.[177] It is evident that he saw in Collins precisely the same position that he saw in Hobbes and Toland, given that in their correspondence he recycled the same arguments that he had made previously. For example, when he argued against the idea that consciousness could be a simple quality of matter, he stated that 'No *individual* or *single Quality* of one Particle of Matter, can be the *individual* or *single Quality* of another Particle'.[178] Thus, he also disproved what

> Mr. *Hobbes* suggests in his *Physicks* ... that *All Matter* is essentially *endued with an obscure actual Sense and Perception*, but that there is required a Number and apt Composition of Parts to make up *a clear and distinct Sensation or Consciousness*. For from this Notion it would follow, that the resulting *Sensation or Consciousness* at last, being but One distinct *Sensation or Consciousness* (as is that of a Man:) the *Sensation or Consciousness* of every One of the constituent Particles, would be the individual *Sensation or Consciousness* of All and Each of the rest.[179]

Precisely as he did in his Boyle Lectures, Clarke referred here to chapter 25 of *Concerning Body*, 'Of Sense and Animal Motion', where he believed that Hobbes made the case that our sense and perception, and hence our consciousness, were products of pressure on our organs.[180] For Collins as for Hobbes, therefore, consciousness became entirely material as well as necessitated, consisting merely of the outcome of motions; Clarke's response made it clear that he saw Collins as another follower of Hobbes.[181] Elsewhere in the correspondence he ridiculed Collins's statement that he 'often admired that Gravitation should be esteemed a Matter of such Difficulty among Philosophers' and his consequent attempt to explain it by the fact that 'all Matter is in constant Motion, and perpetually striking one Part against another'.[182] Collins's arrogance in pretending to provide a simple explanation for gravity, that Newton might have missed, seemed to Clarke equal to Hobbes's vain ambitions:

> I suppose the rest of the World will no less *admire* at *you*, for imagining that by so slight an *Admiration* you could at once set aside all the Propositions in that most excellent Book [*Principia*] ... Not much unlike to this, was Mr. *Hobbes*'s fancying that he had confuted all the Propositions in *Euclid*, by *admiring* at *Euclid*'s Definitions of Lines and Surfaces: And all Men ever since, that understand the first Elements of Geometry, have *admired* at *him* for fancying so.[183]

Collins might or might not have shared Hobbes's self-esteem, but for Clarke they posed almost the same threat, as did the deists that Clarke had previously identified in his Boyle Lectures; they were all bold enough to think that they invented their own new theories. Expressing similar concerns, a tract entitled *The First Principles of Modern Deism Confuted* (1707) sought to demonstrate the immateriality and immortality of the soul against Collins and his 'Clubb of Heroes, whose Names will be had in Honour by those who abhor Christianity'.[184] Again, Hobbes was linked to the deists through the idea that phantasms are mere sensations and that matter can think.[185]

It is evident that Hobbes was on Clarke's and Collins's minds, and not only because of his potentially subversive materialism and determinism. While Clarke quoted Hobbes's saying that '*Arguments* seldom work on Men of Wit and Learning, when they have once engaged themselves in a contrary Opinion', Collins used this quote to remark sarcastically that it would perhaps be better to leave Clarke's argument unanswered and not 'disturb his particular Satisfaction in the Force of his Argument'.[186] He did answer, of course, and in his answer, he also attacked Clarke with the same Hobbesian logic:

> When Reason is on our side, we cheerfully submit to its Dictates ... but when we are not able to answer Difficulties alledged against our *Schemes*, then we contend that Reason is weak, and from its supposed Weakness infer, That our

Inability to clear up Difficulties and answer Objections, ought not to hinder our Assent to *them*.[187]

Here Collins, too, appropriated the Hobbesian idea that a man is against reason when reason is against a man (and not for the last time, as we will see later); and he used it not only to expose Clarke's unreasonableness but also to remind his readers that assent had to be given only to ideas that could pass the test of reason.

What is most striking in this episode is the fact that Collins took Hobbes's side against Clarke unequivocally in his private correspondence. In a letter from May 1707 to William Simpson, Baron of the Court of Exchequer, Collin wrote:

> I am obliged to you for consulting Mr Hobbes & for your care in sending my letter after Mr Clark to Norwich. When upon my arrival here I looked into Mr Hobbes's Physicks I was amazed how a man of Mr Clarks sense could in so gross a manner mistake him, but upon turning over some other Adversaries of Mr Hobbes on the same argument ... I find they understand Mr Hobbes just in the same manner as Mr Clark does. They knew not how to answer him but by first misrepresenting him, & I fancy Mr Clark is either guilty of the same fault or else has contented himself to represent Mr Hobbes out of other mens works.[188]

So, already in his early writing career, Collins defended Hobbes's philosophy as well as his reputation, albeit privately, after consulting his *Concerning Body*. This letter is an extremely significant piece of evidence because it shows that deists and freethinkers, who might have been reluctant to link themselves to Hobbes openly, still recognised his ingenuity. Furthermore, what Collins provided in this letter is a sharp observation about Hobbes's reception and indeed about the way that Hobbes's critics often misrepresented his ideas deliberately to make their own points; the fact that Collins knew that shows that he was well-read in the works of both Hobbes and his adversaries which he claimed to have consulted. It seems that Collins believed that Clarke had done a serious injustice to Hobbes, whereas he actually got Hobbes right. Therefore, the letter gives us good reason to believe that Collins knew and approved of the fact that at that point his theory was indeed close to Hobbes's, or at least that they were both subjected to similar unjust criticisms.

Also in 1707, Collins published *An Essay Concerning the Use of Reason in Propositions*, wherein he defined reason as 'that faculty of the Mind whereby it perceives the Truth, Falshood, Probability or Improbability of Propositions'.[189] Broadly speaking, Collins adopted the Lockean view of reason, but as Toland did, he went further than Locke in making reason superior to revelation and questioning the idea that there could be mysteries or things above reason. He also used the familiar argument that parts of the scripture were later additions, especially some names of places from the times of Moses and Joshua, as well as the accounts of their deaths.[190] Thus, as Collins's biographer argues, the *Essay* effectively continued the deist controversy that started a decade earlier with *Christianity Not Mysterious*.[191] Finally, in this work Collins presented a distinctively Hobbesian notion of liberty as a lack of external impediments:

> Every man may observe in himself, a Power to do or forbear several Actions, according to the Determination of his Mind: if the Mind determins the doing of an Action, there is in some Cases no outward Impediment to hinder him from acting according to that Determination; and not only no outward Impediment, but the forbearance of the Action would have been equally in his Power, if the Mind had determin'd a forbearance.[192]

This, for Collins, would be a state of freedom. Accordingly, 'True Liberty therefore is consistent with Necessity, and ought not to be oppos'd to it, but only to Compulsion'.[193] In early eighteenth-century England, Collins became the leading exponent of a Hobbesian theory of liberty and necessity.[194] The next chapter discusses this in depth and shows that Collins came especially close to Hobbes a decade later in *A Philosophical Inquiry Concerning Human Liberty* (1717).

Pillar of cloud and fire

John Toland's *Hodegus: Or, the Pillar of Cloud and Fire Not Miraculous* was written in 1710 and published in 1720.[195] In many ways, it represents the general spirit of Toland's project, both in its goal and its strategy. The work analyses the story in Exodus 13 of the pillar of cloud and fire that guided the Israelites in the desert, by day and night, and that is traditionally interpreted as a form of God's revelation. It begins with Toland's usual anticlerical approach, accusing the clergymen who 'often us'd violence, to deterr others from the study of the antient Jewish books'.[196] As he did in his previous works, Toland argued that the priests had made the Old Testament look incomprehensible, and its stories more miraculous than they actually are. Not only did Toland engage with the Old Testament closely and literally, but he also sent a clear message to his readers that they should be able to engage in such free inquiries on their own. To prove his point, Toland concluded his study of the pillar of cloud and fire that this was an ordinary use of fire, simply 'carry'd in proper machines of mere human contrivances, which might well be call'd *ambulatory Beacons*'.[197] This fire was the most visible guide available, by virtue of its natural smoke during the day and its natural flames during the night; there was no miracle, no prodigy, and no providence. This method, Toland added, was very fitting for an army, and it had been common among other nations as well. Toland's analysis was therefore meant to 'do justice to Moses', by portraying him as a successful general, knowledgeable about the state-of-the-art military tactics.[198]

Toland used multiple sources from within and outside the scripture to make textual as well as historical claims to prove that stories of revelation had been exaggerated. This was a serious work of philological scholarship, including numerous references to some of the original key words in Hebrew. In line with his consistent agenda from the 1690s, and following Hobbes and Blount, Toland recommended an accurate and natural reading of the scripture. In one passage in *Hodegus*, Toland applied this approach in a way that is particularly reminiscent of Hobbes. Toland argued that the angel of God, who is mentioned in Exodus 14, 'and about which the Christian Divines of all nations are divided', was 'a mere mortal man, the Guide of the Israelites in the Wilderness; and the overseer or director of the portable Fire'.[199] As a typical freethinker, Toland knew he was being provocative in stating that: 'This will probably occasion certain people to make a noise: but so long as I am persuaded Truth's on my side, I shall be as much pleas'd, as they are sure to be angry'.[200] To show that, Toland investigated the word 'angel' and concluded that it simply signified a person. Indeed, this is what Hobbes had done in *Leviathan*, and for very similar reasons. Toland's main argument in this passage was that the word 'angel' in itself did not indicate that it referred to anything other than a mortal man. He explained rightly that the Hebrew word (מלאך) can simply signify a human messenger. Moreover, the context shows that this specific angel, who carried the pillar, did something that could be, and indeed was, done by men.[201] Toland went further to identify this human angel as Hobab, (possibly) Moses' brother-in-law. As Toland revealed, this finding was so important to him, that he even considered naming this work 'Hobab'.[202]

In chapter 34 of *Leviathan*, Hobbes similarly investigated the significa-tion of the word 'angel'. He stated that 'By the name of ANGEL, is signified generally, a *Messenger*; and most often, a *Messenger of God*'.[203] Hobbes examined the Old Testament to show that an angel is always 'some image raised (supernaturally) in the fancy, to signifie the presence of God in the execution of some supernaturall work'.[204] Among the examples he used, the one that received most attention is that of the pillar. There, Hobbes con-cluded, the angel was God Himself, in the form of the pillar, which there-fore signified God's presence. This interpretation appears to be relatively traditional, but Hobbes's overall goal was to show that 'there is no text … from which we can conclude, there is, or hath been created, any permanent thing (understood by the name of *Spirit or Angel*,) that hath not quantity … and, in summe, which is not (taking Body for that, which is some what, or some where) Corporeall'.[205] Hobbes was denying the existence of incorporeal substances, this time in the shape of angels, especially such with 'Wings, as usually they are painted, for the false instruction of common people'.[206] This argument brings to mind Toland's argument in *Letters to Serena* where he ridiculed the way in which the stars were commonly painted as human faces. If in 1695 Toland admired Hobbes's treatment of the scripture in inferring that God was corporeal, now he followed Hobbes to assert in his own radical way that angels, too, were corporeal. For Toland, as for Hobbes, materialism and biblical criticism were, once again, combined weapons deployed in an anticlerical war.

Toland's project—perhaps the entire deist project—can be summed up in his hope 'that the Bible will ever preserve its dignity; and that the Truth will triumph at last, over all the prejudices of the ignorant or the interested'.[207] It can be concluded that for someone like Toland, who aspired more than anything to fight a corrupt and dangerous clergy that maintained ignorance and superstition, Hobbes had much to offer. Toland developed the project that he started in the 1690s until the 1710s, with the same investigative approach and the same anticlerical tone. His materialism, too, was indebted to Hobbes, and the motive might have been similarly anticlerical: to insist that matter in motion is all there is, much like Hobbes did, was another way in which fables about supposedly unintelligible mysteries, such as angels, could be refuted. A work like *Hodegus*, therefore, shows beyond doubt that Toland recruited Hobbes for his lifelong political battle against priestcraft.

Notes

1 W. Nicholls, *A Conference with a Theist* (London, 1696), sig. A5r.
2 M. Craig, *A Satyr Against Atheistical Deism with the Genuine Character of a Deist* (Edinburgh, 1696), pp. 12–15. For another similar attack on deism, Hobbes, and Spinoza, especially regarding their questioning of the integrity of the scripture, see W. Lowth, *A Vindication of the Divine Authority and Inspiration of the Writings of the Old and New Testament* (Oxford, 1692), sigs. A6v–A8r.
3 H. Prideaux, *A Letter to the Deists* (London, 1696), p. 6.
4 Ibid., p. 10.
5 Ibid., p. 13.
6 Ibid., pp. 14–15.
7 Ibid., p. 15.
8 Ibid., p. 17.
9 Ibid., pp. 19–20. Hobbes actually rejected this implication in Lev 31, pp. 564–66.
10 F. Gastrell, *The Certainty and Necessity of Religion in General, or, the First Grounds & Principles of Humane Duty Establish'd* (London, 1697), p. 28.

11 J. Harris, *The Notion of a God, Neither from Fear nor Policy* (London, 1698), p. 3.

12 Ibid., p. 4.

13 Ibid., p. 7.

14 Ibid., pp. 16–17.

15 Ibid., pp. 23–24.

16 Harris, *Immorality and Pride, the Great Causes of Atheism* (London, 1698), p. 19.

17 W. Stephens, *An Account of the Growth of Deism in England* (London, 1696), pp. 3–4.

18 Ibid., p. 5.

19 Ibid.

20 Ibid., p. 6.

21 Ibid., p. 7.

22 Ibid., p. 5. On the *Account*, see for example Champion, *Pillars of Priestcraft Shaken*, pp. 17–18; M. Goldie, 'John Locke, the Early Lockeans, and Priestcraft', *Intellectual History Review*, 28:1 (2018), pp. 125–44.

23 R. Willis, *Reflexions upon a Pamphlet Intituled, an Account of the Growth of Deism in England Together with Some Considerations about the Christian Religion* (London, 1696), p. 7.

24 Collins, *In the Shadow of Leviathan*, pp. 320–44, on p. 337. See also Parkin, *Taming the Leviathan*, pp. 397–402.

25 J. Locke, *An Essay Concerning Humane Understanding* (London, 1690), p. 270, hinted at the possibility of thinking matter, asserting that '[w]e have the *Ideas* of *Matter* and *Thinking*, but possibly shall never be able to know, whether Matter thinks, or no'.

26 Ibid., pp. 264–68. According to Locke, there is a distinction between intuitive and demonstrative knowledge, or immediate and mediate knowledge: when two ideas seem to agree or disagree in themselves ('self-evident'), the knowledge is intuitive; when the agreement or disagreement needs to be assessed through an intermediate idea ('proof'), used as a common measure, the knowledge is demonstrative. This assessment is the work of reasoning. Yet whereas Locke rejected things that are contrary to reason for being inconsistent with clear and distinct ideas, the deists went further to reject mysteries, or things above reason, as well. See J. Toland, *Christianity Not Mysterious*, 2nd edn (London, 1696), pp. 11–15; A. Collins, *An Essay Concerning the Use of Reason in Propositions, the Evidence Whereof Depends upon Human Testimony* (London, 1707), pp. 3–6; M. Tindal, *Christianity as Old as the Creation: Or, the Gospel, a Republication of the Religion of Nature* (London, 1730: T101186), pp. 180–84 (these works are discussed in depth below). For a recent argument that Locke 'opened the floodgates' of the re-evaluation of the Christian faith that influenced the freethinkers, see J. A. T. Lancaster, 'From Matters of Faith to Matters of Fact: The Problem of Priestcraft in Early Modern England', *Intellectual History Review*, 28:1 (2018), pp. 145–65.

27 J. Locke, *The Reasonableness of Christianity, as Delivered in the Scriptures* (London, 1695), sig. A2r.

28 Ibid., p. 286.
29 Goldie, 'John Locke, the Early Lockeans, and Priestcraft', p. 132.
30 M. Goldie, 'John Locke and Anglican Royalism', *Political Studies*, 31:1 (1983), pp. 61–85; Goldie, 'Priestcraft and the Birth of Whiggism'; Goldie, 'John Locke, the Early Lockeans, and Priestcraft'.
31 Locke, *Reasonableness of Christianity*, e.g., p. 43.
32 Locke, *A Second Vindication of the Reasonableness of Christianity* (London, 1697), sig. a2r.
33 Ibid, and p. 376. It is plausible that the *Reasonableness* was aimed partly against Toland, whose *Christianity Not Mysterious* Locke had apparently read prior to its publication. There is also some evidence for Locke's ambivalence about Toland. In 1697 the Irish philosopher William Molyneux described Toland in his correspondence with Locke as 'a candid free thinker, and a good scholar' and reported that he found 'the clergy alarm'd to a mighty degree against him'. Locke and Molyneux expressed a positive yet cautious view of Toland at first, but Locke later wrote that Toland 'is a man to whom I never writ, and, I think, I shall not now begin'. J. Locke *et al.*, *Some Familiar Letters between Mr. Locke, and Several of His Friends* (London, 1708), pp. 190, 222. See also J. C. Biddle, 'Locke's Critique of Innate Principles and Toland's Deism', *Journal of the History of Ideas*, 37:3 (1976), pp. 411–22; J. Marshall, *John Locke: Resistance, Religion and Responsibility* (Cambridge, 1994), pp. 408–10; Champion, *Republican Learning*, pp. 73–75; D. Lucci, *John Locke's Christianity* (Cambridge, 2020).
34 Locke, *Second Vindication*, p. 471.
35 Locke, *Mr. Locke's Reply to the Right Reverend the Lord Bishop of Worcester's Answer to His Second Letter* (London, 1699), p. 422.
36 F. Waldmann, 'John Locke as a Reader of Thomas Hobbes's *Leviathan*: A New Manuscript', *The Journal of Modern History*, 93:2 (2021), pp. 245–82, on p. 273.
37 Toland denied the charge of deism when it was clearly meant as an insult, identical to atheism: 'But to what purpose should I study here or elsewhere, were I an Atheist or Deist, for one of the two you take me to be? What a contradiction to mention Virtue if I believ'd there was no God, or one so impotent that could not, or so malicious that would not reveal himself?' J. Toland, *A Collection of Several Pieces of Mr. John Toland*, ed. P. Desmaizeaux, 2 vols (London, 1726), vol. 2, p. 302. For Toland, the charge was unfounded: 'When Mr. Toland us'd to be traduc'd in Ireland for Deism with many other Opinions, and his Friends demanded of his Accusers where they made those Discoveries in his Writings, the ready Answer always was, that truly they had never read the Book, and by the Grace of God never would'. Toland, *An Apology for Mr. Toland in a Letter from Himself to a Member of the House of Commons in Ireland* (London, 1697), p. 21. See also Sullivan, *John Toland*, pp. 235–73.
38 Champion, *Republican Learning*, esp. p. 6
39 A. Boyer, *The Political State of Great Britain, Vol. XXIII* (London, 1722), p. 342; quoted also in Champion, *Republican Learning*, p. 69.

40 For Toland's Spinozism see, for example, Israel, *Radical Enlightenment*, pp. 609–14; I. Leask, 'The Undivulged Event in Toland's *Christianity Not Mysterious*', in Hudson, Lucci, and Wigelsworth (eds), *Atheism and Deism Revalued*, pp. 63–80.

41 Toland, *Christianity Not Mysterious*, p. xxvi.

42 Ibid. Cf. Lev 47, p. 1116. See also Toland, *Nazarenus*, 2nd edn (London, 1718), p. 72.

43 Toland, *Christianity Not Mysterious*, esp. pp. 151–69.

44 Hunter, *Decline of Magic*, p. 55.

45 Toland, *Christianity Not Mysterious*, p. 166. As Hobbes argued: 'I referre also all those Doctrines, that serve them to keep the possession of this spirituall Soveraignty after it is gotten. As first, that the *Pope in his publique capacity cannot erre*. For who is there, that beleeving this to be true, will not readily obey him in whatsoever he commands?' Lev 47, p. 1,108.

46 Toland, *Christianity Not Mysterious*, pp. 166–67.

47 Ibid., p. 49.

48 Ibid., p. 121.

49 Ibid., pp. 122–23.

50 Ibid., p. 6.

51 Ibid., pp. vii–viii.

52 Tillotson, *The Works of the Most Reverend Dr. John Tillotson*, 2nd edn, 2 vols (London, 1717), vol. 1, pp. 11–21, on p. 19.

53 See 'The *Oracles* and the critics of deism' in Chapter 1.

54 Champion, *Republican Learning*, pp. 69–78.

55 Tillotson, *Works*, vol. 1, p. 17.

56 Ibid., p. 18.

57 Ibid., p. 19.

58 Ibid.

59 While most of Tillotson's arguments for the reasonableness of Christianity were not particularly unusual for the Anglicans, they were very effective in the radical hands of people like Toland. Tillotson continued to serve as an inspiration for eighteenth-century deists and freethinkers. For example, Anthony Collins stated that 'all the *English Free-Thinkers* own [Tillotson] as their Head' for being a man of '*Learning* and *Good Sense*', for emphasising the natural and moral elements of religion, and for questioning the integrity of the general councils and other priestly meetings. Finally, Collins quoted from the same passage which Toland quoted in *Christianity Not Mysterious*, where Tillotson 'wonder'd that People can with patience endure to hear their Teachers and Guides talk against Reason'. A. Collins, *A Discourse of Free-Thinking, Occasion'd by the Rise and Growth of a Sect Call'd Free-Thinkers* (London, 1713: T31966), pp. 171–76, on pp. 171, 176. Tindal, *Christianity as Old as the Creation*, p. 75, praised Tillotson similarly as someone 'than whom none better understood human Nature'.

60 J. Harrington, *The Oceana of James Harrington and His Other Works*, ed. J. Toland (London, 1700), p. 46. In another sermon, Tillotson attributed the

saying '*[t]hat when reason is against a man, then a man will be against reason*' to '*one*, who hath done more by his *Writings* to debauch the Age with Atheistical principles than any man that lives in it'. Tillotson, *Works* (London, 1696), p. 36. There is every reason to believe, therefore, that both Tillotson and Toland knew that Hobbes was the source of this useful phrase.

61 L. P. [J. Toland], *Two Essays Sent in a Letter from Oxford to a Nobleman in London* (London, 1695), p. 29.

62 Ibid., p. 31.

63 Ibid.

64 Ibid., p. 35. Toland also mentioned Balthasar Bekker, the Calvinist preacher known for his denial of demons.

65 Ibid., p. ii.

66 Ibid.

67 Ibid., p. ii–iii.

68 Ibid., p. iii.

69 J. Harris, *The Atheist's Objections, Against the Immaterial Nature of God, and Incorporeal Substances, Refuted* (London, 1698), p. 50.

70 Toland, 'A Catalogue of Books … As Truly or Falsely Ascrib'd to Jesus Christ, His Apostles, and Other Eminent Persons', in *Collection of Several Pieces*, vol. 1, pp. 350–403.

71 Champion, *Republican Learning*, p. 196, and pp. 49, 192–97.

72 Lev 33, pp. 600–602.

73 Toland, *Amyntor: Or, a Defence of Milton's Life* (London, 1699), pp. 57–58.

74 Ibid., 58.

75 Ibid., 49.

76 Ibid., 68. See also Champion, *Republican Learning*, pp. 202–203; N. Keene, ' "A Two-Edged Sword": Biblical Criticism and the New Testament Canon in Early Modern England', in A. Hessayon and N. Keene (eds), *Scripture and Scholarship in Early Modem England* (Aldershot, 2006), pp. 94–115.

77 Anon., *Visits from the Shades* (London, 1704), p. 34.

78 Ibid., p. 32.

79 Ibid., p. 34.

80 Ibid., p. 33.

81 S. H. Daniel, 'Toland, John (1670–1722), Freethinker and Philosopher', *ODNB* (2004), available at: www.oxforddnb.com/view/10.1093/ref:odnb/978019 8614128.001.0001/odnb-9780198614128-e-27497 (accessed 21 July 2023).

82 Toland, *Letters to Serena* (London, 1704), p. 129.

83 Ibid., pp. 77, 81.

84 Ibid., p. 78.

85 Ibid., p. 92.

86 Lev 12, p. 172.

87 Toland, *Letters to Serena*, pp. 129–30.

88 Ibid., p. 159.

89 Ibid., pp. 160–61.

90 B. de Spinoza, *The Collected Works of Spinoza*, vol. 1, ed. and trans. E. Curley (Princeton, 1985), p. 544.

91 For Toland's explicit pantheism, see his *Socinianism Truly Stated* (London, 1705) and *Pantheisticon* (London, 1751); see also 'Toland's later works' in Chapter 3. A plausible early clue for Toland's pantheism can be found in Toland, *Two Essays*, p. 47, in the form of a quote from Virgil ('jovis omnia plena': all is full of God), also used in Blount, *Anima Mundi*, p. 6. See Sullivan, *John Toland*, pp. 115, 175; Berman, 'Disclaimers as Offence Mechanisms', p. 271; but also R. Rappaport, 'Questions of Evidence: An Anonymous Tract Attributed to John Toland', *Journal of the History of Ideas*, 58:2 (1997), pp. 339–48.

92 Toland, *Letters to Serena*, p. 161.

93 S. Duncan, 'Toland, Leibniz, and Active Matter', in D. Garber and D. Rutherford (eds), *Oxford Studies in Early Modern Philosophy, VI* (Oxford, 2012), pp. 249–78, on p. 256. See also M. C. Jacob, *The Newtonians and the English Revolution, 1689–1720* (Ithaca, NY, 1976), p. 232.

94 Hobbes's plenism is formulated in *Concerning Body*, where he turned to 'the taking away of the vacuum'. There, Hobbes gave a detailed account of the world's structure, according to which the world consists of three types of bodies: visible (the earth and the stars), invisible (atoms), and finally 'that most fluid ether, which so fills all the rest of the universe, as that it leaves in it no empty place at all'. In the later *Decameron physiologicum*, Hobbes asserted explicitly with regard to the creator, 'who being infinite, there can be no place empty where He is, nor full where He is not'. Although Hobbes did not go all the way to identify God—a corporeal spirit—with the ether or the plenum, this is a valid implication of his account. Hobbes, *English Works*, vol. 1, pp. 414, 426; Hobbes, *English Works*, vol. 7, p. 89. A. Lupoli, 'Power (Conatus-Endeavour) in the "Kinetic Actualism" and in the "Inertial" Psychology of Thomas Hobbes', *Hobbes Studies*, 14 (2001), pp. 83–103, esp. p. 99, suggests along these lines that Toland's theory provided a solution for a Hobbesian problem. Lupoli argues that according to Hobbes's atomism and his theory of hardness, fluids—including the ether or the *'primum fluidum'*—are essentially motionless and therefore powerless: 'As to the origin of motion … Hobbes never offered a metaphysical solution, always dropping the most obvious and convenient hypothesis. *Viz.* the hypothesis that identifies the *primum fluidum* with the Corporeal God and that attributes to a single original matter an autokinetic power—a Toland-type hypothesis ahead of time'. See also Shapin and Schaffer, *Leviathan and the Air-Pump*, pp. 80–109; Malcolm, 'Hobbes and Roberval', in *Aspects of Hobbes*, pp. 156–99; G. M. Ross, *Starting with Hobbes* (London, 2009), pp. 148–54; G. Gorham, 'The Theological Foundation of Hobbesian Physics: A Defence of Corporeal God', *British Journal for the History of Philosophy*, 21:2 (2013), pp. 240–61.

95 Wigelsworth, *Deism in Enlightenment England*, pp. 75–86.

96 S. Clarke, 'A Demonstration of the Being and Attributes of God' and 'A Discourse Concerning the Unchangeable Obligations of Natural Religion, and the Truth and Certainty of the Christian Revelation', in *The Works of Samuel Clarke*, 4 vols (London, 1738), vol. 2, pp. 513–733.

97 Ibid., p. 532.

98 Ibid., pp. 532–43.

99 Ibid., p. 531.

100 Ibid., p. 562.

101 Ibid, pp. 561–63. To prove his point, Clarke cited large parts from chapter 1 of *Leviathan*, 'Of Sense', and from chapter 25 of *Concerning Body*, 'Of Sense and Animal Motion', where Hobbes argued that 'the immediate cause of sense or perception consists in this, that the first organ of sense is touched and pressed' and that 'the pressure of the uttermost part proceeds from the pressure of some more remote body, and so continually, till we come to that from which, as from its fountain, we derive the phantasm or idea that is made in us by our sense'. Hobbes, *English Works*, vol. 1, p. 390.

102 Clarke, *Works*, vol. 2, p. 521.

103 Ibid., p. 600.

104 Ibid., p. 601.

105 Ibid.

106 Ibid.

107 Ibid., pp. 602–607, on pp. 606–607.

108 Ibid., p. 672.

109 Ibid.

110 Tindal, *Christianity as Old as the Creation*, p. 353.

111 C. Gildon, *The Deist's Manual: Or, a Rational Enquiry into the Christian Religion* (London, 1705), sig. A5r.

112 Ibid., pp. 193–94.

113 Ibid., p. 197.

114 Ibid., pp. 210–30.

115 Ibid., p. 218.

116 Ibid., p. 219.

117 Ibid., pp. 220–28, on p. 224.

118 Unlike Hobbes, Gildon saw society as a product of the divine design, hence a divine institution. See also Parkin, *Taming the Leviathan*, pp. 406–407.

119 B. W. Young, 'Tindal, Matthew (bap. 1657, d. 1733), Freethinker and Religious Controversialist', *ODNB* (2004), available at: www.oxforddnb.com/view/10.1093/ref:odnb/9780198614128.001.0001/odnb-9780198614128-e-27462 (accessed 21 July 2023).

120 G. Hickes, 'A Preliminary Discourse', in W. Carroll, *Spinoza Reviv'd* (London, 1709), sig. d3v. On the comparison that was made by Carroll and others between the *Rights* and *De jure ecclesiasticorum*, a text from 1665 that was attributed to Spinoza but apparently written by Lodewijk Meyer or someone else in his circle, see Colie, 'Spinoza and the early English deists', p. 35; Israel, *Radical Enlightenment*, pp. 607, 620–21; Malcolm, *Aspects of Hobbes*, pp. 45–46.

121 Tindal, *An Essay Concerning Obedience to the Supreme Powers, and the Duty of Subjects in All Revolutions* (London, 1694); Tindal, *An Essay Concerning the Laws of Nations, and the Rights of Soveraigns* (London, 1694); Tindal, *An Essay Concerning the Power of the Magistrate, and the Rights of Mankind in Matters of Religion* (London, 1697); Tindal, *A Letter to a Member of Parliament,*

Shewing, That a Restraint on the Press Is Inconsistent with the Protestant Religion, and Dangerous to the Liberties of the Nation (London, 1698).

122 Tindal, *Essay Concerning the Power of the Magistrate*, p. 2.

123 Ibid., p. 1.

124 Ibid, p. 16.

125 See J. Locke, *A Letter Concerning Toleration and Other Writings*, ed. M. Goldie (Indianapolis, 2010). Tindal, *Essay Concerning the Power of the Magistrate*, p. 2, stated that he attempted to promote the subject of toleration even though it was 'wholly exhausted by the three incomparable Letters concerning Toleration'. Tindal also wrote to Locke in a letter from January 1697: 'I have sent you this Essay, in which I can not pretend to say anything new on the subject of Toleration: For I am very sensible its as impossible to add to what the Author of the letters concerning that subject has said on it, as it is to defend Persecution'. Locke, *The Correspondence of John Locke*, ed. E. S. De Beer, 8 vols (Oxford, 1976–1989), vol. 5, pp. 749–50.

126 Tindal, *Essay Concerning the Power of the Magistrate*, pp. 3–10.

127 Ibid., pp. 18–20.

128 Ibid., pp. 23–24.

129 Ibid., pp. 110–11.

130 Ibid., pp. 112–13.

131 A. Barber, '"Why Don't Those Lazy Priests Answer the Book?" Matthew Tindal, Censorship, Freedom of the Press and Religious Debate in Early Eighteenth-Century England', *History*, 98 (2013), pp. 680–707, on p. 683.

132 Collins, *In the Shadow of Leviathan*, pp. 361–63; for a different view, see D. Levitin, 'Matthew Tindal's *Rights of the Christian Church* (1706) and the Church-State Relationship', *The Historical Journal*, 54:3 (2011), pp. 717–40, who places this work in a context of patristic scholarship and a legal tradition that followed the writer Christopher St Germain.

133 Collins, *In the Shadow of Leviathan*, p. 361.

134 Tindal, *The Rights of the Christian Church Asserted*, 2nd edn (London, 1706), p. 151. According to Hobbes, 'the Kingdome of Christ is not of this world' based on John 18:36, and 'therefore neither can his Ministers (unless they be Kings,) require obedience in his name'. Lev 42, p. 780. See also J. Champion, '"My Kingdom Is Not of This World": The Politics of Religion after the Restoration', in N. Tyacke (ed.), *The English Revolution c. 1590–1720: Politics, Religion and Communities* (Manchester, 2007), pp. 185–202; J. R. Wigelsworth, '"God Can Require Nothing of Us, but What Makes for Our Happiness": Matthew Tindal on Toleration', in Hudson, Lucci, and Wigelsworth (eds), *Atheism and Deism Revalued*, pp. 139–55.

135 Tindal, *Rights*, pp. 13–20.

136 Ibid., p. 20.

137 Ibid., p. 21.

138 Barber, 'Why Don't Those Lazy Priests Answer the Book?', pp. 690–91.

139 Tindal, *Rights*, p. 21.

140 Hobbes, *On the Citizen* 6.11, p. 80.

141 Tindal, *Rights*, p. 28.

142 See also Tindal, *A Defence of the Rights of the Christian Church* (London, 1707), p. 9.

143 On this point Tindal could seem more of a Spinozist than a Hobbist. Spinoza stated in 1674 that the difference between Hobbes and him was 'that I always preserve the natural right in its entirety, and hold that the sovereign power in a state has a right over a subject only in proportion to the excess of its power over that subject'. Israel, *Radical Enlightenment*, p. 259, and pp. 619–22. Israel's judgement on Tindal's Spinozism is based largely on his contemporary critics, such as George Hickes, but as we shall see, Hickes made an equally strong case on Tindal's Hobbism. Furthermore, it is arguable that the views of Hobbes and Spinoza on the question of the right (of the state) concerning sacred matters (ius circa sacra) were closer than is usually believed. See M. Lærke, *Spinoza and the Freedom of Philosophizing* (Oxford, 2021), pp. 216–33.

144 Tindal, *New High-Church Turn'd Old Presbyterian* (London, 1709), p. 5. Cf. S. Parker, *A Discourse of Ecclesiastical Politie* (London, 1670), p. 308, and pp. 135–70 ('A Confutation of the Consequences That Some Men Draw from Mr. Hobs's Principles in Behalf of Liberty of Conscience'). See also Parkin, *Taming the Leviathan*, pp. 252–58.

145 G. Hickes, *A Letter to the Author of a Late Paper, Entituled, a Vindication of the Divines of the Church of England, &c.* (London, 1689), pp. 5–6; Hickes, *Some Discourses upon Dr. Burnet and Dr. Tillotson* (London, 1695), p. 48. For a similar argument on Hobbes, see A. Seller, *The History of Passive Obedience Since the Reformation* (Amsterdam, 1689), sig. A3v.

146 Hickes, *Two Treatises, One of the Christian Priesthood, the Other of the Dignity of the Episcopal Order* (London, 1707), p. ix.

147 Ibid., p. xiii.

148 Ibid., p. xvii.

149 Ibid., p. xix.

150 Ibid., p. cv.

151 Ibid., p. clxxxviiii. Cf. Tindal, *Rights*, pp. 247–48.

152 Hickes, *Two Treatises*, p. ccxxx. Cf. Tindal, *Rights*, pp. 413–14.

153 Hickes, *Two Treatises*, pp. 268–69.

154 Hickes, *Three Short Treatises* (London, 1709), sig. A5r.

155 Bulman, *Anglican Enlightenment*, pp. 1–3, 139–40, 279–81; Bulman, 'Hobbes's Publisher', pp. 358–61.

156 L. Addison, *A Modest Plea for the Clergy* (London, 1677), esp. pp. 12–17.

157 Hickes, *Three Short Treatises*, sig. A5v.

158 Ibid., sig. A8r.

159 C. Leslie, *The Second Part of the Wolf Stript of His Shepherds Cloathing* (London, 1707), p. 25.

160 Ibid., p. 1.

161 Ibid., p. 3.

162 Ibid., p. 4.

163 Ibid., p. 5.

164 Ibid., pp. 7, 14.

165 Goldie, 'The Reception of Hobbes', pp. 612–15.
166 Accounts include O'Higgins, *Anthony Collins*, pp. 69–76; J. P. Ferguson, *The Philosophy of Dr. Samuel Clarke and Its Critics* (New York, 1974); J. W. Yolton, *Thinking Matter: Materialism in Eighteenth-Century Britain* (Minneapolis, 1983); Wigelsworth, *Deism in Enlightenment England*, pp. 86–95; W. L. Uzgalis, 'Introduction', in *The Correspondence of Samuel Clarke and Anthony Collins, 1707–08* (Peterborough, 2011), pp. 9–36; J. Agnesina, *The Philosophy of Anthony Collins: Free-Thought and Atheism* (Paris, 2018), pp. 47–62; and see n. 194 below.
167 The full title summarised the main argument: H. Dodwell, *An Epistolary Discourse Proving, from the Scriptures and the First Fathers, That the Soul Is a Principle Naturally Mortal; but Immortalized Actually by the Pleasure of God, to Punishment; or, to Reward, by Its Union with the Divine Baptismal Spirit. Wherein Is Proved, That None Have the Power of Giving this Divine Immortalizing Spirit, Since the Apostles, but Only the Bishops* (London, 1706).
168 Clarke, *Works*, vol. 3, p. 721.
169 Ibid., p. 722.
170 Ibid., p. 730.
171 Ibid., pp. 751–52.
172 Ibid., pp. 759–60.
173 Ibid., pp. 760, 771.
174 Ibid., p. 863.
175 Ibid., p. 851.
176 Ibid., pp. 904–905.
177 Ibid., vol. 2, p. 563.
178 Ibid., vol. 3, p. 795.
179 Ibid., p. 796.
180 In the subsection that Clarke cited here, Hobbes made a modified claim that 'all bodies are not endued with sense', because only living creatures have a memory of motions and thus an ability to judge 'a perpetual variety of phantasms', which constitutes a sense properly speaking. When Clarke referred to this subsection in his Boyle Lectures, he argued that Hobbes admitted there that '*sensation may be something more*' but that this was just 'a last subterfuge to recur to, when he should be pressed with the forementioned Absurdities, unavoidably consequent upon the Supposition of Sensation being only Figure and Motion'. Hobbes, *English Works*, vol. 1, pp. 393–94; Clarke, *Works*, vol. 2, p. 562.
181 Similarly, when refuting Collins's idea that thinking could be a mode of motion, Clarke added: 'If to this you will reply … that *Thought* may be the *Result* of some *particular Motion*; I answer in the Words of Mr. *Hobbes*, that no *Result* of Motion can ever be any thing else but *mere* Motion still … And consequently all the foregoing Arguments hold equally good, against one Notion as against the other'. Clarke, *Works*, vol. 3, p. 839. So here again Clarke answered Collins by utilising—and rejecting—a Hobbesian notion which he thought was essentially identical to Collins's view.

182 Ibid., p. 812.
183 Ibid., pp. 847–48.
184 J. Witty, *The First Principles of Modern Deism Confuted* (London, 1707), p. xvi.
185 Ibid., pp. 198–99, 222.
186 Clarke, *Works*, vol. 3, pp. 824, 862. Cf. Hobbes, *English Works*, vol. 5, p. 435.
187 Clarke, *Works*, vol. 3, p. 854.
188 Collins, *The Correspondence of Anthony Collins (1676–1729), Freethinker*, ed. J. Dybikowski (Paris, 2011), pp. 193–95.
189 Collins, *Essay Concerning the Use of Reason*, p. 3.
190 Ibid., pp. 22–23.
191 O'Higgins, *Anthony Collins*, pp. 51–61.
192 Collins, *Essay Concerning the Use of Reason*, p. 47.
193 Ibid., p. 50. For example, Cf. Lev 21, pp. 324–26: 'LIBERTY, or FREEDOME, signifieth (properly) the absence of Opposition'; 'Liberty, and Necessity are consistent; as in the water, that hath not only liberty, but a necessity of descending by the Channel; so likewise in the Actions which men voluntarily doe'.
194 O'Higgins, *Anthony Collins*, pp. 96–110; J. A. Harris, *Of Liberty and Necessity: The Free Will Debate in Eighteenth-Century British Philosophy* (Oxford, 2005), pp. 41–63; P. Russell, *The Riddle of Hume's Treatise: Skepticism, Naturalism, and Irreligion* (Oxford, 2008), pp. 225–38; Thomson, *Bodies of Thought*, e.g., pp. 129–30, 230.
195 J. Toland, *Tetradymus. Containing 1. Hodegus ... 2. Clidophorus ... 3. Hypatia ... 4. Mangoneutes* (London, 1720).
196 Ibid., p. 4.
197 Ibid., p. 7.
198 Ibid., p. 11. See also Champion, *Republican Learning*, p. 177.
199 Toland, *Hodegus*, pp. 28–29, 46.
200 Ibid., p. 46.
201 Ibid., pp. 47–48.
202 Ibid., pp. 51–52. For example, Toland based his judgment, which is not unreasonable, on Numbers 10:29: 'Moses said unto Hobab ... we are journeying unto the place of which the Lord said, I will give it you: come thou with us'.
203 Lev 34, p. 622.
204 Lev 34, p. 624.
205 Lev 34, p. 626.
206 Lev 34, p. 626.
207 Toland, *Hodegus*, p. 60.

3

The age of freethinking (1711–1723)

The doctrine of freethinking was first formulated properly in the 1710s, the decade that witnessed what we may call the freethinking controversy. Where deists argued that religion could be understood by reason alone in order to undermine priestcraft, freethinking similarly (if not synonymously) meant that individuals should reason for themselves on all matters, religious or otherwise. The main actors in these debates were to a large extent still Collins and Toland, as well as Shaftesbury. Subsequently, in the early 1720s, the radical periodicals of John Trenchard and Thomas Gordon, the *Independent Whig* and *Cato's Letters*, signalled that these doctrines found their way to the heart of the public sphere. In these decades, too, Hobbes was a major source of inspiration for these writers, who continued to express careful admiration to his thought.

Shaftesbury and early freethinking

Perhaps the first notable treatment of English freethinking can be found in Shaftesbury's *Characteristicks of Men, Manners, Opinions, Times* (1711). Anthony Ashley Cooper, third earl of Shaftesbury (1671–1713), was the grandson of the Whig politician, the first earl of Shaftesbury, and a philosopher in his own right. His philosophy combined ethics and aesthetics and tended towards stoicism. Shaftesbury refuted Hobbesian and Lockean ideas including natural unsociability, egoism, scepticism, and voluntarism.[1] He believed in the existence of moral principles and a moral sense that are not based on self-interest nor on the promise of reward and punishment, but that are part of a harmonious cosmos, pre-ordained by a benevolent God, in which virtuous individuals are designed to promote the good of one another.[2]

Shaftesbury's framework was theistic. He was associated by some with the deist project, but he himself seemed ambivalent to it. In his essay *The Moralists*, deism is discussed in a dialogue between the sceptic Philocles and his interlocutor Palemon, who states that he is 'averse … to the Cause of Theism, or Name of Deist, when taken in a sense exclusive of Revelation' but concedes that 'the Root of all is Theism' and that he does not have 'patience to hear the Name of Deist (the highest of all Names) decry'd, and set in opposition to Christianity', explaining: 'As if our Religion was a kind of Magick, which depended not on the Belief of a single supreme Being. Or as if the firm and rational Belief of such a Being, on philosophical Grounds, was an improper Qualification for believing any thing further'.[3]

Shaftesbury did not see freethinking as harmful to religion, and he supported it openly. In *A Letter Concerning Enthusiasm*, he wondered 'who shall be Judg of *what* may be freely examin'd, and *what* may not? *Where* Liberty may be us'd; and *where* it may not?'[4] The sovereign should limit hurtful conduct, but in matters of reason, liberty and politeness would ultimately provide the answers: 'Justness of Thought and Style, Refinement in Manners, good Breeding, and Politeness of every kind, can come only from the Trial and Experience of what is best. Let but the Search go freely on, and the right Measure of every thing will soon be found'.[5] Shaftesbury developed these themes in the miscellanies that he included in the *Characteristicks*. For him, our thinking should only be restricted by our own thoughts and not by fear of an external authority, so we are entitled to examine freely and rationally every matter until we decide to quit; he referred to those who believed otherwise as wretched '*Half-thinkers*'.[6] He argued that 'above all other enslaving Vices, and Restrainers of *Reason* and *just Thought,* the most evidently ruinous and fatal to the Understanding is that of SUPERSTITION, BIGOTRY, and *vulgar* ENTHUSIASM'.[7] He attacked without naming those 'who first brought *Reason* and *Free-Thought* under disgrace, and made the noblest of Characters, that of a *Free-Thinker,* to become invidious'.[8] Shaftesbury's support of freethinking was intellectual, even aesthetic: freethinking had a crucial role in appreciating the beauty of morality and nature. His version of freethinking was therefore careful and polite, and less aggressive in its hostility to the church. This was the judgement of the nineteenth-century Whig historian Thomas Macaulay, who wrote on Shaftesbury:

> His life was short: but he lived long enough to become the founder of a new sect of English freethinkers, diametrically opposed in opinions and feelings to that sect of freethinkers of which Hobbes was the oracle. During many years the Characteristics continued to be the Gospel of romantic and sentimental unbelievers, while the Gospel of coldblooded and hard-headed unbelievers was the Leviathan.[9]

Scholars today tend to accept the distinction between Shaftesbury and other freethinkers: while his deistic inclinations are often acknowledged, Shaftesbury has been portrayed recently as a proponent of an elitist civil

religion which 'could have a Christian foundation' and of 'a moral theory grounded in human nature'.[10] Indeed, he denounced 'Epic[urians],
Pyrr[honians], Hobbists, Witts, Libertines, Half-Believers' as well as 'free-
talking about matters of Religion & of Establishd Rites of Worship ... if it
be not still with a certain Economy & Reserve: if it be vehemently ... ridi-
culingly & with Contempt'.[11] Furthermore, in 1698 Shaftesbury wrote that
by 'Building a Political Christianity', Hobbes had 'done but very ill Service
in the Moral World', although he praised Hobbes in 1709 as 'a genius, and
even an original among these latter leaders in philosophy'.[12] Also in 1709,
he distinguished himself from Tindal, and added: 'In general truly it has
happened, that all those they call *Free-Writers* now-a-days, have espoused
those Principles, which Mr. Hobbes set a foot in this last Age'.[13]

To contemporaries, however, Shaftesbury was not necessarily very different from Hobbes nor the other freethinkers. One of the earliest responses
to Shaftesbury was a little-known satire on freethinking, entitled *Free-
Thinkers. A Poem in Dialogue* (1711), which is often attributed to Anne
Finch, Countess of Winchilsea.[14] The poem portrays two young men who
fit the commonplace caricature of freethinking: they are licentious, pleasure-
seeking, and cunning drunkards. As one of them declares:

> 'Tis hop'd you'll pardon, we Free-thinkers
> Are unconfin'd, and *lawless Drinkers*,
> And whatsoever suits, or pleases,
> Or for our Profit, or our Ease is,
> We never baulk it, nor ill breeding
> Is now esteem'd, this Frank proceeding.[15]

The freethinkers in the poem oppose any authority and law: they are
'Scorning all Ties, Divine or Civil', and their 'first Rule's Self-preservation'.[16]
Their interlocutor, a monarchist, describes them as dangerous revolution-
aries who 'make us think, there's no Inferiors, But all were born upon the
Level, And equally should sway, and Revel'.[17] These freethinkers have several intellectual ties. While Shaftesbury wrote about the problem of '*Panick*'
as a 'Passion, which can hardly be without some mixture of Enthusiasm,
and Horrors of a superstitious kind', the poem's freethinkers enjoy 'To hear
all *Beings*, prov'd *Mechanick*, And *Nature*, rescu'd from the *Panick*'.[18]
Discussing another character of a freethinker who is familiar to their interlocutor, the latter describes this freethinker as one who talks about Lycurgus,
Solon, Cato, and Brutus, who 'Knows all Republican Defences', who thinks
that 'kings were made but for the *People*'—and who is 'old Dog, at Hobbs
and Toland'.[19] Thus, the poem links Hobbes, Toland, and Shaftesbury with
the figure of the new freethinker, and what is even more striking is that
Hobbes and Toland alike are cast here as sources of modern republicanism.[20]

Freethinking formulated

The writer who did more than anyone else to establish the doctrine of freethinking in England was Anthony Collins. Collins's *Discourse of Free-Thinking, Occasion'd by the Rise and Growth of a Sect Call'd Free-Thinkers* (1713) was described as the manifesto of the freethinkers' club whose meetings took place in London coffeehouses.[21] He took some inspiration from Shaftesbury, whom he knew personally. On the title page of the *Discourse* there were two quotes from the *Characteristicks*: first, ''Tis a hard Matter for a Government to settle Wit'; second, 'Fain would they confound Licentiousness in Morals with Liberty in Thought, and make the Libertine resemble his direct Opposite'.[22]

The goal of the *Discourse of Free-Thinking* was to prove the right to think freely, which Collins derived from the right to know the truth. He defined freethinking rather methodically, as 'The Use of the Understanding, in endeavouring to find out the Meaning of any Proposition whatsoever, in considering the nature of the Evidence for or against it, and in judging of it according to the seeming Force or Weakness of the Evidence'.[23] It is our right—and in fact, our duty—to think freely, for our own sake as well as for the sake and progress of the whole society. Freethinking, Collins argued, was particularly necessary to avoid 'the grossest Absurdities imaginable both in Principle and Practice'.[24] These absurdities included the unreasonable notions that were held first by pagans and then by Christians, such as 'Infallibility in a single Person, or in a Council, the Power of the Priest to damn and save', and 'the Worship of Images, Pictures, Saints, and Relicks'.[25] The aim of freethinking, then, is to expose superstitious beliefs that otherwise cause dangerous and unnecessary fears. Collins asserted that priests did not necessarily teach the truth as such but doctrines that serve their own interests, hence the differences between the teachings of the various sects in Christianity, and consequently the need for free and individual inquiries. Thus, Collins took the deistic criticism of the church and channelled it into a programme of freedom of thought and belief and of religious toleration. He sided with those who were accused of deism and other heterodoxies: '*If any good Christian happens to reason better than ordinary, they*'—the priests, that is—'*presently charge him with Atheism, Deism or Socinianism*: as if good Sense and Orthodoxy could not subsist together'.[26] Those who were charged with deism, atheism, or Socinianism—often interchangeable labels—were simply Christians who thought reasonably enough.

The primary problem with which the *Discourse* dealt was therefore the restraint of thought, namely, 'somewhat which hinders me from thinking'— first and foremost clerical persecution that Collins saw as the primary obstacle to individual as well as collective progress.[27] This was true for arts and sciences as well as for religious matters: whereas priestly impositions maintained the rule of ignorance on all fronts, liberty of thought enabled the development of learning and knowledge of both the movement of earth and the existence of God.[28] In this context, Collins, too, mentioned Galileo, who 'even in the last Age, was imprison'd for asserting the Motion of the Earth'.[29] Moreover, thinking is the only way for us to know God's will, and therefore the free use of thinking is perhaps most needed in the reading of the bible, which came directly from God.[30] The bible, Collins explained, covers an exceptionally wide range of topics, including natural, civil, and ecclesiastical histories, in addition to different sciences, the understanding of each of which is required for the understanding of all the others. Ultimately, a sincere individual reflection is necessary for the understanding of both the scripture and God: 'How is it possible for any Man to enter into the Meaning of the several Passages of Scripture, which seemingly exhibit to us an Idea of God after a human manner, without the most refin'd Metaphysicks, and the deepest thinking and philosophizing on the Nature and Attributes of God?'[31] Biblical criticism, it followed, was an exercise in textual interpretation—historical, philosophical, and philological—which had to be accessible to laity and clergy alike. But this was not all. Collins added that 'the *Morality* of the *Holy Scripture* is not to be precisely and distinctly understood, without an antecedent Knowledg in *Ethicks*, or the *Law of Nature*'.[32] Natural law is the basis of our moral duties, and we should therefore examine even the moral lessons of the scripture in light of the natural law, by virtue of our God-given reason. Thus, Collins's advocacy of freethinking was coupled with natural theology. Truth would never be contrary to reason nor—and here Collins, too, departed from Locke—above reason; revelation was, in fact, unnecessary for the knowledge of morality.[33] Finally, toleration of opinions as well as practices that conformed to the natural law and to the well-being of the society was crucial for freethinking, just as freethinking was crucial to sustain religious toleration.[34]

At first glance, Collins conceptualised liberty of thought as an unconstrained way of thinking, reasoning, and inquiring, enabled by religious toleration. In this sense, he integrated a Hobbesian idea of liberty as the lack of external impediments, which we have already seen that he adopted—liberty of thought was opposed to restraint of thought—with an idea of liberty of conscience that he could have borrowed from a range of sources, especially from his close friend Locke, and arguably even more directly from Bayle.[35] Notably, Collins's idea of liberty of conscience included not only freedom of opinion—conscience and opinion were almost synonymous for him, as for Hobbes—but also the freedom to choose a religion as well as freedom of worship.[36] Collins's conception of liberty of thought also built on the notion of liberty of philosophising, most associated with Spinoza;

indeed, he encouraged his readers explicitly to philosophise even on the most sacred issue, namely, the nature of God.[37] But Collins's conceptualisation of liberty was broader still. Thinking freely, for him, was not only a lack of censorship—this condition was necessary but not sufficient. It was also, and perhaps primarily, thinking without errors, prejudice, and ignorance. It was thinking without superstition, which is nothing short of 'an Evil which either by the means of Education, or the natural Weakness of Men, oppresses almost all Mankind'.[38] For Collins, as for Toland, the problem was therefore one of systematic oppression and not mere interference: he accused the clergy, and sometimes the magistrates as well, of tyranny over the bodies and especially the minds of humankind. It is not an exaggeration to claim that Collins's main enterprise throughout his entire writing career was to expose the multiple ways in which the clergy attempted to achieve such control over the minds of the laity, including wrongful education and multiple methods of imposture.[39] To sum up, liberty of thought consisted of a lack of concrete interference with private and public inquiry in the shape of persecution, censorship, and most extremely inquisition, but also a lack of continuous attempts, especially by clerics, to control, shape, and narrow the minds of human beings.[40]

Collins replied in his *Discourse* to six possible objections to freethinking. One objection could be that not all men are qualified to think freely; Collins answered that this right should nevertheless remain untouched for those who are capable.[41] A second objection is that allowing freethinking might lead to greater diversity of opinions and hence to disagreement and social disorder; Collins answered that although diversity of opinion could cause some confusion, restraining freethinking would only bring greater social disorder, like a remedy which is worse than the disease. In ancient Greece, he argued, different philosophical strands disagreed on the most crucial issues, such as the immortality of the soul and the relationship between the gods and the world, but 'no ill effect follow'd this Diversity of Opinions' precisely 'because Men generally agreed in that mild and peaceable Principle of allowing one another to *think freely*, and to have different Opinions'.[42] The third objection is that freethinking could pave the way for atheism; Collins replied that whereas ignorance is the foundation of atheism, freethinking is the cure, and in any case, it is more likely that the restraint of freethinking would pave the way for superstition and enthusiasm.[43] While denying that there is any atheist at all except for some '*rare Monster*' in the shape of Psalm's fool, who is an 'idle, unthinking, shallow Fellow', Collins translated from Hobbes's *De homine*, that '*they who are capable of inspecting the Vessels of Generation, and Nutrition, and not think them made for their several Ends by an understanding Being, ought to be esteem'd destitute of Understanding themselves*'.[44] The fourth objection is that the priests can think freely for the laity and therefore should be relied upon, as are lawyers and physicians in their own areas of expertise; Collins replied that precisely as with law and physics, the study of divinity should be open to all. Furthermore, unlike law or physics, in matters of divinity individuals have to hold their own beliefs and cannot have anyone else think for them: 'PRIESTS have no interest to lead me to true Opinions, but only to the Opinions they have listed themselves to profess, and for the most part into mistaken Opinions'.[45] Fifth, it could be objected against freethinking that sometimes it is necessary to deceive people deliberately for their own good; Collins replied that the imposition of ideas upon people, especially in the name of religion, only led humankind to unprecedented cruelty and brutality.[46] Finally, the sixth objection that Collins mentioned is that the freethinkers themselves are wicked and infamous men, to which he answered somewhat stoically that those who use their understanding are those who lead the most virtuous lives.[47]

The *Discourse* also offered a list of the greatest freethinkers of all time, among them were ancient figures such as Solomon, Socrates, Plato, Aristotle, Epicurus, Cicero, and Seneca, and modern thinkers, including Bacon, Tillotson—and Hobbes.[48] The way in which Collins recruited Hobbes for his justification of freethinking is a good example of the complex way in which Hobbes was generally perceived by freethinkers and deists. Collins praised Hobbes as 'a great instance of Learning, Virtue, and Free-Thinking' despite his 'several false Opinions, and his High-Church Politicks'.[49] He then quoted some parts that were favourable to Hobbes from Clarendon's *A Brief View and Survey* (1676), a book which was mostly critical of Hobbes. For example, it was argued, '*Leviathan* contains in it good Learning of all kinds, politely extracted, and very wittily and cunningly digested in a very commendable Method, and in a vigorous and pleasant Stile'; 'among the excellent Qualitys, Parts, and Facultys with which Mr. HOBBES is plentifully endow'd, his Order and Method, and his clear Expressions, his Conceptions in weighty, proper, and significant Words, are very remarkable and commendable'; and 'his whole Book discovers a Master Faculty in making hard things easy to be understood'.[50] In short, Hobbes's easy and clear way of writing, his wit, and even his personal integrity are enough to make him a man of virtue and thus a proper freethinker.

Elsewhere in the *Discourse*, Collins told the story about John Fell, dean of Christ Church and bishop of Oxford, who made several alterations in Anthony Wood's *History and Antiquities of the University of Oxford*, which first appeared in Latin in 1674, before its printing. Collins mentioned that Fell 'struck out several Passages wherein WOOD had done justice to Mr. HOBBES, and inserted others in their stead, derogatory to his Fame and Character'.[51] Collins immediately added that 'these Frauds are very common in all Books, which are publish'd by *Priests* or *Priestly Men*'.[52] He linked this instance to other forms of clerical corruption, including the '*Declamations against Reason*': in a typically Hobbesian manner, and in the fashion of other deists, Collins exposed the priests' manipulations of reason, that is, '*their Arts and Methods of discouraging Examination* into the Truths of Religion; and *their encouraging Examination* when Authority is against them, or when they think that Truth is clearly on their side'.[53]

Hobbes's freethinking was closely related to his clashes with the clergy, and in this respect, Collins found Hobbes exceptionally inspirational. In his later *Discourse Concerning Ridicule and Irony in Writing* (1729), Collins wrote similarly that the 'Clergy have ever treated Mr. *Hobbes* with the greatest Mockery, Ridicule and Raillery', as with the case of John Eachard, whose satirical dialogues on Hobbes were particularly successful. But Hobbes, as Collins showed, had coped with that with typical wit: 'upon its being told him, that *the Clergy said* Eachard *had crucify'd* Hobbes', Hobbes replied: 'Why then don't they fall down and worship me?'[54] Furthermore, Collins reported that this quality of Hobbes was appreciated by Charles II, to whose education Hobbes famously contributed:

> The King himself, who had very good natural Parts, and a Disposition to banter and ridicule every Body, and especially the *Presbyterians* ... had in his *Exile* an Education, and liv'd, among some of the greatest *Droles* and *Wits* that any Age ever produc'd ... The Duke of *Buckingham* brought *Hobbes* to him to be his *Tutor*, who was a *Philosophical Drole*, and had a great deal of *Wit* of the *drolling* kind.[55]

It is likely that the rhetoric that Hobbes used in his writings, especially on religious matters, inspired the freethinkers no less than their content.[56] To be sure, freethought was not a common attribute of Hobbes who was perceived as someone who allowed the sovereign a certain degree of control over subjects' thoughts. Yet Collins's case shows that deists and their allies could still relate to Hobbes and even use him to promote the liberties in which they were interested.

Once again, the responses were quick to appear. The writer Richard Steele was so distressed by the new freethinkers that he declared in 1713 that 'if ever Man deserved to be denied the common Benefits of Air and Water, it is the Author of a *Discourse of Free-Thinking*'.[57] The most famous and thorough response to the *Discourse of Free-Thinking* was that of Richard Bentley, who had already attacked Hobbes and the deists in the first Boyle Lecture in 1692. In his *Remarks upon a Late Discourse of Free-Thinking* (1713), Bentley argued that 'under the specious show of *Free-thinking*, a *Set* and *System of Opinions* are all along inculcated and dogmatically taught; *Opinions* the most *Slavish*, the most abject and base, that Human Nature is capable of'.[58] By 'free', Bentley argued, the freethinkers actually meant '*Bold, Rash, Arrogant, Presumptious*, together with a strong Propension to the *Paradox* and the *Perverse*'.[59] Bentley turned the table on Collins's argument: it is not the clerics who teach their opinions as unshakable truths but the freethinkers who present their outrageous irreligious doctrines as superior principles: 'There is nothing plainer through his whole Book, than that He himself makes Singularity, Whim, and Contradiction to be the specific Difference, and an Essential part in the Composition of a *Free-thinker*'.[60] Freethinking, Bentley argued, was merely a cover for stating the opposite of the common views—not only those of the clergy but those of most of mankind—by people who were simply not qualified to comment on divinity studies. This was the strength of Bentley, who, as a classical scholar, could expose the inaccuracies of Collins's scriptural interpretations. The criticism, then, was that the so-called liberty of the freethinkers was actually opposition for its own sake and a constant effort to differ from mainstream views. This point was common to most critiques that were aimed at Collins. Moreover, argued the critics, the freethinkers' liberty signified in reality the absence of *all* restrictions, and the worst part was that they refused to accept restrictions not only on thought but also on speech and writing.[61] This was not inaccurate: indeed, it was not only freedom of thought but also freedom of expression—even of opinions opposite to those of the establishment and particularly the church—that Collins sought to defend.[62]

The critics also wondered what Hobbes was doing on Collins's list of the greatest freethinkers, which one of them called 'very odd and whimsical, very unfair and disagreeable'; according to this critic, 'if he means *Free Thinkers* in Opposition to the Embraces of true Religion', then Collins might as well 'content himself with *Epicurus* of Old, and Mr. *Hobbes* of late'.[63] Bentley, of course, did not miss this link either:

> O the glorious Nation you would be! If ... *Free-thinkers* appointed Tutors to your young Nobility and Gentry. How would Arts, Learning, Manners and all Humanity flourish in an Academy under such preceptors? Who instead of your Bible should read *Hobbes*'s *Leviathan*; should *instill* early the sound doctrines of the Mortality of the soul, and the sole Good of a voluptuous Life.[64]

Bentley was right: in the academy of the freethinkers and deists, *Leviathan* was indeed an obligatory book. Furthermore, as Bentley identified, Hobbes's theory informed Collins's views on the questionable immortality of the soul and existence of free will. Collins's Hobbesian philosophy of materialism and determinism, that began to develop in the mid-1700s, reached its peak in 1717.

Liberty and necessity

In *A Philosophical Inquiry Concerning Human Liberty* (1717), Collins
approached the question of liberty and necessity in a distinctively Hobbesian
manner. Collins defined man's liberty as the *'power to do as he wills, or
pleases* ... unless prevented by some restraint or compulsion', clarifying that
this definition includes actions as well as thoughts.[65] Thus, only compulsion
or restraint constrained liberty. He insisted that his concept of liberty was
consistent with the certainty of actions and hence with divine prescience;
on the other hand, since God's prescience supposes the predetermined existence of all future things, it cannot be reconciled with free will. Thus, human
actions are determined by pleasure and pain; liberty and necessity are reconciled; and free will is rejected.[66] Joseph Priestley, who followed Collins
in converting to determinism, mentioned in the preface to his edition of the
Philosophical Inquiry that 'Mr. Hobbes ... was the first who, in this, or
any other country, rightly understood, and clearly stated, the argument; but
he wrote nothing *systematical*, and consequently nothing that could be of
much use to a student. For this purpose this treatise of Collins is excellent'.[67]

In a number of places Collins came particularly close to Hobbes, even to
the letter. In the *Philosophical Inquiry* he developed his position by replying
to six possible objections, just as he did in his *Discourse of Free-Thinking*.
Some of these objections are identical to the ones that bishop Bramhall made
with regard to Hobbes's view of liberty and necessity, and in several places
Collins simply repeated Hobbes's answers. First, he replied to the objection
that if men cannot avoid doing what they do, then punishments are unjust.
His response was that the end of punishment should be understood as prevention of crime or deterrence, adding that the punishment is just so long
as the crime is voluntary, 'for the law very justly and rightly regardeth only
the will, and no other preceding causes of action'; this was an extract from
Hobbes.[68] Collins borrowed an example word for word from Hobbes to
argue for deterrence: if stealing is punishable by death, then enforcing it on a
thief would deter others from doing so and hence would be just. It may also
be objected, Collins continued, that punishment is useless if one's actions
are determined; but, he replied, the threat of punishment is in itself a cause
which can determine one's will and is therefore rather useful.[69] Similarly,
he replied to a third objection that praise and blame are useless, arguing
that giving reasons to people, or indeed blaming or praising them, can also
determine one's will in one way or another and hence are not useless; this
was also Hobbes's answer.[70] Next, Collins replied to a fourth objection
according to which if the period of human life is determined, then medicine
would be pointless, arguing that it would be part of the chain of necessary
causes—exactly as Hobbes had argued with regard to 'arts, arms, books,

instruments, study, medicines, and the like'.[71] The fifth objection was that it is unclear 'how a man's conscience can accuse him, if he knows he acts necessarily'; Collins answered that even if one's conscience cannot prevent an action from being done, one may still come to regret it 'by the absence of the pleasure of the sin'—exactly as Hobbes had argued that the necessity of actions does not take away the possibility of repentance or grief.[72] Collins completed this section by considering a sixth and final objection: 'That if all events are necessary, it was as impossible (for example) for Julius Caesar not to have died in the Senate, as it is impossible for two and two to make six'; he was willing to accept this implication.[73]

The *Philosophical Inquiry* presented available ideas of determinism in an orderly fashion and thus became an important and influential work which shaped the views of Voltaire, Franklin, and others on the subject.[74] Thus, like Blount, Collins had an important role in formulating and transmitting ideas—in this case, especially from Hobbes—to a wide and often more radical audience. Although Collins did not mention Hobbes in this work, the resemblance of his position to Hobbes's, as well as his direct borrowings from Hobbes's answers to Bramhall, leave no room for doubt about the significance of this influence. As with Toland's active matter, which could be a development of Hobbesian plenism, Collins's idea of God's prescience provided further justification for Hobbesian determinism. It was this kind of views that had the potential to show that no further divine intervention was needed—precisely what Clarke, and the orthodoxy, feared.

Toland's later works

While Collins was building his freethinking persona, Toland produced several works which were, in some respects, the culmination of his enterprise. In one of them, he revealed that he had been 'no less confidently than falsely reported, to have had a hand in the *Discourse of Free-Thinking*', praising Collins nevertheless as 'a very worthy Gentleman and a stanch Englishman'.[75] Indeed, Toland had already dedicated one of his works to Collins: *Adeisidaemon* (*The Unsuperstitious*, 1709), a work which aimed to clear Livy of the charge of credulity and superstition, and to suggest more broadly, in a similar manner to Bayle and Collins, that the superstitious might be more destructive of society than the atheist.[76] Furthermore, Toland was as unapologetic about his friendship with Collins as he was about 'being intimate with Turks and Jews, with Christians of most denominations, with Deists and Sceptics, with men of wit or worth in every nation of Europe, and with some out of it'.[77] In the following years, Toland would express not only his freethinking inclination but also his sympathy to other religions and his consequent case for broad toleration and even for naturalisation of the Jews.[78]

Perhaps the most important work of Toland from his later years, and certainly the most relevant to our discussion here, is *Nazarenus* (1718), a work which, according to Justin Champion, 'epitomizes the form and content of the deist attack in England', and which reinforced Toland's long-standing reputation as 'the sham Gospeller' or 'Mr. Gospelscorn'.[79] In this work, Toland completed the biblical scholarship that he had started in *Amyntor*, which was discussed in the previous chapter. He presented himself 'only' as 'a historian, resolv'd to make no Reflections but what my facts will naturally suggest, which facts are generally collected from the *Bible* and the *Fathers*', but he also clarified that he was 'not wanting, when there's occasion for it, to chalk out the methods, whereby the errors of simple or designing men may be seasonably confuted'.[80] The highlight of this work was his announcement of a 'NEW GOSPEL', the apocryphal Gospel of Barnabas, 'never before publicly made known among Christians'.[81] By seeking to establish the authenticity of this gospel, which 'may be as old as the time of the Apostles', Toland intervened once again in 'a cultural discourse that held at its heart notions of sacred authenticity and originality'.[82] Toland made this discovery already in 1709, and around that time he sent an early version of this work in a scribal form to Prince Eugene of Savoy and his assistant Baron Hohendorf, men who shared his anticlerical commitments and whose Viennese libraries are known to have contained exceptional collections of clandestine and radical literature, including copies of *Leviathan*.[83]

In *Nazarenus*, there is an apparent connection to Hobbes, as we have seen in Toland's previous works, although in this case Hobbes is not mentioned. Justin Champion has summarised this point: 'Much of the strategy deployed by Toland for his public audiences (both lay and clerical)—constructing an ersatz erudition and exploiting a forensic reading of orthodox biblical scholarship to authorise an alternative account of scriptural truth—can be traced back to the writing of Thomas Hobbes'.[84] This was also the critics' view. The independent tutor Jeremiah Jones, one of the prominent critics of Toland's biblical interpretation, complained in 1719 on the various methods of those who attempted '*to render the Canon of Scripture uncertain*', thereby 'making many reject the Revelation it self', including: 'The preferring some *sorry Versions before the Originals*, and consequently correcting and altering the Originals by these Versions' and '*The great Freedoms that have been taken with the Sacred Text*, by a groundless Supposition of Corruptions, and Contradictions therein'.[85] He then accused:

> The unguarded Discourses of diverse Learned and Ingenious Men on those Heads, have supplied the Enemies of Christianity with Arguments against it,

and been many Ways improv'd by evil Minds to its Dishonour. These are the Weapons with which *Hobbs*, *Spinoza*, *Toland* and the *Club of Deists*, or *Freethinkers* (as they love to be call'd,) have fought against all Reveal'd Religion, and 'tis but too well known, how easily weak and degenerate Minds have been influenc'd, and imposed upon by their Sophistry.[86]

Jones particularly disagreed with the argument that the gospels had been concealed by different private churches or people for a long time. This theory was introduced by Henry Dodwell in his *Dissertationes in Irenaeum* (1689) and was cited at length by Toland in *Amyntor* to suggest that the canon had not been finalised before the second century, which called into question the authenticity of at least some supposedly canonical writings.[87] The link to Hobbes was clear, claimed Jones, because he too referred to the books 'of the New Testament, of which the copies were not many' before their canonisation.[88] Both Hobbes and Toland suggested the Council of Laodicea of the fourth century as a possible date for the formation of the canon, as we have seen, but even that was quite suspicious in their eyes; for Jones, on the other hand, by that point there had been '*almost an universal agreement concerning the Canon*'.[89]

As Jones believed, Toland certainly used his biblical scholarship as a weapon to undermine the canonicity of the scripture, even when he did so under a considerably pious pretence in publicly printed works such as *Amyntor* and *Nazarenus*. Furthermore, Toland's promotion of the Gospel of Barnabas served his vision of public religion. The newly discovered gospel recorded the beliefs of the Nazarenes, or Ebionites, whom Toland considered as 'the oldest Christians'.[90] They were a sect of Jewish Christians, for whom Jesus was a 'mere man', though 'divinely conceiv'd', whereas Paul was '*a transgressor of the Law*', that is, 'an intruder on the genuin Christianity ... substituting his own pretended Revelations to the doctrines of those with whom CHRIST had convers'd'.[91] There was a clear theological continuity between Judaism and Christianity: while the Jewish Christians continued to observe their laws, they accepted Jesus as the 'perfecter of the Law'.[92] Furthermore, the Gospel of Barnabas was nothing short of 'Mahometan Gospel': some of the beliefs that it describes are common to Islam as well—for example that Jesus was not crucified but it might have been Judas instead—and it even mentions Muhammad 'as the design'd accomplisher of God's economy towards man'.[93] Thus, through this gospel, Toland attempted to bind together the three monotheistic religions, in a similar manner to Stubbe's *Account*, in order to establish a vision of natural and tolerant religion which conformed to the eternal moral law and the precepts of Noah.[94] The Nazarenes were not condemning nor condemned in their time, Toland insisted, as the original teaching of the gospels is toleration in accordance with natural law.[95] The 'Mahometans', who could also be considered originally as a Christian sect, should thus 'be tolerated at London and Amsterdam, as the Christians of every kind are so at Constantinople and thro-out all Turkey'.[96]

Nazarenus attempted to go back to primitive Christianity to recover the original true religion: 'The Religion that was true yesterday is not false to day; neither can it ever be false, if ever it was once true'.[97] It was typically anticlerical in the assertion that answers to inquiries into scripture and religion were to be found in the texts themselves and not in nonsensical appeals to apostolic tradition, citing as evidence the fact that from the early debates 'every side and sect pretended they were the onely true Christians'.[98] Furthermore, Moses, Jesus, and Muhammad were portrayed in political terms: Toland even confessed that it is the 'Respublica Mosaica, or the Commonwealth of Moses, which I admire infinitely, above all the forms of Government'.[99] This point would be made much more subversively in manuscript. Indeed, the deists' scepticism was often expressed beyond the printed form, and especially orally during gatherings in freethinking venues such as coffeehouses.[100] Toland, too, circulated his ideas in printed, scribal, and oral forms, and was far more explicitly heterodox in writings that were not meant for the general public.

A notable case study is the *Traité des Trois Imposteurs*, a clandestine text that was in circulation during the seventeenth century, printed in The Hague in 1719, and had numerous versions published throughout the eighteenth century around Europe. Toland is believed to have been intimate with key figures behind its production and even involved in the circulation of one of its versions. The work, often considered deistic, presented Moses, Jesus, and Mohammed as impostors, and all religions as human constructions and fruits of human imagination, manipulated by priests and rulers as a political device to control the ignorant masses. Thus, the work effectively rejected all organised religion, although some of its English variants seem to betray a more optimistic tone, in that the religious leaders are also portrayed as good legislators who could reform public religion.[101]

It is widely accepted that the *Traité* was largely influenced by Spinoza: it was also known as *L'Esprit de Spinosa*, with another version titled *La Vie et L'Esprit de Mr Benoît de Spinosa*. At the same time, it was clearly also indebted to Hobbes. Numerous references to Hobbes were made, echoing for example his views on the psychological analysis of religion, the fear of men that led them to invent demons, false gods, and meaningless spirits, and the corporeality of spirits as well as of God, taken primarily from chapters 12 and 45 of *Leviathan*.[102] Hobbes was particularly useful for the topic of religious impostors and legislators: referencing *Leviathan*, the text made the point that '[t]he ambitious who have always been great masters in the art of deceiving, have followed this route when they gave laws; & to oblige the People to submit itself voluntarily they have persuaded it that they had received them from a God or a Goddess'.[103] Indeed, in the original passage in *Leviathan*, Hobbes mentioned not only the example of Numa Pompilius, which is also borrowed in the *Traité*, but also Muhammad, who 'to set up his new Religion, pretended to have conferences with the Holy Ghost, in forme of a Dove'.[104] This text is therefore an important demonstration of how Hobbes's ideas were integrated into the attacks of freethinking circles on religion as a whole, also—and perhaps more radically—in clandestine manuscripts. Thus, as Malcolm notes, '[t]hanks to the enormous popularity of this treatise (in its various forms), some of Hobbes's most radical ideas about the nature of religion were thus propagated throughout Europe'.[105]

Going back to Toland, in 1720 he published his ultimate esoteric work, *Pantheisticon*, which portrayed a secret society of pantheists. The work, which was published in Latin first, and in English only in 1751, was clearly not meant for a wide audience: as Toland asserted, quoting Seneca, 'We shall be in Safety ... if we separate ourselves from the Multitude; for the Multitude ... is a Proof of what is worst'.[106] The pantheists constitute a society of philosophers, located in London as well in some other European capitals, who discuss every issue 'in the Silence of all Prejudices', and only among themselves: '*We must talk with the People, and think with Philosophers*'.[107] Their view of the world is that '*All Things are from the Whole, and the Whole is from all Things*', whereas God is 'the Force and Energy of the Whole'.[108] The pantheist philosophy is similar to Toland's materialist and plenist view in *Letters to Serena*, for example, in arguing that 'all Things ... are in Motion' and that thought, too, 'is a peculiar Motion of the Brain', and also in believing in the 'Ethereal Fire environing all Things'.[109] This philosophy, however, seems to go further than the Hobbesian influence that Leibniz recognised previously and come closer to the views of Giordano Bruno and Spinoza, while in ethics, the pantheists derive inspiration from classical sources, and primarily from Cicero.[110] The pantheists' convictions should also be familiar to readers of Toland, although here they are expressed more freely: 'they ruminate on the Law of Nature, that true and never deceiving *Reason*' and thereby 'dispell all Darkness, exempt themselves from trifling Cares, reject all pretended Revelations ... explode forged Miracles, unreasonable Mysteries, ambiguous Oracles, and lay open all Deceits, Tricks, Fallacies, Frauds, old Wives Tales, whereby a thick Cloud envelops *Religion*, and a pitchy Night overspreads *Truth*'.[111] It should come as no surprise, then, that the members of the society declare collectively 'let us detest all *Priest-craft*'.[112] Yet, according to Toland, in public the pantheists are not required to reveal their private truths, ''till they are at full Liberty to think as they please, and speak as they think'.[113] Thus, Toland was playing a twofold and quite ambiguous game, by revealing—albeit only to an elite audience—a philosophy, and perhaps even a private view, that presumably had to be kept a secret.[114]

Toland died in 1722. His epitaph, which he composed for himself, contained the following lines:

> He was an assertor of Liberty
> A lover of all sorts of Learning
> A speaker of Truth
> But no mans follower, or dependant,
> Nor could frowns, or fortune bend him
> To decline from the ways he had chosen.[115]

A devout freethinker at his death, Toland left a fascinating legacy. He was, in fact, a follower of many—the aim here was to highlight the various ways in which he followed Hobbes. But his work was certainly original, first and foremost in the way in which it advanced and combined multiple tools and resources—historical, theological, philosophical, and political—and spoke to multiple audiences, to deconstruct the clerical institutions that perpetuated falsehood and tyranny. As he once simply confessed: 'I hate PRIEST-CRAFT, and that's my crime'.[116]

Popularising freethought

In the early 1720s, John Trenchard (1668/9–1723) and Thomas Gordon (*c.* 1691–1750) produced two periodicals, the *Independent Whig* (1720–1721) and *Cato's Letters* (1720–1723). These highly influential and aggressively anticlerical periodicals were part of 'the most widely read and important polemical works of the reign of George I' and were especially popular in London coffeehouses.[117] The *Independent Whig* 'can be roughly described as deistic', as David Berman argues, due to its 'hostility to priests and the supposed authority of priests' as well as its 'glorification of reason and reasonable religion'.[118] Indeed, this spirit was stated clearly in the subtitle which was added to later editions: *A Defence of Primitive Christianity, and of Our Ecclesiastical Establishment, Against the Exorbitant Claims and Encroachments of Fanatical and Disaffected Clergymen.*

A third anonymous contributor to the *Independent Whig* is presumed to have been Collins.[119] One of the essays that was possibly written by Collins is entitled 'Reasons Why the High-Church Priests are the Most Wicked of All Men', and another is entitled 'A Letter to a Clergyman, Shewing the Impossibility of Assenting to What We Do Not Understand'.[120] The latter made the point that propositions that are not understood cannot be assented to: this is true for mysteries as it would have been true had God published his book in Welsh.[121] This point is close to both Collins's and Toland's positions. In the *Essay*, Collins argued that a blind person cannot perceive colours and hence cannot assent to a proposition on them: 'When he is told that his Face is red or white, he understands no more than if he was told his Face was Cousheda ... The case is just the same when we hear two Chinese discourse'.[122] Collins made a similar point elsewhere by using a made-up word: that if God's attributes were not understood to us, as he believed that archbishop William King thought, then the proposition 'Be ye Holy as I am Holy' would mean the same as 'Be ye Holy as I am Rabba'.[123] This is identical to Toland's way of arguing against mysteries in 1696: 'Could that Person justly value himself upon being wiser than his Neighbours, who having infallible Assurance that something call'd *Blictri* had a Being in Nature, in the mean time knew not what this *Blictri* was?'[124]

Another series of essays by the same author is entitled 'Of High-Church Atheism'. There it was argued that the clergy's constant warning about growing atheism was false, or 'a mere Chimera of the High Priests', designed to serve their own goals: 'For while People are alarmed with the Fears of Atheism, they are disposed to fall into all the pretended Measures of the Priest to suppress it, and to become zealous for him, who never fails to make use of the Panic or Madness of the People (which is his Opportunity) to establish Doctrines and Practices for his own Advantage'.[125] The author claimed, therefore, that atheism was not as common as the priests wanted to present it. If anything, the priests were the ones who could be accused of 'practical atheism' for destroying true religion and introducing practices that were destructive of public peace, such as persecution—but also other practices such as 'the Danger of Cuckoldom' by a priest 'who, by his Power of Confessing and Absolving the Woman, has so glorious an Opportunity'.[126]

Religion was moral conduct; atheism, insomuch as it existed, was immoral conduct; and all other sorts of atheism were simply a clerical exaggeration if not invention. As proof, this essay made the point that religion was intrinsic to human nature as well as to society: 'That Religion, or the Worship of a Deity, is natural to Man, is confessed by Mr. Hobbes himself in his *Leviathan*, wherein he endeavours to assign the natural Causes thereof'.[127] Moreover, religion 'esteemed necessary to Government by Princes and States, who, whether they themselves have believed any Religion or no, have established Forms of Religion ... as knowing its powerful Operation on the Minds of Men'.[128] This argument followed Hobbes's account of religion in chapter 12 of *Leviathan*. Yet, in advocating toleration, it denounced as atheistic the Hobbesian notion that the civil magistrate should be the legislator in religious matters, because 'it roots out all Religion, by taking away Mens Right to follow their Consciences therein; which constitutes the very Essence of Religion'.[129] This combination of picking elements from Hobbes's theory and rejecting some of his political conclusions was characteristic of freethinkers such as Collins, but this was a more interesting take on Hobbes: he was both used to deny atheism and attacked for possibly paving the way for it.

Trenchard and Gordon were Whigs, republicans, or 'commonwealthmen' whose primary goal was to show 'the Advantage and the Beauty of Civil and Ecclesiastical Liberty, and the odious Deformity of Priestcraft and Tyranny'.[130] They believed that Christianity in its true and uncorrupted form was natural religion, made up of virtue and morality. They were 'theorists of civil religion', as Ashley Walsh shows, in which 'a national established church could restrain priestcraft by dis-incentivising the fabrication of superstitions', and the clergymen could fulfil a positive pastoral function.[131] They were also sympathetic to deism:

> In China, all Men of Consideration, all of any Eminence for Learning or Dignity, are Deists. I wish that in Spain and Italy, and in many other Countries called Christian, as much civil Felicity, and as many Marks of Prosperity, were found, as in China: It were indeed better for Mankind, that all fiery Catholics and Bigots, every-where, were converted into rational and sober Chineses. To be Followers of Christ is the best Choice, and the sure Road to Happiness: But to follow Priests and Bigots in most Countries, and in most of their Ways, is not to follow Christ, or Happiness, or common Sense.[132]

They rejected the derogatory use of such labels, stating that it was unjust 'to suppose a Man is a Deist, and therefore a Republican; or a Republican, and therefore a Deist'.[133] In fact, it was argued, it was possible that 'after all, there were then no Deists, or Signs of Deism; but that this Charge was invented by Priests and Bigots, who are always notoriously addicted to forge Falshoods and Calumny against those who differ from them in their Dreams and Forms'.[134] Hence, it should come as no surprise that the *Independent Whig* and *Cato's Letters* made various approving references to the writer who was himself 'suspected of Infidelity' even though he was 'no Republican', namely, Hobbes.[135]

Trenchard and Gordon described Hobbes as 'a great philosopher' in a number of places in their periodicals.[136] They may well have been inspired by his idea of the kingdom of darkness when they argued, for example, that the priests, who used 'words without meaning' and 'the Nonsense of Metaphysicks', were responsible for the corruption of language in order to maintain confusion and instability.[137] Similarly, they cited Hobbes's idea that 'Ignorance is a middle State between Knowledge and false Learning' to argue against deriving ideas from 'foolish books' and 'false speculations', as Hobbes argued against relying blindly on the authority of old books and writers.[138] In both cases, the main target was Aristotelian and scholastic philosophy, or vain philosophy, and its clerical abuse. One who is supposedly learned in this sense is worse off than one who is yet to be taught, because for the former 'all the Avenues and Passages to Wisdom are destroyed or locked up, and he is so puzzled, perplexed, and confounded in a Maze of improved Nonsense and Absurdity, that he never can get through it, or out of it', or more metaphorically:

> The Acquisitions in such Learning have been aptly compared to the Fluttering and Rumbling of a Swallow falling down a Chimney, who, when he is at bottom, flies about, and hurries backwards and forwards to every Window, and every Corner of the Room, to make his Escape; but never thinks of the Way by which he came in, and so becomes an easy Prey to the first Enemy which assaults him.[139]

This metaphor, too, is taken directly from Hobbes.[140] The idea, once again, was to free reason from the harmful influence of the clergy, starting with the correction of speech and education. To promote this cause, the *Independent Whig* relied on Hobbes, who made this case when he rejected meaningless words, including incorporeal substances. Hobbes's rejection of incorporeal substances was of course why he was suspected of infidelity—but this very allegation, it could be argued, was in itself part of a clerical campaign to suppress reason.

This connection was made explicit time and again. In March 1720, the *Independent Whig* targeted the 'The Advantageous Situation of the Clergy, strangely inconsistent with their common Cry of Danger'. Trenchard argued against the persecuting tendencies of the high clergy and their attempts to suppress knowledge and free examination while pretending to defend truth and religion. The clergy had the upper hand in society, and still they kept demanding more and more privileges from the secular power of the state while attempting to restrict the liberties of the laity. Thus, 'They take Advantage, and make their Market, of all Factions and Disturbances in States, and apply them to their own Benefit', and what is more, 'Every Event of Life contributes to their Interests: They Christen; they Educate; they Marry; they Church; they Bury; they Persuade; they Frighten; they Govern; and scarce any thing is done without them'.[141] Furthermore, persecution was not common in early Christianity and yet Christianity flourished successfully; if there were causes for the corruption of religion they were not to be found in the laity. Then, Trenchard added,

> A great Philosopher tells us, when Reason is against a Man, a Man will be against Reason. I therefore much fear, if these my Friends and Patrons should continue to hold forth, and exert their Eloquence, against private Judgment, Freedom of Inquiry, and a daily and diligent Search after a religious Knowledge of the Holy Scriptures, that the World may mistake their Endeavours, and imagine that all these good Things make against them.[142]

This was, of course, a familiar citation from Hobbes. It was used again by Gordon in *Cato's Letters* in 1721, while providing a Hobbesian account of human nature. His argument was that human judgement is often 'liable to be corrupted and weighed down by the Biasses that Passion, Delusion, and Interest hang upon it', and therefore cannot always be trusted.[143] Humans tend to think of themselves as right regardless of whether they are actually right, which leads to conflicts, and 'it proceeds that Men, who are so naturally alike, become morally so unlike, that sometimes there is more Resemblance between a Man and a Wolf, than between one Man and another'.[144] Gordon believed that humans were motivated by their passions, that they pursued pleasure and profit, and that they were easily affected by the minutiae of life. Pride, therefore, was a key motive. Elsewhere, Gordon argued that men had a natural passion for superiority, and he echoed Hobbes arguing that 'Nature has made them all equal, and most Men seem well content with the Lot of Parts which Nature has given them'.[145] In short, humans are stimulated by 'Ambition, Revenge, Lust, and Avarice', and from there follow the 'vicious Pursuits of Men'.[146] The crux of the argument is that human judgement is dictated by human interests:

> Wrong, with Advantages attending it, will be turned into Right, Falsehood into Truth; and, as often as Reason is against a Man, a Man will be against Reason: And both Truth and Right, when they thwart the Interests and Passions of Men, will be used like Enemies, and called Names.[147]

There it was again, the same Hobbesian phrase that had been used consistently since the 1660s to support liberty and toleration in an anticlerical context, now at the heart of the Whig mainstream of the eighteenth century. Gordon's goal here was to issue a warning, and in the spirit of *Cato's Letters*, the usual suspects were the priests: 'Let it abate our Confidence in particular Men, who may make our Trust in them the Means of their misleading us ... Let us remember what the World has ever got by implicit Faith of any Kind whatsoever'.[148] To reveal the interests behind judgements was to uncover all that was truly untrue and thereby to liberate the readers' reason—and their nation. As Gordon explained in typical shrewdness, the most deceitful and dangerous notions of all were 'the Infallibility of the Pope, and the Irresistibleness of Tyrants':

> that is, that one Man, living in the hourly Practice of Error, or Vice, or Folly, and often of them all, shall judge for the whole Earth, and do what God has not done; that is, fashion the Minds of all the human Race like his own, and make them his Sacrifices, where he cannot make them his Slaves: And that another Man shall have a divine Right to represent God and govern Man, by acting against God and destroying Man.[149]

This was the criticism of Trenchard and Gordon in a nutshell. As they seem to have acknowledged, it had much in common with Hobbes's criticism; much more ecclesiastically than politically, to be sure. Finally, Gordon and especially Trenchard followed Hobbes closely in one more important respect. In a number of essays composed between 1721 and 1723, Trenchard expressed an outright materialistic and deterministic view: 'Every thing in the Universe is in constant Motion, and where-ever we move, we are surrounded with Bodies, every one of which must, in a certain Degree, operate upon themselves and us', he wrote in one essay.[150] Trenchard's position was identical to that of Hobbes and Collins: in two essays 'Of Liberty and Necessity', he reiterated their views, while replying to Clarke's *Remarks upon a Book, Entituled, a Philosophical Enquiry Concerning Human Liberty* (1717) which had been written in response to Collins's treatise of the same year.[151] Trenchard's position was that everything that happens has material causes, and that in this there is no difference between body and mind. Thinking is a mechanical process that is determined by external causes, namely, physical motions that affect the brain, precisely in the same way that seeing is determined by objects that strike the eye. Furthermore, Trenchard followed Collins in arguing that systems of matter are 'compounded Bodies' that 'attain new Qualities and Powers which they had not before', and that this is sufficient to explain the necessary operations of both body and mind.[152]

At one point, Trenchard acknowledged his debts. In an essay with the telling title 'That Whatever Moves and Acts Does So Mechanically and Necessarily', he argued that '[i]t is justly observed by Mr. Locke, and by Mr. Hobbes and others before him, that we have no innate Ideas, nor can reflect upon them before we have them; that is, we cannot think before we have something to think upon', thus describing the process of thinking as a sensation followed by a reflection: 'the first seems to me as necessarily to produce the latter, as Wind sails a Ship, or the winding up of a Clock sets it in Motion'.[153] Since the human body works in a purely mechanical manner, the idea of free will is rejected. For Trenchard, this position was reconciled with the notion of God as the first cause. It is absurd, he argued, to believe that 'one Being shall make another, create the Matter of which it was made, give it all the Faculties that it has' and 'yet leave it at Liberty to act against them all'.[154]

Not only did Trenchard defend here the Hobbes-Collins view of liberty and necessity, but his rhetoric, too, was anticlerical throughout. He argued repeatedly that though there might be causes that we do not understand, this in itself is not a reason to conclude that they are immaterial or supernatural: 'And it is still more ridiculous to use the Word Spirit (of which we have no sort of Idea), to account for other Things, of which we have very little or no Idea neither'.[155] The fact that people came to think this way is a result of the priestly 'art of deceiving', which took advantage of superstitious men to invent 'fantastical Stories of Conjurers and Witches, of Spirits, Apparitions, Fairies, Demons, and Hobgoblins, Fortune-tellers, Astrologers, and the Belief in Dreams, Portents, Omens, Prognostics, and the several Sorts of Divinations'.[156] Thus, these priests—the heathens and the Catholics, originally—employed natural phenomena that had not yet been understood, such as 'Eclipses, Meteors, epidemical Plagues, Inundations, great Thunder and Lightnings, and other amazing Prodigies, and seeming Menaces of Nature', for nothing short of the oppression of the vulgar, indeed, the oppression of mankind.[157] Superstition relied on the natural and even medical weakness and susceptibility of men and their ignorance of natural causes. Trenchard started to develop this line of argument already in his *Natural History of Superstition* (1709), a work that has been described as both Hobbist and deist, wherein the idea was summarised well: 'It requires less pains to believe a Miracle, than to discover it to be an Imposture'.[158]

For Trenchard, just as for Hobbes, Toland, and Collins, materialism or naturalism went hand in hand with anticlericalism. Thinking materially was, in this sense, thinking freely: 'I could never subscribe to Opinions, because others held them before me; nor will I send into the Clouds for Solutions, which lie under my Nose ... neither shall I regard the Calumnies and uncharitable Censures of those who dare not peep out of their dark Dungeons, and would measure all Truth by imbibed Prejudices'.[159] Trenchard drew one more implication from this outlook: God 'has so formed at once the whole Fabrick of Heaven and Earth, as to produce all the Events which he intended', because 'He certainly is a more skilful Artificer, who can make a Watch which will go for a thousand Years, and then break to Pieces at a stated Time, than another who makes one which must be wound up every Day, and mended every month'.[160] By asserting that God need not mend His creation continuously, Trenchard took the position that Clarke had attributed to the deists; it was the same position that Leibniz took against Clarke and Newton, and that would be defended once more by Tindal, as we shall see.[161] Even if his position was not original, Trenchard had a remarkable stage which was not as philosophical and exclusive as that of the others; thus, his importance lies in the fact that he could popularise the positions that had previously been formulated by others, while his clear and witty manner of writing made them both accessible and amusing.

Critics paid close attention to these developments. One of them was the theologian Edmund Law, whose *An Essay on the Origin of Evil* (1731) was the translation of archbishop William King's *De origine mali*. This work dealt with the question of theodicy and was aimed against Bayle, Leibniz, Collins, and others; it soon 'became the major treatment of the subject in English'.[162] In his notes, Law described Hobbes as Collins's predecessor.[163]

With regard to the denial of free will, he noted that '[t]he most remarkable Defenders of this Opinion, among the Moderns, seem to be *Hobbs*, *Locke* (if he be consistent with himself) *Leibnitz*, *Bayle*, [John] *Norris*, the *Authors* of the *Philosophical Enquiry concerning human Liberty*, and of *Cato's letters*'; for all of them, 'he that can *do* what he wills ... is free, even tho' he be necessarily determin'd to will'.[164] An unmistakeable tradition of anticlerical determinism which had started with Hobbes was now associated with Collins, Trenchard, and Gordon, the greatest freethinkers of early eighteenth-century England.

Hobbes and the freethinkers were perceived to be so intimately related, that critics deployed the ultimate freethinking-Hobbesian phrase in their satires. Jonathan Swift, for example, suggested that infidelity led to immorality, or vice versa: 'And thus, Mr *Hobbs*'s saying upon Reason may be much more properly apply'd to Religion: That, *if Religion will be against a Man, a Man will be against Religion*'.[165] Another critic wrote: 'I appeal to these Patrons of Reason, and Free-Thinking, I desire them to knock at their Consciences, if they are not past feeling, and ask them ... whether the true Reason of their profess'd Opposition to Religion, be not (what Mr. *Hobbs* long ago confess'd) because Religion is against them'.[166] The best way to fight the freethinkers was to use their own weapons—and that, it became evident, included their favourite Hobbesian arguments.

Notes

1   P. Sagar, *The Opinion of Mankind: Sociability and Theories of the State from Hobbes to Smith* (Princeton, 2018), esp. pp. 39–42, 81–86, on p. 86, establishes the stark contrast between the political premises and conclusions of Shaftesbury and Hobbes, arguing that Shaftesbury preferred 'not an overawing absolutism founded on fear, but a well-governed classical republic carefully managing its commercial affairs to ensure the interests of citizens were directed toward moral virtue rather than luxury, providing the safe space in which refined members could practice the rigors of rational self-direction and moral cultivation'. T. Stuart-Buttle, *From Moral Theology to Moral Philosophy: Cicero and Visions of Humanity from Locke to Hume* (Oxford, 2019), pp. 89–117, explains Shaftesbury's opposition to Locke, especially Locke's moral theology.
2   See L. E. Klein, *Shaftesbury and the Culture of Politeness: Moral Discourse and Cultural Politics in Early Eighteenth-Century England* (Cambridge, 1994).
3   A. A. Cooper, third earl of Shaftesbury, *Characteristicks of Men, Manners, Opinions, Times*, ed. D. Den Uyl, 3 vols (Indianapolis, 2001), vol. 2, p. 119.
4   Ibid., vol. 1, p. 7.
5   Ibid. Klein, *Shaftesbury and the Culture of Politeness*, pp. 197–98, clarifies that Shaftesbury referred to discursive liberty as 'a condition of unlimited interpersonal interaction'.

6 Shaftesbury, *Characteristicks*, vol. 3, p. 183.

7 Ibid., p. 186.

8 Ibid., p. 190.

9 T. B. Macaulay, *The History of England from the Accession of James II*, ed. H. Trevelyan, 5 vols (Cambridge, 2011), vol. 4, p. 645.

10 Walsh, *Civil Religion*, p. 194; Rivers, *Reason, Grace, and Sentiment*, p. 15; but see also A. O. Aldridge, 'Shaftesbury and the Deist Manifesto', *Transactions of the American Philosophical Society*, 41:2 (1951), pp. 297–382.

11 Quoted in Klein, *Shaftesbury and the Culture of Politeness*, p. 157. At the same time, a central tool to secure critical thinking, intellectual liberty, and toleration was ridicule, even of religious matters. For example, Shaftesbury, *Characteristicks*, vol. 1, pp. 7–8. See also R. Carroll, *Uncivil Mirth: Ridicule in Enlightenment Britain* (Princeton, 2021), pp. 20–51.

12 B. Whichcote, *Select Sermons of Dr. Whichcot*, ed. Shaftesbury (London, 1698), sig. A4v; Shaftesbury, *The Life, Unpublished Letters, and Philosophical Regimen of Anthony, Earl of Shaftesbury*, ed. B. Rand (London, 1900), p. 414; Rivers, *Reason, Grace, and Sentiment*, pp. 88–89; Walsh, *Civil Religion*, p. 52.

13 Shaftesbury, *Several Letters Written by a Noble Lord to a Young Man at the University* (London, 1716), p. 38. This is not to argue that Shaftesbury was always more inclined to moderation than someone like Tindal. Stuart-Buttle, *From Moral Theology*, pp. 111–12, shows that for Shaftesbury, unlike Tindal, Christianity was opposed to (rather than reconcilable with) reason and philosophy and therefore 'unnatural'.

14 J. Keith and C. T. Kairoff, 'Works Excluded from This Edition', in *The Cambridge Edition of the Works of Anne Finch, Countess of Winchilsea. Volume 1: Early Manuscript Books* (Cambridge, 2019), pp. cliv–clvi, question the attribution of this poem to Finch.

15 [A. Finch,] *Free-Thinkers: A Poem in Dialogue* (London, 1711), p. 5.

16 Ibid., pp. 23, 28.

17 Ibid., p. 10.

18 Shaftesbury, *Characteristicks*, vol. 1, p. 10; [Finch,] *Free-Thinkers*, p. 4.

19 [Finch,] *Free-Thinkers*, p. 12. According to the OED, 'to be (an) old dog at' means 'to be experienced in or adept at'.

20 Champion, *Republican Learning*, p. 249, outlines a relationship between Hobbes and Toland's somewhat elitist version of republicanism: 'Following Hobbes and Spinoza, Toland argued that the vulgar were incapable of rational conduct because they had been led astray by the corrupting influence of the Church. ... A consequence of this was that Parliament and nobility, as bearers of reason and virtue, were the best agencies of republican reform'.

21 O'Higgins, *Anthony Collins*, p. 91.

22 A. Collins, *Discourse of Free-Thinking*, title page. Cf. Shaftesbury, *Characteristicks*, vol. 1, p. 13; vol. 3, p. 187.

23 Collins, *Discourse of Free-Thinking*, p. 5.

24 Ibid., p. 13.

25 Ibid.

26 Ibid., p. 84.

27 Ibid., p. 15.

28 Ibid., p. 8.

29 Ibid., p. 14.

30 Ibid., pp. 10–12.

31 Ibid., pp. 11–12.

32 Ibid., p. 12.

33 See also Collins, *Essay Concerning the Use of Reason*, pp. 24–25.

34 D. Lucci, 'Deism, Freethinking and Toleration in Enlightenment England', *History of European Ideas*, 43:4 (2017), pp. 345–58. See also J. Dybikowski, 'Anthony Collins' Defense of Freethinking', in G. Paganini, M. Benítez, and J. Dybikowski (eds), *Scepticisme, clandestinité et libre pensée—Scepticism, Clandestinity and Free-Thinking* (Paris, 2002), pp. 299–326.

35 O'Higgins, *Anthony Collins*, p. 49. See also Collins, *In the Shadow of Leviathan*, pp. 181–211.

36 Collins, *A Philosophical Inquiry Concerning Human Liberty* (London, 1717), pp. 103–104, defined conscience as 'a Man's own opinion of his actions with relation to some rule'. Cf. Lev 29, p. 502: 'private Consciences ... are but private opinions'.

37 Israel, *Radical Enlightenment*, pp. 614–19; S. Hutton, 'Liberty of Mind: Women Philosophers and the Freedom to Philosophize', in J. Broad and K. Detlefsen (eds), *Women and Liberty, 1600–1800: Philosophical Essays* (Oxford, 2017), pp. 123–38, on p. 125. See also Miller, ' "Freethinking" and "Freedom of Thought" '; Champion, *Republican Learning*, esp. pp. 247–48; Lærke, *Spinoza and the Freedom of Philosophizing*.

38 Collins, *Discourse of Free-Thinking*, p. 35.

39 For example, Collins, *Priestcraft in Perfection* (London, 1710), esp. pp. 46–47, aimed to prove that the clergy forged the twentieth article of faith of the Church of England, according to which '*The Church hath power to decree Rites and Ceremonys, and Authority in Controversys of Faith*'. As Collins hoped his reader would conclude, the forgery of the article showed 'how uncertain Tradition is', and this instance was in no way the only one: 'Ought we not rather to suppose, that where they have had an Opportunity, they have laid out their natural Talents in Alterations, Interpolations and Rasures of those Books'.

40 In this sense, Collins conceptualised liberty both as non-interference and as non-domination. I develop this argument in E. Carmel, 'Anthony Collins on Toleration, Liberty, and Authority', *History of European Ideas*, 48:7 (2022): 892–908. For these concepts of freedom, see Q. Skinner, *Liberty Before Liberalism* (Cambridge, 1998).

41 Collins, *Discourse of Free-Thinking*, pp. 99–100.

42 Ibid., p. 102.

43 Ibid., pp. 104–106.

44 Ibid., p. 104. Cf. Hobbes, *Thomae Hobbes malmesburiensis opera philosophica quae latine scripsit omnia*, ed. W. Molesworth, 5 vols (London, 1839–1845), vol. 2, p. 6.

45 Collins, *Discourse of Free-Thinking*, pp. 107–109, on p. 109.

46 Ibid., pp. 111–14.

47 Ibid., pp. 118–22.

48 Ibid., pp. 150–52, Collins stated sarcastically that Solomon would be considered an atheist 'in our days' for verses like Ecclesiastes 3:20, '*all are of the Dust, and all turn to Dust again*'. This verse was also used together with other biblical sources to implicitly question the immortality of the soul by Blount, who seems to have copied that from Hobbes. Cf. Lev 44, p. 986; Blount, *Oracles of Reason*, p. 118.

49 Collins, *Discourse of Free-Thinking*, p. 170.

50 Ibid., p. 171. Cf. E. Hyde, earl of Clarendon, *A Brief View and Survey of the Dangerous and Pernicious Errors to Church and State, in Mr. Hobbes's Book, Entitled Leviathan* (Oxford, 1676), pp. 2, 16–17, 21.

51 Collins, *Discourse of Free-Thinking*, p. 96. This episode is documented by Wood and Aubrey. It is reported that Hobbes learned about Fell's intervention and sent an epistle to Wood in response; Wood showed it to Fell, who then asked him to tell Hobbes 'that he was an old man, had one foote in the grave, that he should mind his latter end, and not trouble the world any more with his papers'. Hobbes then saw the king and asked him for permission to defend himself, to which the king agreed, and so Hobbes's response was distributed in Oxford coffeehouses and stationery shops. When it reached Fell, the latter 'fretted and fumed' and rushed into inserting a response of his own at the end of Wood's *History*. See Aubrey, *Brief Lives*, vol. 1, pp. 343–46; A. Wood, *The Life and Times of Anthony Wood*, ed. A. Clark, 5 vols (Oxford, 1891–1900), vol. 2, pp. 291–94.

52 Collins, *Discourse of Free-Thinking*, p. 96.

53 Ibid., p. 97.

54 Collins, *A Discourse Concerning Ridicule and Irony in Writing* (London, 1729), pp. 13–14. See J. Eachard, *Mr. Hobbs's State of Nature Considered in a Dialogue between Philautus and Timothy* (London, 1672); Eachard, *Some Opinions of Mr. Hobbs Considered in a Second Dialogue between Philautus and Timothy by the Same Author* (London, 1673).

55 Collins, *Discourse Concerning Ridicule*, p. 43.

56 R. D. Lund, *Ridicule, Religion and the Politics of Wit in Augustan England* (Farnham, 2012), pp. 31–60.

57 R. Steele, *The Guardian*, ed. J. Calhoun Stephens (Lexington, 1982), p. 49.

58 R. Bentley, *Remarks upon a Late Discourse of Free-Thinking* (London, 1713), p. 4.

59 Ibid., p. 11.

60 Ibid., pp. 11–12.

61 See for example J. Swift, *Mr. C–ns's Discourse of Free-Thinking, Put into Plain English, by Way of Abstract, for the Use of the Poor* (London, 1713), p. 15; Steele, *The Guardian*, pp. 47–49.

62 Beiser, *Sovereignty of Reason*, p. 258.

63 W. Whiston, *Reflexions on an Anonymous Pamphlet, Entituled, a Discourse of Free Thinking* (London, 1713), pp. 40–41.

64 Bentley, *Remarks upon a Late Discourse*, pp. 18–19.

65 Collins, *Philosophical Inquiry*, pp. 113–14 (references are to the 1717 edition unless mentioned otherwise).

66 Collins, *Essay Concerning the Use of Reason*, pp. 45–50; Collins, *Philosophical Inquiry*, esp. pp. 82–84. For example, cf. Hobbes, *English Works*, vol. 5, pp. 15–20, 450–51.

67 Collins, *A Philosophical Inquiry Concerning Human Liberty. Republished with a Preface by Joseph Priestley* (Birmingham, 1790), pp. iii–iv.

68 Collins, *Philosophical Inquiry*, pp. 93–94. Cf. Hobbes, *English Works*, vol. 5, p. 151. The answers to these objections appear also in Hobbes, *English Works*, vol. 4, pp. 251–60. See also O'Higgins, *Anthony Collins*, pp. 104–106.

69 Collins, *Philosophical Inquiry*, p. 95.

70 Ibid., pp. 98–101, Collins also repeated Hobbes's example of Cato the Younger who was praised for being 'good by nature, because he could not be otherwise'. Cf. Hobbes, *English Works*, vol. 5, pp. 154–55.

71 Collins, *Philosophical Inquiry*, pp. 101–103; Hobbes, *English Works*, vol. 5, p. 155.

72 Collins, *Philosophical Inquiry*, pp. 103–104. Cf. Hobbes, *English Works*, vol. 5, p. 200.

73 Collins, *Philosophical Inquiry*, p. 104.

74 O'Higgins, *Anthony Collins*, pp. 107, 110, 219–20.

75 Toland, *Nazarenus*, p. xxiii (references are to the 1718 edition unless mentioned otherwise).

76 J. Toland, *Adeisidaemon* (The Hague, 1709).

77 Toland, *Nazarenus*, p. xxiii.

78 J. Toland, *Reasons for Naturalizing the Jews in Great Britain and Ireland* (London, 1714).

79 Anon., *The Entertainer: Containing Remarks upon Men, Manners, Religion and Policy* (London, 1720), sig. A4v; C. Davenant, *The Political and Commercial Works of That Celebrated Writer*, ed. C. Whitworth, 5 vols (London, 1771), vol. 4, pp. 240–42; Champion, 'Deism', p. 444; J. G. A. Pocock, *The Machiavellian Moment: Florentine Political Thought and the Atlantic Republican Tradition*, 3rd edn (Princeton, 2016), p. 449.

80 Toland, *Nazarenus*, p. 5.

81 Ibid., p. ii.

82 Ibid., p. 17; Champion (ed.), *Nazarenus* (Oxford, 1999), p. 66.

83 Toland, *Nazarenus*, p. ii; Champion, *Republican Learning*, e.g., pp. 169–70, 237–38; Malcolm, *Aspects of Hobbes*, p. 489.

84 J. Champion, '"Syllables Governe the World": Biblical Criticism, Erudition, Heterodoxy and Thomas Hobbes', in R. Armstrong and T. Ó hAnnracháin (eds), *The English Bible in the Early Modern World* (Leiden, 2018), pp. 183–212, on p. 188.

85 J. Jones, *A Vindication of the Former Part of St. Matthew's Gospel* (London, 1719), 'Preface' (unnumbered). This text was reprinted posthumously as part of Jones, *A New and Full Method of Settling the Canonical Authority of the New Testament*, 3 vols (Oxford, 1798), vol. 3.

86 Jones, *Vindication of the Former Part*, 'Preface'.
87 Ibid., pp. 217–29, esp. pp. 221–23. Cf. Toland, *Amyntor*, pp. 69–80.
88 Lev 33, p. 600.
89 Jones, *New and Full Method*, vol. 1, p. 28. See also Keene, 'A Two-Edged Sword', pp. 100–104.
90 Toland, *Amyntor*, p. 64; Toland, *Nazarenus*, p. iii.
91 Toland, *Nazarenus*, pp. 16–17, 29.
92 Ibid., p. 39.
93 Ibid., pp. ii, 16.
94 Ibid., pp. 65–66.
95 Ibid., p. 40.
96 Ibid, p. 5. See also Jacob, *Henry Stubbe*, pp. 158–60; J. Sheehan, *The Enlightenment Bible: Translation, Scholarship, Culture* (Princeton, 2005), pp. 40–43; Keene, 'A Two-Edged Sword', pp. 108–11; Champion, *Pillars of Priestcraft Shaken*, pp. 120–32; Lucci, 'Deism, Freethinking and Toleration', pp. 347–51.
97 Toland, *Nazarenus*, p. 65. Beiner, *Civil Religion*, p. 54n40, notes: 'Hobbes in effect anticipates the "Ebionite" view offered in John Toland's *Nazarenus*. ... If Toland's Ebionite view is correct, then Hobbes is simply steering Christianity back to the (pre-Pauline) self-understanding of Jesus and his immediate followers'.
98 Toland, *Nazarenus*, p. 81.
99 Ibid., Appendix I, p. 1.
100 Hunter, *Decline of Magic*, esp. p. 56.
101 Champion, 'Legislators, Impostors, and the Politic Origins of Religion'. See also Jacob, *Radical Enlightenment*, pp. 215–20; Champion, *Republican Learning*, pp. 170–73; Champion, *Pillars of Priestcraft Shaken*, pp. 1–2.
102 A. Anderson, *The Treatise of the Three Impostors and the Problem of Enlightenment: A New Translation of the Traité des Trois Imposteurs (1777 Edition)* (Lanham, 1997), e.g., pp. 14, 16.
103 Anderson, *Treatise of the Three Impostors*, p. 17. Cf. Lev 12, p. 176.
104 Anderson, *Treatise of the Three Impostors*, p. 22; Lev 12, p. 178.
105 Malcolm, *Aspects of Hobbes*, pp. 491–93, on p. 493.
106 Toland, *Pantheisticon*, 'To the Reader' (unnumbered).
107 Ibid., pp. 14, 57–58.
108 Ibid., pp. 15, 17.
109 Ibid., pp. 21–22.
110 See for example Jacob, *Newtonians and the English Revolution*, pp. 245–50; K. A. East, *The Radicalization of Cicero: John Toland and Strategic Editing in the Early Enlightenment* (Cham, 2017).
111 Toland, *Pantheisticon*, p. 62.
112 Ibid., p. 65.
113 Ibid., p. 108.
114 See Jacob, *Radical Enlightenment*; S. H. Daniel, *John Toland: His Methods, Manners, and Mind* (Kingston, 1984), pp. 211–25; J. Champion, 'John Toland: The Politics of Pantheism', *Revue de synthese*, 116:2–3 (1995), pp. 259–80; Rivers, *Reason, Grace, and Sentiment*, pp. 50, 71–76; Champion,

Republican Learning, pp. 240–44; Champion, *Pillars of Priestcraft Shaken*, pp. 193–95.

115 Quoted in Daniel, *John Toland*, p. 13.

116 Toland, *The Second Part of the State Anatomy* (London, 1717), p. 22.

117 C. Robbins, *The Eighteenth-Century Commonwealthman* (Cambridge, MA, 1959), p. 115.

118 D. Berman, 'Anthony Collins' Essays in the *Independent Whig*', *Journal of the History of Philosophy*, 13:4 (1975), pp. 463–69, on p. 464.

119 Berman, 'Anthony Collins' Essays', attributes ten essays in the *Independent Whig* to Collins, based on numerous reports on Collins's authorship as well as their resemblance to his works; Gordon, as the editor, only mentioned the initial of the writer of each essay, and the essays in question received the initial C., while the others are signed by T. (Trenchard) or G. (Gordon). Walsh, *Civil Religion*, pp. 60–61, questions Collins's authorship.

120 J. Trenchard and T. Gordon, *The Independent Whig*, 7th edn, 4 vols (London, 1741–1747), vol. 1, no. 17 and 19.

121 Ibid., no. 19, p. 165.

122 Collins, *Essay Concerning the Use of Reason*, pp. 9–10.

123 Collins, *A Vindication of the Divine Attributes* (London, 1710), pp. 24–25. See also Berman, 'Anthony Collins' Essays', p. 469.

124 Toland, *Christianity Not Mysterious*, p. 128.

125 *Independent Whig*, vol. 2, no. 42, p. 100.

126 Ibid., p. 102.

127 Ibid., p. 96.

128 Ibid., p. 98.

129 Ibid., no. 44, p. 113.

130 Trenchard and Gordon, *Cato's Letters: Or, Essays on Liberty, Civil and Religious, and Other Important Subjects*, 6th edn, 4 vols (London, 1755), vol. 4, no. 138, p. 281.

131 Walsh, *Civil Religion*, pp. 59–79, on p. 61.

132 *Independent Whig*, vol. 3, pp. 315–16. Pocock, *Machiavellian Moment*, pp. 468, 476, argues that Cato (namely, Trenchard and Gordon) 'declares that England (or Britain) is a republic, of that peculiarly happy kind which has a king as its chief magistrate', adding that 'it is interesting to see that republicanism and deism alike carried on the English and Puritan crusade against a clergy enjoying separate or *jure divino* authority'. See also M. P. McMahon, *The Radical Whigs, John Trenchard and Thomas Gordon: Libertarian Loyalists to the New House of Hanover* (Lanham, 1990); G. Tarantino, *Republicanism, Sinophilia, and Historical Writing: Thomas Gordon (c. 1691–1750) and His 'History of England'* (Turnhout, 2012).

133 *Independent Whig*, vol. 3, p. 316.

134 Ibid., p. 296.

135 Ibid., p. 296. See also Gordon, *An Examination of the Facts and Reasonings in the Lord Bishop of Chichester's Sermon* (London, 1732), pp. 44–45, 59–60.

136 *Independent Whig*, vol. 1, no. 11, p. 88 and no. 30, p. 258; *Cato's Letters*, vol. 1, no. 33, p. 257.

137 *Cato's Letters*, vol. 4, no. 126, p. 180. See I. Higgins, 'Remarks on *Cato's Letters*', in D. Womersley, P. Bullard, and A. Williams (eds), *Cultures of Whiggism: New Essays on English Literature and Culture in the Long Eighteenth Century* (Newark, 2005), pp. 127–46, on p. 133; G. L. McDowell, 'The Language of Law and the Foundations of American Constitutionalism', *The William and Mary Quarterly*, 55:3 (1998), pp. 375–98, on p. 392.
138 *Independent Whig*, vol. 1, no. 30, p. 258.
139 Ibid., pp. 258–59.
140 Lev 4, pp. 56–58.
141 *Independent Whig*, vol. 1, no. 11, p. 85.
142 Ibid., p. 88.
143 *Cato's Letters*, vol. 2, no. 47, p. 97.
144 Ibid.
145 Ibid., no. 43, p. 71. Cf. Lev 13, p. 188: 'almost all men think they have [wisdom] in a greater degree, than the Vulgar … But this proveth rather that men are in that point equall, than unequall. For there is not ordinarily a greater signe of the equall distribution of any thing, than that every man is contented with his share'.
146 *Cato's Letters*, vol. 2, no. 47, p. 99.
147 Ibid., p. 100. On the similarity between Cato and Hobbes on the issue of human nature, see also V. B. Sullivan, *Machiavelli, Hobbes, and the Formation of a Liberal Republicanism in England* (Cambridge, 2004), pp. 227–57.
148 *Cato's Letters*, vol. 2, no. 47, p. 103.
149 Ibid., pp. 101–102.
150 *Independent Whig*, vol. 2, no. 53, p. 211. See also *Independent Whig*, vol. 2, no. 53, pp. 209–19; *Cato's Letters*, vol. 4, no. 110–11, pp. 38–57; no. 116, pp. 86–95.
151 Clarke, *Remarks upon a Book, Entituled, a Philosophical Enquiry Concerning Human Liberty* (London, 1717), p. 43, argued: 'If the Reasons or Motives upon which a Man acts, be the immediate and efficient Cause of the Action: then either abstract Notions, such as all Reasons and Motives are … are themselves Substances; or else That which has it self no real Subsistence, can put a Body in Motion'. While for Clarke any of these possibilities would be absurd, for Trenchard it is certainly plausible that these so-called 'abstract Notions' are in fact 'Species of Thinking' which are caused physically and necessarily, including passions, and which is what sets a body in motion (even if we do not know exactly how). *Cato's Letters*, vol. 4, no. 111, pp. 55–56.
152 *Cato's Letters*, vol. 4, no. 116, p. 90.
153 Ibid., pp. 86–87.
154 Ibid., no. 111, p. 52.
155 Ibid., no. 116, p. 89.
156 *Independent Whig*, vol. 2, no. 53, pp. 216, 211.
157 Ibid., p. 212.
158 Trenchard, *The Natural History of Superstition* (London, 1709), p. 35, and pp. 9–10. See Champion, *Pillars of Priestcraft Shaken*, pp. 160–61; Hunter, *Decline of Magic*, p. 54.

159 *Cato's Letters*, vol. 4, no. 116, pp. 94–95.

160 Ibid., p. 95.

161 Newton clarified in his *General Scholium* of 1713—plausibly against the deists and their like—that God 'rules all things', hence 'the lord of all'. In the correspondence of Leibniz and Clarke from 1715–16, Leibniz made the analogy of God as the watchmaker to argue that the world operates by 'the beautiful pre-established Order' which does not need to be repaired from time to time; to suggest otherwise would be to imply that God created an imperfect machine and thus that He is an imperfect creator: 'Sir Isaac Newton, and his Followers, have also a very odd Opinion concerning the Work of God. According to their Doctrine, God Almighty wants to wind up his Watch from Time to Time: Otherwise it would cease to move'. I. Newton, *Philosophical Writings*, ed. A. Janiak (Cambridge, 2004), pp. 90–92; Clarke, *Works*, vol. 4, pp. 587–88.

162 B. W. Young, 'Law, Edmund (1703–1787), Bishop of Carlisle and Theologian', *ODNB* (2004), available at: www.oxforddnb.com/view/10.1093/ref:odnb/9780198614128.001.0001/odnb-9780198614128-e-16141 (accessed 21 July 2023). See also Miller, ' "Freethinking" and "Freedom of Thought" '.

163 W. King, *An Essay on the Origin of Evil*, trans. with notes E. Law, 2nd edn, 2 vols (London, 1732), vol. 2, p. 329n55.

164 Ibid., p. 232n42.

165 J. Swift, *A Letter to a Young Gentleman, Lately Enter'd into Holy Orders* (London, 1721), p. 29. Tillotson, *Works* (1696), p. 36, also made this point.

166 J. Hildrop, *Reflections upon Reason* (London, 1722), p. 19.

4

The last battle (1724–1740)

The heyday of English deism witnessed the appearance of Collins's and Tindal's last and highly controversial works. Subsequently, new works reformulated and even radicalised similar anticlerical ideas, wherein Hobbesian ideas played a significant role. Two writers are particularly notable: Alberto Radicati di Passerano, the Italian nobleman who was in exile in London, and Thomas Morgan, who started his career as a dissenting minister. Radicati described himself as a Christian freethinker; Morgan, a Christian deist. Thereby, these infamous labels started to be embraced publicly and, naturally, continued to draw the attention of prominent critics until the early 1740s. The consistent attacks of William Warburton on the deists and freethinkers were especially striking, not least because they did much to identify—and indeed almost to canonise, albeit unintentionally—an entire lineage of intellectual heterodoxy from Hobbes to Morgan.

Collins's later works

The last productive period for Collins was between the years of 1724 and his early death in 1729. His two most significant works from this period were *A Discourse of the Grounds and Reasons of the Christian Religion* (1724) and *The Scheme of Literal Prophecy Considered* (1726). In these works, Collins argued that it was not evident that the prophecies about the Messiah in the Old Testament referred to Jesus—they predicted a temporal, not spiritual deliverer—and so that these prophecies were not fulfilled literally. If the prophecies did not predict Jesus, then Jesus' miracles were not proofs for his being the Messiah either. These works required an advanced level of biblical scholarship and relied on a variety of sources, including Jewish anti-Christian titles which Collins held in his library. He also appealed directly to the authority of Hobbes, Spinoza, and Richard Simon, who 'have been severely censur'd, as giving up or attacking the Bible, for asserting, that some few interpolations, tho' not relating to the essentials of religion, have been made therein'.[1]

In *A Discourse of the Grounds and Reasons*, Collins refuted the theologian William Whiston, but not before he dedicated an entire preface to defend the right of Whiston, whose controversial inquiries of the bible had complicated him before, to write and publish his views. Collins reaffirmed his conviction that 'it is every man's mutual right and duty to think for himself, and to judge upon such evidence as he can procure to himself, after he has done his best endeavours to get information'.[2] Precisely because we need sufficient information to make our judgments, Collins derived from the right to think freely also the right to profess one's views freely to attempt to convince others, as a necessary means for the formation of knowledge and the discovery of truth.[3] Where Whiston argued that the Hebrew texts had been corrupted and had to be restored, Collins agreed that these texts had difficulties providing the necessary proof for Christianity, but he objected that Whiston's attempt to restore them would simply result in 'a mere WHISTONIAN BIBLE'.[4] Collins employed his own textual criticism: unlike Whiston's, however, it questioned the prophecies as well as the scripture.

The replies to the *Discourse*, particularly by Edward Chandler, bishop of Coventry and Lichfield, led Collins to publish the *Scheme*, where he reiterated his previous convictions, while defending once again the right to liberty of opinion and belief. Chandler called for the magistrate to 'supress the Atheism and Looseness of the Times'.[5] Collins commented that the tactic of 'calling in the aid of the Civil Magistrate … is not only unlike a scholar and lover of truth, in a matter that ought to be determin'd by the force of argument, and as dishonourable as using a sword and pistol, against a man who has a sword only, but irrational, and anti-christian'.[6] He added the words that the dissenting minister Samuel Chandler used in his own reply to Collins: 'If the scheme of our *modern Deists* be founded in truth, I cannot help wishing it all good success'.[7]

Having faced several opponents who called to censure his works, Collins argued not only that he had the liberty to publish them but also that censuring them fell outside the scope of the civil authority. His argument was that human authority is destructive in matters of opinion, such as religious matters, as opposed to civil or social ones. In the *Scheme*, he proposed two principles that would ensure liberty. The first is a 'universal liberty' of 'opinions and practices not prejudicial to the peace and welfare of society', the lack of which would lead to '*Hobbism*, or, what is worse, *Popery*'; the second is that only the law of nature should be enforced by the civil magistrate, whereas 'indifferent things' should be left to individual judgment.[8] As we will see, Collins developed this political idea significantly in 1727.

John Rogers, chaplain to the Prince of Wales and future George II, published in 1727 *The Necessity of Divine Revelation* against the deists, and especially against Collins. The debate was still on the sufficiency (or lack thereof) of natural reason and hence on the status of natural theology. Rogers's 'Conclusion against the *Deist*' was that miracles that had worked did provide 'all the Proof that any reasonable Man can expect, or require, that the Gospel is a divine Revelation'.[9] Furthermore, he refuted the idea that one is able to use one's reason sufficiently to always come to a true understanding of religion and morality, because human reason is 'subject to those Weaknesses and Imperfections we feel in ourselves, and observe in others'.[10] If humans relied only on their unequal and defective rational abilities, the result would be nothing more than 'an utter Confusion of all Morality'.[11] It is so wrong to think that humans are or ever will be directed by pure reason, that 'a Scheme, whose Success depends upon so groundless a Supposition, must be given up as chimerical'.[12] Despite Collins's proposal, or the 'Libertine Scheme', divine revelation was very much still needed as our guiding rule.[13]

Rogers had another target here: 'Mr. *Hobbs*, who thought somewhat deeper than these Gentlemen' and yet was 'as little a friend to Revelation as these Gentlemen'.[14] According to Rogers, Hobbes made the civil magistrate the ultimate standard of morality, and hence he made the supreme authority human rather than divine. However, Rogers objected, human laws are simply not good enough; some things even 'the wisest Constitution cannot ascertain'; and human princes are themselves 'not exempt from Weakness and Passions'.[15] The fear of the sovereign, Rogers continued, cannot be a sufficient motive 'where Men can presume themselves cunning enough to elude the Notice of human Justice, or rich enough to bribe, or strong enough to defy the Execution of it'.[16] Humans are simply too flawed to be trusted with the direction of all future actions:

> Upon the whole; we have consider'd the Expedients which have undertaken to supply Mankind with a Rule of Morality, equal to the Purposes of social Life, without having Recourse to divine Revelation. It is evident, that no Rule cou'd answer this End, unless it cou'd obtain a general Acknowledgment … Before this can appear possible, the Bulk of Mankind must be supposed to apprehend clearly, and reason justly, without Prejudice, Passion, or Partiality; a Supposition manifestly contrary to Fact, and fit only for *Utopia*.[17]

So, Hobbes, who rightly did not trust unaided reason, placed the civil magistrate precisely where infidels such as Collins placed reason and natural religion, namely, as the ultimate source of morality. Hobbes—'this great Father of modern Infidelity'[18]—was only a little better than Collins and his friends, because he realised that men had to submit to some authority—he just chose the wrong authority and in doing so proved to be utopian (in the derogatory sense of the term).[19] Common to all of these infidels is that they disregarded the only true authority, the only true source of morality, that is, divine revelation. Hobbes and the deists offered two sources of authority that were equally delusional, and so Rogers called his readers to be equally wary:

> In the mean Time, what has occurr'd in these Reflections, will, I hope, determine you not to give up an Institution, which directs so rational a Service of the Deity, and enforces, by the noblest Prospects and Motives of Action, so pure, so useful a System of Morality, so conducive to the personal and civil Interests of Mankind, either for that wild, impracticable Project of Natural Religion, to which our modern Deists invite you, or for what Mr. *Hobbs*'s Magistrate shall be pleas'd to devise for you.[20]

Rogers put Hobbes and the deists together as the enemies of divine revelation, indeed the great infidels of the time.

Not only did Rogers argue against Collins's sceptical views, he also argued against the liberty to voice such views that he found to be so destructive of society: 'The Liberty of private Judgment in Religion', he wrote, 'I acknowledge to be an inherent Right of every Man'; but, he added, 'there appears no general Obligation either of Reason or Religion, which requires a Man to publish his Sentiments'.[21] The liberty to hold private opinions is granted; the liberty to publish them does not automatically follow. This was a commonplace Anglican criticism. Rogers concluded that any heretic who attempts to publish a subversive scheme 'may be consider'd as the Aggressor, an Invader of settled Rights, a Disturber of publick Peace' and so stopping such an aggressor 'is not persecuting him, but protecting those to whom Protection is due'.[22] Collins replied in *A Letter to the Reverend Dr. Rogers* of 1727, which has remained very little-known in the literature.[23] Most crucial for Collins in this text was, once again, the question of freedom of thought, and his last defence of it revealed new sides of his politics.

Collins's Hobbesian moment

Collins began his *Letter* by attacking Rogers that his book was 'grounded on Principles absolutely destructive of Peace, Humanity, Liberty, Property, Truth, Revelation, and the Christian Revelation in particular'.[24] Collins made his case for religious toleration and freedom of the press in opposition to Rogers, who believed that these principles would lead to '*Licentiousness and Confusion*'.[25] Toleration was the right path because it would conform to the true moral spirit of the New Testament, contribute to the inquiry of the truth, and preserve the quiet and peace of society.[26] Collins defended his right to publish his previous works, reminding Rogers that this was not, in fact, against any law, and that 'It does not contradict any Law to call in question the *Genuineness* or Authority of a *Text* of *Scripture*'.[27] The law does not—and should not—apply to the religious realm.

This was Collins's typical position since the 1700s. What is particularly interesting in this tract is how Collins contrasted liberty with authority. While he took upon himself to represent the side of liberty, he attributed to Rogers the side of authority, that is, the idea that religious matters too should be determined by an authority. In arguing that the civil magistrate had to restrain the publication of texts such as Collins's, Rogers advocated the idea that there should be 'human Judge in matters of Religion', that the magistrate, as a puppet of the clergy, should be 'the Judge of Doctrines', and that the civil law should be 'the means to settle and maintain Opinions'.[28] In sum, Rogers made religion a matter of authority. Collins accused Rogers that his idea is based 'on *Hobbian* Principles, by which the Civil Magistrate is impower'd to chuse a Religion ... for his Subjects, and to compel them by Violence or Laws to support it, and acquiesce under it'.[29] For Collins, Rogers displayed a longing for coercive uniformity—a common derogatory meaning of 'Hobbism'. Yet, according to Collins, it is wrong to let humans set the rules in matters of religion because 'History shows them for the most part, if not always, to be the Effect of Party, Power, Faction, Enthusiasm, and Interest'.[30]

Collins identified authority in this context—that is, the authority of those who aim to determine religious truths for others—with infallibility, or rather a pretence to infallibility. His strong opposition to authority was anticlerical, and he emphasised that the greatest danger came from those who demanded absolute and blind trust and threatened those who would not trust them with the most severe sanctions: 'In fine, it is a manifest Proof of Imposture, for any Man or Body of Men, to set up for *Infallibility* or *Authority* in matters of Speculation, and to forbid Men to use their own Senses and Reason, which are given them for their Direction'.[31] The problem was therefore not authority per se but more accurately unjustified, arbitrary, and tyrannical authority in religious matters. For Collins, one can attain knowledge in religion only by way of private judgment and not authority because no authority, not even that of the magistrate, could evidently be the only true one: 'And if you prove your *Authority*, I shall readily own your *Infallibility* in like manner'.[32]

The *Letter* was a fierce defence of liberty and an attack on arbitrary authority. Just like 'Hobbism' and 'Popery', the idea of authority served Collins throughout the *Letter* as a straw man, a position which even he admitted that was not fully embraced by Rogers. In this sense, 'authority' was used by Collins almost pejoratively, in a manner that is not all that different from the way in which Collins's opponents mocked the 'liberty' of the freethinkers, which for them was mere anarchy. Yet, Collins objected to *false* or *abused* authority, primarily in matters of religion. His position regarding the civil authority, however, was more complex.

Collins's guiding principle was that the magistrate 'should *restrain* Men from vicious Actions, and from injuring one another, and give them *liberty* in all things that have no such tendency, and particularly liberty in all matters of mere Religion'.[33] For this reason, as we have seen, he made a distinction between the law of nature and personal issues. Natural law forbids crimes, ensures honesty and justice, and preserves the peace of society; personal matters, including religion, concern the individual alone and are not harmful to society. The civil sovereign has full authority in the social realm which is dictated by the natural law—but the question remains as to who decides what precisely falls under which category. As Rogers remarked sarcastically: 'he expresly allows a civil Magistrate, tho' under this Restraint, that nothing be inforced by civil Sanctions but only the Law of Nature. But I am afraid some Free-thinker or other will assert this to be a Personal Matter too, and then the Magistrate will have nothing to do with it'.[34] The result, then, would be anarchy. But there was another option, namely, that Collins's proposal would grant a considerable power to the civil sovereign, more than Collins had ever suggested before. As Rogers also observed: 'who must be Judge of this Law of Nature to be enacted? If whatever the Magistrate shall think or pronounce the Law of Nature, is to be enacted and acknowledg'd as such, we had e'en as good leave him to his own Discretion without this Restraint'.[35]

Collins confirmed this implication in his reply to Rogers. He established that the law of nature is a social matter and is therefore to be enforced by the sovereign, and added importantly: 'the Magistrate, being the Person who is to make Laws for the Government of the Society, is unavoidably the Judge, what is the *Law of Nature* or Reason, or whether Murder, Adultery, Thievery, etc. are Matters injurious to *Society*. And he is regularly under no Controul, but his own Reason, and has *Liberty of Conscience*'.[36] Even though the magistrate relies eventually on his reason, there could be ways to help improve his reasoning: 'it is highly proper, that the Principles and Rules by which a good Magistrate should conduct himself, should be laid before him … It is not fitting, that he alone of all Mankind, should be destitute of the Assistance of other Mens Reason, to understand aright his Duty'.[37] One way of providing the magistrate with good advice would be to write discourses, such as Collins's of course.[38] In this context, Collins invoked Fénelon, as he, too, advised the king to rule in accordance with the common good and the law of nature and not to interfere in religious matters.[39]

Having said that, Collins confirmed that the magistrate is the judge of what constitutes the law of nature and what actually is harmful to society and that the magistrate is regularly under no control in this respect. Now, if the magistrate is the one who enforces the law of nature *and* the one who interprets what the law of nature actually entails, and if this authority is unchecked, then this makes the magistrate very powerful. To put the point another way, what happens if the magistrate decides that a religious matter becomes a social one and therefore merits intervention? There seems to be nothing in Collins's theory to exclude this possibility. Indeed, he supported 'restraining [men], whenever they profess or practise any thing contrary to the Peace of Society, or injurious to their Neighbour'.[40] The question, then, is whether, and when, religion should be controlled by the sovereign, at least publicly, to assure peace and order.

At one point in the *Letter*, Collins came close to conceding that the power of the sovereign *could* apply to religious matters if the sovereign sees fit. He hinted at such a possibility when he remarked that the magistrate has 'the Liberty of acting according to his Conscience (which must be always his immediate Rule of Action) and of establishing *Popery* or *Mahometism* upon Penaltys, even the Penalty of Death, if he thinks it his Duty to do so'.[41] The rest of this paragraph is intriguing:

> Nor is offering Reasons to the *Mahometan*, or *Popish*, or any other *Magistrate*, to induce him to Moderation, Forbearance, and Toleration; to persuade him to let Truth and Reason have fair play; to convince him that it does not belong to him, or is not a part of his Commission, to make a Religion for his People; and to prove to him, that it is both his Interest and Duty, not to take away the natural Right of Men, in judging for themselves in matters of Religion, but to protect them in the Enjoyment of that valuable Property, as in the Enjoyment of their other Propertys; in the least inconsistent with allowing the Magistrate to act according to his Conscience.[42]

Here Collins repeated his basic argument, advising any magistrate to allow religious freedom and toleration, but seems to have left open the possibility that magistrates could decide otherwise according to their liberty of conscience. It is of course hard to conclude what Collins meant exactly based on single paragraphs of this work. Yet, it is at least a plausible interpretation that, for Collins, although there are things that would not be desirable for the sovereign to do, there is nothing that he or she could not do by definition. While it is arguable that the liberty of conscience that Collins attributed to the magistrate is the essence of any supreme authority, it is still remarkable that Collins—unlike Locke, for instance—did not add any explicit caveat to this right.[43]

In religious matters, both Collins and Locke believed that the sovereign must be highly restricted, but when it came to civil matters, Collins left the magistrate with no apparent restrictions. Furthermore, Collins's sovereign would ultimately remain entirely free to determine the limits of the civil authority, with no binding duty to uphold Collins's distinction between personal and social matters. In other words, Collins was less concerned to limit the civil authority or to assure that it would not act arbitrarily—at least not as concerned as Locke was or as Collins himself was with regard to any kind of clerical authority. Therefore, on the issue of the power of the civil sovereign, Collins seems to have ended up with a position that was closer to Hobbes than to Locke, namely, that the civil sovereign is the judge of what poses a threat to civil order, which ultimately may or may not include religious matters. This might seem surprising, not least given Collins's critical reference to Hobbism in this context. What might explain Collins's Hobbesian moment in the *Letter*, such as it was?

One possible explanation is that Collins simply had more urgent worries, and that perhaps he was not a thorough political writer after all. But there is another possibility that is worth considering, namely, that taking away the clerical authority required necessarily strengthening the civil authority. This issue, as we have already seen, often brought the so-called radicals closer to Hobbes than they wished to acknowledge. The ways in which they grappled with this problem resulted in political theories that were more nuanced, even if not free of inconsistencies, than is usually recognised. Liberty and authority were the two foundations of any prosperous society, and it was only the right balance between them that could allow for what Collins cared for the most: religious toleration and freedom of thought.

The correspondence between Collins and Rogers had an interesting epilogue. In 1728, Rogers replied to Collins and others in *A Vindication of the Civil Establishment of Religion*. His goal was to demonstrate the right of the civil magistrate to establish religion, including the right to protect it by civil sanctions, while conceding that civil peace may sometimes require a certain degree of toleration.[44] In response, the philosopher Thomas Chubb published in the same year *Some Short Reflections on the Grounds and Extent of Authority and Liberty*. Chubb was a proud freethinker who endorsed Collins's concept of freethinking almost word by word.[45] His main point in his reply to Rogers was that the civil magistrate should not interfere with religious matters at all: the purpose of society is the public good, and thus authority can be exercised only with regard to things that concern the public. When a government no longer serves the public good, the people have the right to hold it accountable, otherwise 'the End and Purpose of Association would be destroy'd; Liberty would not be secured, but would be changed into Slavery; and the publick Interest into the personal Property of the Governor'.[46]

Chubb, too, had to make some concessions. For example, he admitted that the government may restrain even religious actions that are considered hurtful to society, given that such actions would then be considered civil and would not be restricted simply on the basis of their religiousness.[47] Even with regard to worship, Chubb similarly conceded that 'Governors may so far interpose, as to appoint a *Time* for publick Worship, a *Place* to perform it in, a *Form* or *Mode* of Worship, and a *Person* to minister in Divine Service, these being not of *religious* but of *civil* Consideration only', yet clarifying that 'it will not follow, that they have a Right to *oblige*, or *restrain* any Individual in these Respects'.[48] Chubb ended his tolerationist tract by making a conclusion which was not all that far from Rogers's. He argued that laws which prohibit the publication of religious opinions are unreasonable but then repeated the same caveat: 'Governors cannot in Reason be justified in the making, or in the Execution of them, excepting in those Cases in which Men's natural Rights are concerned, and which Governors are obliged to defend'.[49]

Collins and Chubb were therefore not mere tolerationists: their idea of religious toleration was in the end subordinated to the idea of civil authority that would enforce it, and thus the religious liberties of the individual would ultimately depend on what Collins called the magistrate's liberty of conscience. Civil authority played a central role in liberating humankind from the tyranny of the clergy over the human mind. To be sure, this did not simply translate into an outright Hobbesian position either, despite the parallels. Furthermore, Chubb specifically objected to Hobbes's notions of the defects of reason and the primacy of self-interest. Chubb believed that God would only encourage a reasonable conduct and would not offer any other rule of action but the law of nature. He attacked Hobbes and what he considered 'the fundamental Principle of his Atheism', namely, Hobbes's conception of reason as fragile, subjected to manipulation, and hence unreliable: 'that every one will say that is right Reason, that pleases him best; and call that Sort *Trump*, that he has most of in his Hand'.[50]

For Chubb, our duties are always derived from the nature and reason of things, ordered by God, and not from mighty and unreasonable divine interpositions. On the view that selfishness, for example, and not reason, was our guiding rule, Chubb proclaimed: 'how favourable soever this doctrine may be to *Hobbism*; yet, surely, it is very injurious to the christian religion'.[51] Hobbes, then, was cast as an atheist because of his view of human nature, which was of course common in Anglican and deist critiques alike, and yet Chubb equally rejected the view that God's irresistible power left room for extraordinary interventions. Now it was the human faculty of reason that came to the fore and the rule of God that had to conform to it. The writer who did most to develop this principle in the exact same years was Matthew Tindal.

The bible of deism

Christianity as Old as the Creation: Or, the Gospel, a Republication of the Religion of Nature (1730), known as the bible of deism, marks in many ways the culmination of English deism.[52] In this work, Tindal defended deism against Samuel Clarke while formulating it significantly further. He seems to have been almost proud to endorse deism and freethinking, as we will see, although scholarly views on his self-identification still differ.[53] According to Tindal, natural religion is the original and universal religion, that is, 'the Belief of the Existence of a God, and the Sense and Practice of those Duties, which result from the Knowledge, we, by our Reason, have of him, and his Perfections; and of ourselves, and our own Imperfections; and of the Relation we stand in to him, and to our Fellow-Creatures'.[54] Since God is infinitely happy in Himself, there is nothing that His creatures can add to His happiness, and therefore all they are required to do is to promote their common interest by imitating God in loving their fellow-creatures.[55]

Tindal sought to promote a rational society, and to that end he advocated the view that reason gives us all the information we need for our mutual happiness and that the law of nature applies universally and consistently without exception. Against those who insisted on the special status of revelation, Tindal's argument was that "'tis impossible to have Rules laid down by any *External* Revelation for every particular Case; and therefore, there must be some standing Rule, discoverable by the *Light of Nature*, to direct us in all such Cases'.[56] This was the ultimate justification for God's apparent lack of interference in the course of nature, precisely the position that Clarke had identified with deism: 'Inconstancy, as it argues a Defect either of Wisdom or Power, can't belong to a Being infinitely wise and powerful: What unerring Wisdom has once instituted can have no Defects'.[57] God does not need to change anything in what He instituted, because, assuming that He is perfectly wise, His creation should have no defects in need of correction. Tindal's conclusion, arguably the most explicit one among the deists, was that 'God does not act arbitrarily, or interpose unnecessarily', and thus He does not command 'for commanding-sake'.[58] Therefore, not only should there be no need for revelation, but arguing that there is such a need suggests that there is a defect in God's work, namely, the law of nature. It is those who argued for the need of revelation, and not the deists, who were inconsistent with true Christianity.

For Tindal, as for Clifford, Warren, Blount, Toland, and Collins, revelation was redundant at best or more likely misleading. His main target was priestcraft and the later erroneous additions inserted to Christianity by interested parties. He argued that the deist merely believes that reason was given by 'the common Parent of Mankind' to 'all his Children, even those of the lowest Capacities, and at all Times'.[59] Since reason is common to everyone, no one can claim to have exclusive knowledge in matters of religion, and everyone is equally capable of measuring the truth of any religious principle. By using their reason to reflect critically upon any doctrine, the '*Christian Deists*', as opposed to the rest of the Christians, 'are sure not to run into any Errors of Moment; notwithstanding the confess'd Obscurity of the Scripture; and those many Mistakes that have crept into the Text, whether by Accident, or Design'.[60] In response to Clarke, Tindal argued that if there is any difference between the reason of things and external revelation, the former must take priority:

> If Christianity, as well as *Deism*, consists in being govern'd by the original Obligation of the moral Fitness of Things, in Conformity to the Nature, and in Imitation of the perfect Will of God, then they both must be the same; but if Christianity consists in being govern'd by any other Rule, or requires any other Things, has not the Dr. himself giv'n the Advantage to *Deism*?[61]

Not only must the rule of reason take priority over that of revelation, but it must be the only rule, since 'there can't be Two Independent Rules for the Government of human Actions'.[62] The idea of one rule, namely, that of reason rather than revelation, was parallel to Tindal's idea in the *Rights* of one political power, magisterial and not ecclesiastical. This time, too, it had a familiar Hobbesian ring. Tindal argued against those 'who, on Pretence of magnifying Tradition, endeavour to weaken the Force of Reason; (tho' to be sure they always except their own;) and thereby foolishly sap the Foundation, to support the Superstructure'.[63] But, he added, 'as long as Reason is against Men, they will be against Reason. We must not, therefore, be surpris'd, to see some endeavour to reason Men out of their Reason; tho' the very Attempt to destroy Reason by Reason, is a Demonstration Men have nothing but Reason to trust to'.[64] As several anticlerical writers had done before him, Tindal used this Hobbesian phrase in 1730 to argue against priestcraft which threatened to suppress human reason: 'not despairing, but that the Time may come again, when the Laity shall stifle every Thought rising in their Minds, tho' with ever so much Appearance of Truth, as a Suggestion of Satan, if it clashes with the real, or pretended Opinions of their Priests'.[65]

To sum up, reason is weakened in the name of tradition or revelation, whereas in fact, it is interests and manipulations that make people act unreasonably. People, and priests in particular, tend to think that their own opinions are true simply because they are their own and they serve their own good. If they manage to convince the laity of this, then true religion is in real danger. This danger can be avoided, however, once priestcraft is uncovered and people follow natural reason even to examine the truth of revelation.

Hence, Tindal defended the existence of God, but in attempting to defend a wholly natural and rational religion, he effectively became a freethinker, an identity which he was now happy to embrace:

> I shall not be surpris'd, if for so laudable an Attempt, as reconciling Reason and Revelation, which have been so long set at Variance, I shou'd be censur'd as a *Free-Thinker*; a Title, that, however invidious it may seem, I am far from being asham'd of; since One may as well suppose, a Man can reason without thinking at all, as reason well without thinking freely.[66]

Here, then, a Hobbesian premise was employed in support of freethinking. Both Hobbes and Tindal acknowledged the vulnerability of reason but also its power: human rationality was threatened, and precisely because of that, the need to use it was more urgent than ever. They relied on human reason to combat social chaos, largely caused by the religious establishment challenging the political authority by using claims to a special knowledge of revelation, and they saw natural reason as an answer to the deliberate obscurity of the tradition and the scripture. In one of the most revealing passages of *Leviathan*, Hobbes argued that 'we are not to renounce our Senses, and Experience; nor … our naturall Reason. For they are the talents which he hath put into our hands to negotiate, till the coming again of our blessed Saviour; and therefore not to be folded up in the Napkin of an Implicite Faith, but employed in the purchase of Justice, Peace, and true Religion'.[67] Tindal named precisely the same tools that are required for us to conduct our lives and know our duties: 'our Senses, our Reason, the Experience of Others as well as our own, can't fail to give us sufficient Information'.[68]

This connection was also made by Skelton. In one of the dialogues of *Deism Revealed*, Dechaine the deist and Shepherd the Christian discuss some recent notions of reason, agreeing that the concept of reasoning received growing attention from philosophers at the time. Shepherd reviews and refutes several recent definitions of reason. The first is from chapter 5 of *Leviathan*, wherein Hobbes 'absurdly gives a most whimsical definition of the mere act, drawn from the etymology of the word. He says, *It is reckoning (that is, adding and subtracting) of the consequences of general names agreed upon for the marking and signifying* [of] *our thoughts*'; 'That is', replies Dechaine, 'indeed, a most wild definition'.[69] Shepherd then goes on to Tindal, who 'says, *When we attribute any operation to reason, as distinguishing between truth and falsehood, &c. we mean by it the rational faculties*; and by the *rational faculties* he means, the natural ability to apprehend, judge, and infer'.[70] But this definition still does not satisfy Shepherd, who thinks that it is absurd to include apprehension within reason because 'apprehension is that distinct faculty, by which we previously receive the ideas afterwards to be reasoned on'.[71] For Shepherd, none of the philosophical definitions surveyed captures the essence of reasoning. Not only do they all treat it as a mere act, but they are not even precise as to the particular character of this act in relation to the preceding and subsequent acts in the process. Furthermore, these definitions are similar in that they lack an element that is crucial for Shepherd: they ignore the operation of the human soul, and by concentrating only on the procedural manner of deduction, such accounts are 'in the words of our divines, extremely prejudicial to revealed religion'.[72]

Even when someone like Tindal disagreed with substantial parts of Hobbes's political theory, he nevertheless recognised him as a most resourceful ally in the urgent campaign to undermine the power of priests. Tindal thought that churchmen who criticised Hobbes for the harsh way in which he described human nature, while at the same time sending men to fight in the name of religion, were mere hypocrites. Hobbes was attacked regularly by Anglicans for stripping man of his sociability and putting him in a state of war rather than in a state of mutual love. But, Tindal maintained, it was the religious establishment that twisted God's character and corrupted human nature, morality, and sociability:

> If Man, as our Divines maintain against *Hobbs*, is a social Creature, who naturally loves his own Species, and is full of Pity, Tenderness, and Benevolence; and if Reason, which is the proper Nature of Man, can never lead Men to any Thing but universal Love and Kindness ... how comes it to pass, that what is taught for Religion in so many Places of *Christendom*, has transform'd this mild and gentle Creature into fierce and cruel; and made him act with Rage and Fury against those who never did, or intended him the least Harm?[73]

In some respects, then, Tindal carried on the legacy of Hobbes's anticlericalism and continued to fight the battles that Hobbes could no longer fight. His book received much attention, with more than thirty replies from all sides of the clerical spectrum.[74] The threat, therefore, came to life: a sect of deists and freethinkers, that perhaps originated in the minds of the worried Anglicans as much as it did in reality, now had a dominant philosophical and public voice. This development naturally produced another surge of criticism, which culminated in a number of notable works that 'brought popular Christian apologetic to its highest point of sophistication and force'.[75] Among these were William Law's *The Case of Reason, or Natural Religion, Fairly and Fully Stated* (1731) and Joseph Butler's *The Analogy of Religion, Natural and Revealed, to the Constitution and Course of Nature* (1736). These writers called into question the perfection and clarity that the deists attributed to reason and to nature respectively, thereby reasserting the need of faith and revealed religion. In addition, the theologian Daniel Waterland criticised Tindal in his *Scripture Vindicated* (1730–1732), where he argued

that some events documented in the scripture, such as the fall, were historical facts, and again in *Christianity Vindicated Against Infidelity* (1732).[76]
In the latter, Waterland stated that '*Deism* may perhaps have become fiercer
or bolder than formerly'; he wondered 'whether these licentious Principles
were the proper Produce of our own Soil, or may not be rather said to have
been transplanted hither from Abroad', and then determined: 'Mr. *Hobbes*
has been reputed the first or principal Man that introduced them here, or
however that openly and glaringly espoused them'.[77] Waterland hypothe-
sised that deism spread in Europe first and that Hobbes absorbed this sort of
ideas in his visits to Italy and France. Hobbes, then, was cast as the importer
of deism to England and as one of the later deists' 'chief Instructors'. The
irony was, Waterland added, that deists such as Tindal followed their
instructors so blindly that they were, in fact, the true bigots: 'While they
are afraid of being *guided* by Priests, they consent to be *governed* by Anti-
priests'.[78] Precisely the same point was made by William Law, who attacked
what he called the freethinkers' '*bigotry to ... philosophy*':

> For it may as well be affirmed, that a man departs from the use of his reason,
> because he depends upon *ideas*, *arguments*, and *syllogisms*; as that he departs
> from the use of his reason, because he proceeds upon *prophecies*, *miracles*,
> and *revelations*. And if he uses his reason weakly ... he no more renounces
> his reason, or goes over to another direction, than *Hobbes*, *Spinosa*, *Bayle*,
> *Collins*, or *Toland*, renounce their reason, when they take their own *fancies* to
> be demonstrations.[79]

In 1735, an anonymous fellow of All Souls described the wide range of
unacceptable behaviour practised by the late doctor Tindal in *The Religious,
Rational, and Moral Conduct of Matthew Tindal*. The criticism voiced in
this work moves quite hastily between personal, social, and professional
aspects. One passage sums up its general spirit:

> In short, the Seeds of Infidelity, which Mr. *Hobbs*'s Disappointments had
> caused him to sow, were now growing up into a plentiful Crop; and his
> Doctrines being become the Fashion among too many of the Nobility and
> Gentry, who were desirous to be set free from the Restraints and Fetters of
> Religion, as they esteemed them, the Doctor resolved to be *Alamode*, and to
> cultivate and improve what Mr. *Hobbs* and his Disciples had begun. And there-
> fore he turned downright *Atheist*; tho' he was desirous, that the Generality of
> Mankind should imagine he had stopt short at *Deism*; but he was too reserved
> and cunning to profess himself a *Deist* in an explicit and open manner.[80]

Deism, this writer thought, was merely a cover for downright atheism,
which amounted to immoral behaviour and false views that gained dangerous momentum. This account found the roots for Tindal's so-called deism
in one main character: Mr. Hobbes. Using Hobbes, or deism, to stain a

person's reputation was not an original trick. Nor was it a groundless accusation. It is probable that Tindal realised the connection to Hobbes himself, but he was surely cautious in admitting it.

Radicati, a Christian freethinker

Alberto Radicati di Passerano (1698–1737), who self-identified openly as a Christian freethinker, was in some ways a product of the age of free-thinking studied in Chapter 3.[81] Radicati was an Italian nobleman who was in exile in London between 1728 and 1734. A materialist and a panthe-ist, a biblical interpreter and an enthusiastic advocate of egalitarianism, he 'absorbed the more violent and polemical elements from English deism'.[82] Radicati believed that the religion of nature and the moral precepts of Jesus are the remedies for superstition, and that the prince should oversee the actions of the power-hungry clergy. He studied the works of Machiavelli, Hobbes, Spinoza, and Simon, as well as Blount, Toland, Tindal, and Collins, among others. Radicati published several works in London in the 1730s, some with the same publisher of the *Independent Whig*. His *Philosophical Dissertation upon Death* (1732), wherein he justified suicide, was especially notorious and got him arrested for a short while. In the words of bishop George Berkeley, Radicati was a 'Minute Philosopher', much like Tindal.[83]

Radicati's *Twelve Discourses Concerning Religion and Government*, published in London in 1734, were dedicated to the 'Lovers of Truth and Liberty'. There he argued that the doctrine of Jesus consists of only four principles: poverty, humility, forgiveness, and charity.[84] Radicati told the Parable of the Good Samaritan to show that Jesus commended moral behaviour first and foremost: in the parable, it is the Samaritan who offers help to an injured man while the Jewish priests ignore him. The lesson of this story, Radicati argued, was that 'Christ was fully satisfied, that such as are commonly called Atheists or Deists, whose minds are not spoilt nor perverted by Superstition, are more charitable and infinitely better men than they, whose minds are corrupted by the Vices and Cruelties, which are the natural effects of Superstition'.[85] Even infidels, it was implied, were better than most priests.

Radicati held a clear notion of deism:

> I say Deists, or Atheists; for that name is wrongly given to such as deny Tradition; as if there was no way of coming at the knowledge of a Deity, without believing the most absurd and abominable Fictions … But to say that Deists are Atheists is false; for they that are so called by the Vulgar, and by those whose interest it is to decry them, admit a first cause under the names of God, Nature, Eternal Being, Matter, universal Motion or Soul.[86]

Deists were those who acknowledged God as the first cause but accounted for God in natural or material, rather than superstitious, ways. For Radicati, deism was a viable and justified position and the product of a very long tradition:

> Such were Democritus, Epicurus, Diagoras, Lucian, Socrates Anaxagoras, Seneca, Hobbes, Blount, Spinosa, Vanini, St. Evremond, Bayle, Collins, and in general, all that go under the name of Speculative Atheists; and none but fools or madmen can ever deny it. So that the word Atheist must signify Deist, or nothing. There being no such thing as an Atheist in the world, as the Ignorant imagine, and the crafty Priests would have believed, when they brand with this odious name such as detect their impostures, with design to expose them to the rage and fury of an incensed populace.[87]

The prestigious lineage that Radicati composed here, which included ancient as well as modern figures, from England as well as from Continental Europe, was a group of people that had been long accused of atheism but were, in fact, deists; if anything, they were simply people who believed in a deity and at the same time did not hesitate to expose the machinations of the clergy. Elsewhere, Radicati paid closer attention to the English side of the story.

Similar to the previous work, *A Succinct History of Priesthood*, published in London in 1737, was dedicated to 'the Ever-illustrious, and most Celebrated Sect of FREE THINKERS'. There Radicati took the same line as the *Independent Whig*, arguing that during Anne's reign the clergy were 'incessantly roaring out every where, that the Church was in Danger'; but the political aspirations of the clergy did not materialise fully, and had that been the case, they would have only worsened their situation by prompting another reformation. Radicati concluded:

> [G]ive me leave, my Brethren *Free-Thinkers*, who do in Effect think freely, to make a few Remarks on what I have been advancing, and also upon Religion: For there are People in the World who imagine, that Religion disquiets you horribly, since you are always railing at it so cordially. Formerly indeed it was a very dangerous Matter to attack it so abruptly as you often do: *Hobbes* and *Spinosa* were obliged, as you know, to write with much Caution, in Terms so obscure, that very many People have never been able to comprehend what Designs those Authors could have in composing the *Leviathan*, and *Tractatus Theologico-Politicus*: And you are not ignorant what unhappy Destiny fell to the Share of Servetus and Vanini, together with their Writings.[88]

Both Hobbes and Spinoza, according to Radicati, were freethinkers whose attack on religion was ground-breaking but still cautious, even esoteric. A statement to that effect was made also by Radicati's opponent, Berkeley, who devoted his *Alciphron* (1732) to an attack on the freethinkers: '*Hobbes* allowed a corporeal God; and *Spinosa* held the Universe to be God. And yet no body doubts they were staunch Free-thinkers'.[89] The followers of Hobbes and Spinoza, however, were more liberated in developing what their teachers had started:

> [I]t is owing wholly to the enterprising *Genii* of this Age, that we have seen Religion besieged openly from every Quarter; Its Mysteries are turned into Ridicule by the ingenious Mr. *Toland*: Its Clergy are become contempt-ible to many since they have read that smart Piece, The *Independent Whig*; which having effectually cleared the Way, and given Assault to religious Out-works, its very Foundations were afterwards violently shaken by the cele-brated Performance of Mr. *Collin*[s]'s [*Grounds and Reasons of the Christian Religion*].[90]

These were for Radicati the latest appearances of English deism and free-thinking, which ridiculed mysteries, showed the real face of the clergy, and paved the way for a total reconstruction of religion. Toland, Collins, Trenchard, and Gordon, on this view, were historic innovators if not revo-lutionaries, and what is more, they were among the few who truly under-stood what their predecessors, Hobbes and Spinoza, were trying to do. Nevertheless, even for Radicati, revealed religion was to be rejected totally but not religion as such; the best model, he concluded, was that of a pure and moral religion controlled by the civil magistrate, as he saw executed successfully in the Dutch Republic.[91]

Morgan's anti-churchism

As with Radicati's self-proclaimed Christian freethinking, Thomas Morgan (1671/2–1743) self-identified as a Christian deist. Morgan, who is best known for his three-volume *The Moral Philosopher* (1737–1740), drew considerable attention from his contemporaries, including the prominent critics of deism, but he remains an overwhelmingly neglected figure in intel-lectual history.[92] There are some clear continuities between his work and the works of writers such as Blount, Toland, and Collins, while in some other respects his ideas were distinctly innovative. His Christian deism com-prised, for example, a radically hostile reading of Moses' character which went beyond most of his contemporaries alongside a more traditional belief in Jesus' role in aiding human reason, a topic which set him apart from other deists such as Chubb. Moreover, as Peter Harrison writes, '[w]hile commonly regarded as just another deist Morgan's originality lay in his application of the tools of historical criticism to scripture and to the history of religions'.[93] For these reasons, Morgan exhibits a particularly interesting case of a conscious and complex sort of deism, one which also engaged with Hobbes, whose work Morgan evidently knew well.

Morgan was not always a deist. He ordained a Presbyterian minister in 1716, a role in which he served at a Marlborough congregation until he was dismissed in the early 1720s—apparently between 1720 and 1724—for his heretical views, which at that point were limited to a mild preference of Arianism over Trinitarianism and an opposition to the obligation of the ministry to subscribe to the doctrine of the Trinity.[94] At that time, he described himself as a 'Protestant Dissenter' in an exchange of pamphlets with some rival Presbyterian ministers, including William Tong and Benjamin Robinson, following their *The Doctrine of the Blessed Trinity Stated & Defended* (1719). Morgan's initial letter to the ministers was entitled *The Nature and Consequences of Enthusiasm Consider'd* (1719), and it was included together with its later defences in *A Collection of Tracts, Relating to the Right of Private Judgment, the Sufficiency of Scripture, and the Terms of Church-Communion; upon Christian Principles*, published in 1726.

The ministers who defended the Trinity and the subscription held that the Trinity was clearly derived from the scripture, as the reformed church had confirmed, and that denying this was entirely heterodox. Otherwise, 'Would not Advantage be given to Deists and Antiscripturists, not to say Atheists, to scoff at the Bible', if it turned out that so many Christians, who looked for answers in the scripture, had been wrong all along?[95]

> What Use, may they say, can such a Book be of, or what Likelihood that it is from God? Could he not speak plainly of himself, where 'tis pretended he designed to do so? ... Would not that Book, instead of leading to Life and Salvation, be the most insnaring and dangerous one that can be?[96]

The war on the Trinity, then, was the war on the truth of scripture and Christianity as a whole—a war that, if lost, would lead to the victory of the atheists and deists who had been longing to prove that the scripture did not, in fact, support orthodox Christianity.

Morgan, on the other hand, had not even considered himself a deist at that point, and he, too, believed that the scripture was sufficient to determine the truth. The problem, though, was not with the scripture but the ministers' judgment of the scripture which they presented as certain. Morgan accused the ministers of enthusiasm and tritheism: either they worshipped three different Gods, or they worshipped one God, namely 'the one supreme Being, of absolute, Infinite Perfection, who is the first Cause all Things', in which case their worship shared 'the same Object with all other Christians, and the same Object precisely with even a *Socinian* or *Deist*'.[97] This assertion was met with a fierce response in *The Necessity of Contending for*

Revealed Religion (1720), written by the Independent minister Thomas Bradbury who was on the side of the subscribers. Bradbury denounced Morgan's insinuation about the ministers' tritheism as shameful and alleged that Morgan had written against the ministers' subscribing to the notion of one God. He then attacked Morgan sarcastically: 'so hard it is to please a Man, who is apt to forget himself with the Pen in his hand!'[98] Morgan replied to Bradbury in a postscript to the second edition of *The Nature and Consequences of Enthusiasm Consider'd* (1720), wherein he accused Bradbury of defamation. Bradbury's allegation was entirely false: 'He might with equal Truth and Justice have declared, that the only Thing I wrote against was, their having protested against the Opinions of *Machiavel*, *Hobbes*, or *Spinoza*'.[99] Morgan added his own sarcastic remark: 'but there is no guarding against a Man, who always writes Controversy in a Ferment'.[100] This was the first mention of Hobbes in Morgan's works, even though this statement does not tell us much about his attitude to the philosopher who was detested by his own opponents. It is noteworthy that here we also find one of Morgan's first mentions of deism: it was Bradbury, he stated, who had 'subverted the Christian Revelation, and given it up into the Hands of Deists and Infidels'.[101] Thus, the two opponents, both still ministers at the time, conducted a passionate war of words and accused one another of similar crimes. Not only did Morgan still admit revelation but he also identified deism with infidelity, which he defined as the conviction that 'the Christian Doctrines are in themselves, and laying aside the Testimony of Scripture, irrational, absurd, and ridiculous'.[102] At the same time, by taking the side of the non-subscribers firmly against prominent ministers and especially against their claim for infallibility, he started moving away from the orthodoxy, a process that would eventually lead to his self-professed Christian deism in the 1730s.

Morgan elaborated in a letter to the writer and physician Sir Richard Blackmore, who had previously attacked the Arians together with the atheists and deists.[103] Morgan argued that subscription would not reveal the sincerity of one's belief and that everyone had an equal right to use private judgment with regard to the scripture, not just the defenders of the Trinity. He clarified that 'the Scripture has a clear determinate Sense enough, with respect to the *general Principles and Doctrines*, to which the Revelation is confin'd; and which is sufficient to answer all the Ends and Purposes of *true Religion*'.[104] Beyond that, however, there would always be differences of interpretation and no way to determine with certainty which interpretation is true. Furthermore, enforcing tests of orthodoxy and thereby encouraging blind obedience in some given churches would only cause confusion and chaos: 'It must put the Church into as bad a Circumstance, as *Hobbes*'s State of Nature; and no two Churches upon Earth could maintain Christian

Communion with each other; and even the particular Members of every individual Church must necessarily be divided and torn from one another, from the Catholick Church, and from Christ himself, as often as they should prepare *new Tests*'.[105] In a Hobbesian manner, therefore, Morgan attempted to expose the political manoeuvres of the clergy—and their disastrous outcomes—that lay behind the theological controversies of his time.

For Morgan, individuals could choose to subscribe to Christian doctrines if they believed that they were derived from the scripture and if they used their own reason, but a demand made by other churchmen to subscribe was an illegitimate infringement of liberty. He called those who advocated subscription '*Ecclesiastical Imposters*' who pretended to have an authority they did not truly have and judge in matters that were merely speculative. He added that any obligation to subscribe would in any case need to be grounded in civil law by the civil magistrate, since the goal of the impostors was 'only to engross the Wealth and Preferments of the Church into their *own Hands*, by excluding all who will not list themselves into *their Party*; which being a wicked and *selfish Design*, ought certainly to be eluded by all *lawful Means*'.[106]

Elsewhere, Morgan declared similarly: 'No doubt but the *Clergy*, so far as they are *Civil Officers*, and expect their Pay from the *Crown*, must conform themselves, in Matters of *Religion*, to the *Civil Law*'.[107] There was, of course, a Hobbesian ring to this position. Commenting on this remark, one critic wrote: 'I have not *Leviathan* by me, so cannot direct you to the Chapter, but question not its being there, being a Doctrine *Hobbs* is so full of'.[108] In response, Morgan stated his view that the church could not have an independent authority from the king. Nevertheless, he protested, 'you here very unluckily refer me to *Hobbs*'s *Leviathan*, as a Book which you presume I must have by me; and you give me to understand, that if this be so … it must follow, that the Church is a Leviathan, established upon the Principles of *Hobbism*, which resolve all Religion into the Will of the Civil Magistrate'.[109] The Hobbesian (or rather Hobbist) implication, Morgan stated, was not suggested by himself but by his opponent. At any rate, the two debated Hobbes in considerable depth. Morgan's critic quoted another passage from *Behemoth* to support his case of Morgan's Hobbism and Morgan analysed it further. In the passage, Hobbes wrote that 'we neuer shall haue a lasting peace till … the Ministers know they haue no Authority, but what the Supream Ciuill Power giues them'.[110] Morgan replied sarcastically:

> The *Ministers* then, it seems, know that they have an Authority which is not derived from the Supreme Civil Power, tho' they swear the contrary. A fine Compliment, surely, upon *these Ministers*, for which they will doubtless

vote you their due Thanks; who, according to your Account of them, must
be a Pack of mercenary graceless Wretches, that, to secure the Benefits of a
Civil Establishment, take Oaths every Day, contrary to their Knowledge and
Consciences.[111]

According to Morgan, the idea that the church should be subordinated to
the civil law—and that it was, in fact, at the time—should have been obvious by that point. Priests who still did not believe in that order of things,
even though they were part of the established church, had to be hypocrites
and liars. Putting it this way helped him highlight his anticlerical conviction
but also to turn his opponent's criticism against him, a rhetorical tactic that
served Morgan successfully throughout his writings.[112] This was an interesting way to engage with Hobbes, more subtle than what Collins or Tindal
had done when they were accused of Hobbism for similar reasons. While
both sides attempted to show that it was the other who led to a Hobbesian
conclusion, Morgan at the very least did not disagree with the Hobbesian
idea that his critic attributed to him. After all, he, too, believed that the
problem would not be averted "till the Pretence of Independent Church-
Authority is dropt, and 'till *these Ministers* know that they are Subjects, and
not Rulers; the Servants, Delegates and Sub-Agents, and not the Lords and
Masters of the *Church*, or *Christian People*'.[113]

In the years following his dismissal from the congregation, Morgan
turned to the study of medicine, while continuing to pursue his theological
and philosophical interests. In the late 1720s, he held an extensive exchange
with Thomas Chubb, in which the latter represented the more typical deistic idea of the sufficiency of natural reason for salvation, whereas Morgan
upheld the defects of human nature and hence the necessary role of Christ
in restoring the human faculties that were lost after the fall. It is plausible that it was this exchange that encouraged Morgan to present his own
modified version of deism, namely, his Christian deism, in the subsequent
decade.[114] This is found in what became his most important and contested
work, *The Moral Philosopher* (1737). This work was designed as a dialogue
between Philalethes, who is a 'Christian Deist', and Theophanes, who is a
'Christian Jew'. Philalethes, representing Morgan's position, declared: 'I am
a profess'd Christian Deist. And, therefore, I must take Christianity … to be
a Revival of the Religion of Nature'.[115] He distinguished himself from those
who promoted another sort of religion, 'consisting in speculative Opinions,
doubtful Disputations, external Rituals, arbitrary Laws, and mere positive
Institutions', which he traced back to the Jews and the Old Testament.[116]
Much more explicitly now than before, Morgan asserted that the true kind
of Christianity was not 'such a mysterious, unintelligible Thing' and that
it did 'not so much depend upon Miracles and Prophecies, or on the Sense

and Construction of antient Authors, writ in Languages that we do not well understand' but rather 'on the most plain and necessary Truths, such as are founded in the eternal, immutable Reason and Fitness of Things; and which must, therefore, be always and every where the same'.[117] He reaffirmed his previous position on Jesus and reconciled it with deism: Christianity was the religion of morality and of inward worship of God, and it was Jesus who 'was sent from God to restore, revive, and republish this Religion after it had been lost in the general Superstition, Idolatry, and gross Ignorance of Mankind'.[118] Having established his belief, Philalethes concluded on Morgan's behalf: 'I am a Christian, and at the same Time a Deist, or, if you please, this is my Christian Deism'.[119] It is hard to exaggerate how striking it is that Morgan called himself a deist publicly, even if anonymously, not only because of his orthodox background but also because even the writers who were most associated with deism at the time, including those who actually defended deism against clerical opponents, were still extremely cautious to embrace and advertise this identity. This is also a major reason for the fact that today's scholarship deals with deism primarily as a term of abuse, and rightly so. Yet, Morgan's case demonstrates that the story is much more complex than it may appear and that substantial shifts occurred over time: deistic confessions, which had been made almost only in clandestine form in the late seventeenth century, as we saw in Chapter 1, could be found entirely openly in the mid-eighteenth century.

It is plausible that the *Moral Philosopher* was indebted to the thought of Toland, Collins, and Tindal, and it is highly likely that Hobbes had a considerable impact on Morgan's ideas. Even though Morgan did not cite Hobbes in this work, we have seen that he did refer to him in previous works and was familiar with his writings. On some important issues, such as miracles and the bible, Morgan certainly came close to Hobbes's views, and it is worth considering this connection in more depth.[120]

By the time Morgan wrote the *Moral Philosopher*, he had formulated a distinctly sceptical and critical position towards miracles. There were a number of explanations for this position, given by the character of Philalethes. First, if and when God spoke to a person by inspiration or revelation, only that person could know that with certainty.[121] Second, miracle working, Morgan held, had nothing to do with the truth of doctrines, since even false prophets and their like were reported to have worked miracles, and therefore miracles alone could not prove any doctrine.[122] In a Hobbesian manner, Morgan warned further that men were likely to be either deceiving or mistaken.[123] In this context, he made a distinction between two sorts of religion, namely, the religion of nature and positive religion, which he also called 'the political Religion, or the Religion of the Hierarchy'.[124] Whereas the former is based on the universal rules of truth and reason, the latter

was based on the different teachings of the clergy and thus on tradition
and authority. The problem, of course, was that the clergy, who acted like
jugglers, were motivated by their own interests but always pretended that
their particular teachings were divinely revealed.[125] Morgan's objection to
miracles was derived primarily from his suspicious attitude towards the
clergy—an attitude which he had demonstrated already in his opposition to
the issue of subscription—but he did not rule out completely the possibility
of miracles. Miracles such as those that Jesus and the apostles performed,
he maintained, were aimed to promote the common good by drawing
the attention of their listeners and bringing them 'to consider coolly and
soberly, the Nature and Tendency of the Doctrines they had to propose to
them; and not to take up implicitly with what the Priests and Rulers thought
or said of it'.[126] Jesus and the apostles were themselves teachers of truth and
reason. The issue was thus not only miracles but what could serve as a solid
enough basis for belief: Morgan here echoed Collins's dichotomy between
the scheme of liberty and the scheme of authority, clearly preferring the
former.[127]

There was another layer to Morgan's scepticism about miracles which
he developed in his subsequent works. In the second volume of the *Moral
Philosopher*, for example, he mentioned that many stories had been falsely
thought of as supernatural due to 'Imposture, Ignorance, or Credulity', adding that 'we know not the utmost Power of natural Agents, or how far even
the most common Causes may sometimes concur unobserved by us, which
may make a Thing look extraordinary when there is nothing uncommon in
it'.[128] According to Morgan, what was considered supernatural was most
likely unusual natural phenomena whose true causes remained unknown.
It was therefore human ignorance as well as arrogance, with the help of
self-interested deceivers, that produced false stories of miracles.[129] This may
have been the most Hobbesian point of Morgan's argument; indeed, we
have already seen how Blount and Trenchard, for example, used exactly
the same Hobbesian argument that phenomena such as eclipses could
seem miraculous so long as they were inexplicable.[130] Eventually, Morgan
went even further and reached a conclusion closer to Tindal's: 'It is highly
improbable, and cannot be admitted, that God should work Miracles, or
interpose by an immediate divine Power, out of the Way of natural Agency
and common Providence, but to answer some great End of vast Importance
to Mankind'.[131]

An additional highly controversial point was made in the second volume
of the *Moral Philosopher*. Referring to the Pentateuch, Morgan asserted
that the supposition 'that this Account was written by *Moses* himself, and
was as firmly believed then as it was in the After-Ages' was 'a Thing which
cannot be proved'.[132] This, as we have seen, was one of the most radical

arguments made explicitly by Hobbes, Spinoza, and Blount, among others, although Morgan did not acknowledge any sources here. Yet, for Morgan, unlike his predecessors, this argument was part of a much more profound attack against Moses, whom Morgan portrayed as a sinister politician who led his people to commit cruel and violent acts, for example against the Canaanites.[133] He explained that 'most or all the biblical Books have received great Alterations and Additions from Time to Time, by Revisers or Editors, who have lived at a great Distance from one another'.[134] Some books, for instance, were written only during or after the Babylonian captivity, both Morgan and Hobbes suggested. Morgan also questioned the authorship of the Books of Samuel by Samuel himself since they cover events that occurred after his death, and added: 'it might as well be said, that the Books of *Kings* and *Judges* were wrote by those Kings and Judges themselves … But it is plain, that most of those historical Books, which give an Account of the Lives, Actions, or Works, of such or such Persons, speak of them in the third Person, as any other Historian would'.[135] Not only was this the same claim that Hobbes made famously but also the exact same reasoning that led Hobbes to question Moses' authorship of the Pentateuch and consequently to deny that 'these titles, The Book of *Ioshua*, the Book of *Iudges*, the Book of *Ruth*, and the Books of the *Kings*, are arguments sufficient to prove, that they were written by *Ioshua*, by the *Iudges*, by *Ruth*, and by the *Kings*. For in titles of Books, the subject is marked, as often as the writer'.[136] Interestingly, whereas Hobbes and Spinoza promoted the idea that Ezra the Scribe composed at least parts of the bible, Morgan put forward the possibility that it was Samuel who wrote the history of Israel until his time.[137] In any case, by 1739, the self-professed Christian deist had adopted a careful historical approach to the study of the scripture, which could be indebted partly to Hobbes, and which was certainly in line with the previous works of Blount, Toland, and Collins.

Consequently, numerous critics who were enraged by the *Moral Philosopher* placed Morgan in the same infamous tradition. One review of Morgan's work from 1737 stated that 'it is not improbable that he has gathered all the Principles of his Work, from *Hobbes, Spinoza, Toland, Tindal*, and other such worthies', and in 1739, another critic mocked 'the inimitable Writings of Mr. *Hobbes, Blunt, Toland, Tindal, Collins, Gordon*, and that Prince of Paralogicians, the *Moral Philosopher*'.[138] Also in 1739, John Chapman, the theologian and classical scholar who had written against Collins and Tindal before, attacked Morgan in *Eusebius: Or the True Christian's Defense*. This work, which is considered Chapman's most important and well-received, was commissioned by John Potter, Archbishop of Canterbury, to whom Chapman was chaplain at the time.[139] Chapman attacked Morgan's Christian deism for having destroyed the basis of Christianity by denying the evidence of its divine nature and accepting only natural religion, just as Tindal had done before him.[140] In response to Morgan's definition of Christianity as a revival of the religion of nature, Chapman suggested to define Morgan's view as 'a *Revival* of the *Toland* or *Tindal System*'.[141] According to Chapman, Morgan portrayed the bible as a 'Book so *interpolated* in one place, and *curtail'd* in another, so *difficult*, and *obscure*, and even *unintelligible* in all but *Moral Truths*, and the Cause of so many *Disputes*, and *Divisions* among *Christians*, that according to you we have no other way to settle an infallible *Faith*, but by laying its *Authority* wholly aside, and framing a *Christianity* without it'.[142] On that issue, Chapman's argument against the deists was certainly not innovative.

Regarding the claim that Christians had been long in disagreement even about essential doctrines, especially of revelation, which proved their unintelligibility, Chapman noted that disagreements never revolved around the general truth of doctrines but only around their details, adding: 'it is a lamentable Case, and has often been the Subject of the like tragical Complaints among our good *Christian Deists*, such as *Collins*, *Tindal*, &c.'.[143] As with many other clerical critics of deism, Chapman claimed that in any case there was no justification to distinguish between revealed and natural religion: if human disputes and mistakes could discredit the former, they would equally discredit the latter as well. Indeed, there had been disagreements even about God's existence but that surely was not a sufficient reason to reject this idea altogether: 'For what true *Philosopher* would immediately see no Evidence in *Nature* for a Supreme intelligent Being, because a *Bruno* or *Spinoza* denied it? ... Or no Distinctions of *Moral Good* and *Evil* from a *Cumberland* of *Pufendorf*, because a *Hobbes* or *Protagoras* could discern none?'[144] This was a strong point which touched on an inherent weakness in the argument of writers such as Tindal and Morgan who relied on the universality and infallibility of human reason but were never quite able to show why reason would only lead specifically to the conclusions that were desirable for them. Chapman's choice of Bruno, Spinoza, and Hobbes in this context was of course not coincidental. The implication was that if Morgan insisted on his position—which he clearly did—then he had to admit that his own reasoning would lead to the denial of any controversial notion, including God, and hence to the ultimate heretical, Hobbist view.

One of Morgan's most robust and high-profile critics was William Warburton, future bishop of Gloucester. Warburton had long been an adversary of atheism and deism and thus, not surprisingly, also of Hobbes. As early as 1727, he attacked Hobbes together with François de la Rochefoucauld, describing him as the leader of 'a Sect of Anti Moralists' whose 'senseless and shocking' view of human nature '*painted* it base, cowardly, envious, and *a Lover of its self*' and was therefore opposed to religion.[145] He continued to attack the theory of 'the jolly Philosopher of *Malmesbury*' whose view of human nature made him an advocate of public slavery instead of public liberty and thus 'Antiquity was to be all *proscribed* for the Sake of his *Leviathan*'.[146] In 1736, Warburton refuted the view of 'the Enemies of our holy Faith', which he found especially in Tindal's *Rights of the Christian Church Asserted* and in the *Independent Whig*, namely, 'that the Christian, and all other Churches, in their natural State without coactive Power, are Creatures of the Civil Magistrate'.[147] According to Warburton, these authors reproduced Hobbes's argument. He aimed to denounce them alongside the other great threat to civil peace, namely, the high church view that the church was entirely independent from the state. Accordingly, Warburton claimed that the ideas of the 'Jacobite, and Free-Thinking System Framers' were 'unavoidably drawn, by the Alacrity of their own Heaviness, in to the very Centers of *Malmsbury* and *Rome*, from whence indeed they derived their Birth, but are, I know not why, ungraciously ashamed of their Pedigree'.[148] Warburton sought to offer a middle way between these two extremes by advocating a mutually beneficial alliance between the state and the church. Warburton granted the church an active role in the leadership of civil religion, for example, by receiving representation in Parliament.[149] Yet his reservations about sectarianism and his resulting vision of a state protected established church did create an impression that his position, too, could lead to Erastianism. Indeed, not only did he emphasise the supremacy of the civil magistrate, which meant that the church's actions depended on the magistrate's approval, but he also argued in an almost Hobbesian manner that 'Protection is a kind of Guardianship; and Guardianship implies Obedience and Subjection in the Ward, towards him who is invested with that Character'.[150]

Warburton's case against the deists and freethinkers was developed in *The Divine Legation of Moses Demonstrated, on the Principles of a Religious Deist*, which also provided the context for his confrontation with Morgan. An impressively ambitious work, it helped 'make him a central figure in English life and one whose contribution to its intellectual culture was unavoidable'.[151] Warburton dedicated the first volume (1738) to the freethinkers, explaining, however sarcastically, that they became the patrons of the time: 'For nothing, I believe, strikes the serious Observer with more Surprize, in this Age of Novelties, than that strange Propensity to Infidelity', considering that 'the Advocates of Deism are received with all the Applauses due to the Inventers of the Arts of Life, or the Deliverers of oppressed and injured Nations'.[152] He denounced their complaints about ecclesiastical tyranny and especially about restraints on liberty, which he perceived as outdated and hypocritical, as well as the choice of ridicule and mirth as their favourite method, which he associated primarily with Shaftesbury. He attacked their description of the clergy as 'debauched, avaricious, proud, vindictive, ambitious, deceitful, irreligious, and incorrigible', pointing to the works of Tindal and Collins and to the *Independent Whig*.[153] Collins, Warburton added, even betrayed his close friend Locke after the death of the latter, because Locke proved too devout.[154] This 'Abuse of the Clergy', Warburton added, 'is not only an insult on Religion ... but likewise on Civil Society. For while there is such a Thing as a Church *established by Law*, the *Ministry* of it must needs bear a *sacred* Character, that is, a public one; even on your own Principles'.[155] Indeed, some enlightened Anglican writers like Warburton based their arguments on the freethinkers' premises.[156] To prove that, Warburton quoted none other than Hobbes, who stated in *Leviathan* that the 'Publique Ministers', who are appointed by the sovereign, 'have authority to teach, or to enable others to teach the people their duty to the Soveraign Power, and instruct them in the knowledge of what is just, and unjust, thereby to render them more apt to live in godlinesse, and in peace amongst themselves'.[157] As he demonstrated in the *Alliance*, Warburton did have something in common with this group of writers, namely, the conviction that a condition of harmony between the state and the church was conducive to civil order, and more broadly, that religion could be argued for in terms of social utility. At the same time, he was at pains to distinguish himself from these notorious freethinkers whose assault on religion he could not tolerate and whose oracle, he believed, was 'The Atheist, *Hobbes*'.[158] Similarly, the second volume of the *Divine Legation* (1741) left very little room for doubt about just how much Warburton loathed them all: 'The *Philosopher of Malmsbury* was the Terror of the last Age, as *Tindal* and *Collins* are of this'.[159]

The novel argument of the *Divine Legation* was that Moses did not need to use the promise of future rewards and punishments when he ruled the Jewish people. Warburton argued that this disproved the deistic portrayal of Moses as a human, pagan-like legislator who ruled the Jewish republic merely as a civil society utilising notions that were agreeable to the prejudiced human mind. Although the deists thought that Moses inherited his political knowledge from the Egyptians, Warburton argued, the Egyptians had held the doctrine of future rewards at that time and so it would have been available for Moses to use had he been the kind of legislator that the deists believed he was, but he did not. The conclusion, then, was that Moses was not a fraudulent impostor but was in fact chosen by God and that he knew that God's continual extraordinary providence was true and sufficient for the government of his people.[160]

The *Divine Legation* received many responses from a wide range of critics. Morgan's response was especially intriguing because he was clearly one of the deists who were targeted by Warburton and one of the very few who were still alive and able to answer.[161] Morgan's *A Brief Examination of … Warburton's Divine Legation of Moses* (1742) was also his final work. It can be seen as a summary of the by now familiar case against priestcraft, by which he meant the priestly cheatings and impositions which took advantage of human weakness in order to earn an exclusively sacred reputation.[162] Morgan offered his own history of priestcraft, according to which the civil rulers were also the priests until the practice of setting an interdependent priestly 'mystical Order' emerged in Egypt in the days of Joseph, which gave rise to the bond between superstition and enslavement.[163] Defending the precise view that Warburton attributed to the deists, Morgan argued that by the time Moses came to power, the Jewish people had been completely '*Egyptianized*' and so Moses adjusted his law to that condition and made things even worse because the unrestrained 'Priesthood was more absolute and arbitrary'.[164] Eventually, this history of corruption reached early Christianity which 'was nothing else but Judaism allegorized'.[165] In Hobbesian words, Morgan concluded that when new Pagan influences were brought into it by the Romans and when the early church established its power by violent persecutions of so-called heretics, 'the Man of Sin was thoroughly revealed, the Kingdom of Darkness establish'd, the Light of Truth eclipsed and almost extinguished, and the Devil had nothing to do but to set Priests and People one against another, and give them the Honour of Martyrdom by their own Hands'.[166]

Thus, Morgan was among the last writers who undertook to present the view of the infamous deists. By doing so, he demonstrated the considerable social and cultural change that critical and anticlerical ideas and identities had gone through only within a few decades. What once was solely a pejorative term of abuse seems to have completed a long process of reappropriation when Morgan answered to Warburton, albeit anonymously and sarcastically, in the following way: 'WE the Deists and Free-thinkers of *Great-Britain*, beg leave to approach your learned Person, and, with the profoundest Humility, to return you our most grateful Acknowledgments, and sincerest Thanks … for the signal Honour, and unmerited Favour, of addressing [the *Divine Legation*] to us'.[167] On behalf of the deists, Morgan complimented Warburton's central argument that Moses did not use the notion of future rewards and punishments: 'that *Moses* taught nothing of this Doctrine … we not only grant, but most sincerely thank you, for the Pains you have taken to prove it for us'.[168] Furthermore, he insisted that Warburton's targeting of the deists was merely polemical—that he did so simply to win the support of his brethren and out of spite—while in fact he might have been closer to the deistic view than he had realised. What Warburton could attempt but failed to do to refute the deists, argued

Morgan, was to prove the supernatural immediate providence of God that supposedly demonstrated the divinity of the Mosaic system.[169]

The true mission of the deists, Morgan clarified, was to save 'the true universal Religion of God and Nature': 'Virtue, or moral Rectitude ... and a Veneration for the glorious Perfections of the Deity ... is the Religion of a Deist', and achieving that required exposing 'the sacerdotal Superstition or false Religion', indeed the kingdom of darkness.[170] Such false religion, Morgan summarised sharply, was 'nothing but *Churchism*' according to which 'if the Priesthood cannot thrive and fatten in this World, the People must be damn'd in the next'.[171] Morgan's work was therefore an ultimate display of mid-eighteenth-century anticlericalism, or perhaps antichurchism, to borrow his own term. Morgan might be a forgotten deist, as he has been called recently, but by the early 1740s he had become the most devoted representative of self-identified deism in Britain. Of course, Warburton was not convinced and, for his part, continued in his efforts to fight infidelity. In another work from 1742 he reaffirmed that 'the Tribe of *Free-thinkers*', including '*Toland, Tindal, Collins ... Morgan, Tillard*, and their Fellows' were 'the mortal Foes both of Reason and Religion' who 'injured *Wit* as well as *Virtue*'.[172] Such was the animosity between them that when Morgan died the following year, Warburton did not miss the chance to express his relief, writing to a friend: 'I live in peace, now the redoubtable Dr. Morgan is dead'.[173]

The tradition that Warburton identified with Hobbes and the subsequent deists and freethinkers was about to enter a new phase with a new heretic who drew the fire of the divines, David Hume. Warburton had no doubts with whom Hume's ideas belonged or what future it deserved. Some years later, a work that he wrote with Richard Hurd, future bishop of Worcester, noted:

> Hence it is, that CHUBB, MORGAN, COLLINS, MANDEVILLE, and BOLINGBROKE are names, which nobody hears, without laughing. It is not for me, perhaps, to predict the fate of Mr. DAVID HUME. But if You, Sir, had taken upon You to read his destiny, the Public had, now, seen this Adorer of *Nature*, this *last* hope of his declining family, gathered *to the dull of ancient days*;
>
> Safe, where no critics, no divines molest,
>
> Where wretched TOLAND, TINDAL, TILLARD rest.[174]

It is striking that Warburton referred to this group collectively time and again. His frequent citations demonstrated an in-depth knowledge of their ideas and as a result his campaign against them was focused and effective. Nevertheless, the fact that Warburton went out of his way to name the members of this group and refer to their works repeatedly over the course of his career had also the unintended effect of helping to canonise a tradition he so often hoped and predicted would be either laughed at or entirely forgotten.

Notes

1 A. Collins, *A Discourse of the Grounds and Reasons of the Christian Religion* (London, 1724), p. 112. See also S. Snobelen, 'The Argument over Prophecy: An Eighteenth-Century Debate between William Whiston and Anthony Collins', *Lumen*, 15 (1996), pp. 195–213; Hudson, *Enlightenment and Modernity*, pp. 28–34; G. Tarantino, 'The Books and Times of Anthony Collins (1676–1729)', in A. Hessayon and D. Finnegan (eds), *Varieties of Seventeenth- and Early Eighteenth-Century English Radicalism in Context* (Farnham, 2011), pp. 221–40.
2 Collins, *Discourse of the Grounds and Reasons*, p. v.
3 Ibid., pp. v–xi.
4 Ibid., p. 225. See W. Whiston, *An Essay towards Restoring the True Text of the Old Testament* (London, 1722).
5 E. Chandler, *A Defence of Christianity from the Prophecies of the Old Testament* (London, 1725), sig. A4r.
6 Collins, *The Scheme of Literal Prophecy Considered*, 2 vols (London [The Hague], 1726), vol. 2, p. 392.
7 Ibid., p. 393. Cf. S. Chandler, *A Vindication of the Christian Religion* (London, 1725), p. xiii.
8 Collins, *Scheme*, vol. 2, pp. 413–14.
9 J. Rogers, *The Necessity of Divine Revelation, and the Truth of the Christian Revelation Asserted* (London, 1727), p. 151.
10 Ibid., p. 6.
11 Ibid., p. 8.
12 Ibid., p. 11.
13 Ibid., p. 4.
14 Ibid., pp. 12–13.
15 Ibid., pp. 18–19.
16 Ibid., p. 21.
17 Ibid., p. 23
18 Ibid., p. 13.
19 See Carmel, 'Commonwealth for Galileo'.
20 Rogers, *Necessity of Divine Revelation*, p. 53.
21 Ibid., p. lxiii.
22 Ibid., pp. lxiv–lxv.
23 O'Higgins, *Anthony Collins*, pp. 192–94 is an important exception.
24 Collins, *A Letter to the Reverend Dr. Rogers* (London, 1727), p. 1.
25 Ibid., p. 3.
26 Ibid., pp. 9–10.

27 Ibid., p. 13.
28 Ibid., pp. 4, 10.
29 Ibid., pp. 1–2.
30 Ibid., p. 4.
31 Ibid., p. 42.
32 Ibid., p. 82.
33 Ibid., p. 49.
34 Rogers, *Necessity of Divine Revelation*, pp. lvii–lviii.
35 Ibid., p. lix.
36 Collins, *Letter*, pp. 46–47.
37 Ibid., p. 47.
38 Ibid.
39 Ibid., pp. 47–48. Yet for Fénelon, not quite as for Collins, religion could limit politics in various ways. R. P. Hanley, *The Political Philosophy of Fénelon* (New York, 2020), p. 150, claims: 'For Fénelon, the separation of church and state is ultimately valuable for the way in which it makes possible a system of mutual and reciprocal subordination that enables the Church, in its autonomy, to serve as a check on temporal power'.
40 Collins, *Letter*, p. 37.
41 Ibid., p. 43.
42 Ibid.
43 Locke also thought that the legislative power, which is the supreme authority, should govern the society in accordance with the natural law, but he made significant efforts to assure that the interpretation of the law of nature would be clear and that the supreme power would not turn into 'absolute Arbitrary Power'. While for Locke the supreme authority is subject to explicit '*Bounds*' —and breaking them would make it illegitimate—we do not find a parallel proviso in Collins. J. Locke, *Second Treatise of Government*, ed. M. Goldie (Oxford, 2016), pp. 68–69, 72. See also O'Higgins, *Anthony Collins*, pp. 194.
44 Rogers, *A Vindication of the Civil Establishment of Religion* (London, 1728), pp. iv–vi.
45 For example, T. Chubb, *An Enquiry Concerning Redemption* (London, 1743), pp. 30–31.
46 Chubb, *Some Short Reflections on the Grounds and Extent of Authority and Liberty* (London, 1728), p. 17.
47 Ibid., p. 30.
48 Ibid., p. 32.
49 Ibid., pp. 49–50.
50 Chubb, *The Comparative Excellence and Obligation of Moral and Positive Duties, Fully Stated and Considered* (London, 1730), pp. 18–19. Cf. Lev 5, p. 66: 'when men that think themselves wiser than all others, clamor and demand right Reason for judge; yet seek no more, but that things should be determined, by no other mens reason but their own, it is as intolerable in the society of men, as it is in play after trump is turned, to use for trump on every occasion, that suite whereof they have most in their hand'.

51 Chubb, *A Discourse Concerning Reason, with Regard to Religion and Divine Revelation* (London, 1731), pp. 49–50.

52 Skelton, *Deism Revealed*, vol. 2, p. 265, for example, described Tindal as 'the great Apostle of Deism' and *Christianity as Old as the Creation* as 'the Bible of all Deistical readers ... in comparison of whom, *Toland* is but a pedant, *Collins* a sophister'. Tindal apparently had a plan for another volume for *Christianity as Old as the Creation* which was never published; see D. Berman and S. Lalor, 'The Suppression of *Christianity as Old as the Creation*, Vol. II', *Notes and Queries*, 31:1 (1984), pp. 3–6.

53 Ingram, *Reformation without End*, pp. 64–81, on p. 66, for example, argues that Tindal 'defined himself in terms of what he was not—a persecutory, bigoted, orthodox churchman'.

54 Tindal, *Christianity as Old as the Creation*, p. 13.

55 Ibid., p. 15.

56 Ibid., p. 18.

57 Ibid., p. 20.

58 Ibid., pp. 115–16.

59 Ibid., pp. 362–63.

60 Ibid., p. 371.

61 Ibid., p. 368.

62 Ibid., p. 178.

63 Ibid., p. 179.

64 Ibid.

65 Ibid., p. 180.

66 Ibid.

67 Lev 32, p. 576.

68 Tindal, *Christianity as Old as the Creation*, p. 16.

69 Skelton, *Deism Revealed*, vol. 1, pp. 68–69. Cf. Lev 5, p. 64.

70 Skelton, *Deism Revealed*, vol. 1, p. 69. Cf. Tindal, *Christianity as Old as the Creation*, pp. 180–81.

71 Skelton, *Deism Revealed*, vol. 1, p. 69. A third definition that is considered is Richard Cumberland's, who 'defines right reason to be *affirmation and negation, according to the real nature of things*'. Shepherd thinks that it is not useful because it 'gives us no idea of the extent or power of reason', as the act of reasoning has to be prior to that of affirmation or negation. On Cumberland and Hobbes, see J. Parkin, *Science, Religion and Politics in Restoration England: Richard Cumberland's De Legibus Naturae* (Woodbridge, 1999).

72 Skelton, *Deism Revealed*, vol. 1, p. 70.

73 Tindal, *Christianity as Old as the Creation*, p. 56.

74 Young, 'Tindal, Matthew'.

75 Herrick, *Radical Rhetoric*, p. 11.

76 D. Waterland, *Scripture Vindicated; in Answer to a Book Intituled, Christianity as Old as the Creation. Part I* (London, 1730), e.g., pp. 10–20. For the questioning of the literal interpretation of the story in Genesis, see Tindal, *Christianity as Old as the Creation*, pp. 385–88. See also Ingram, *Reformation without End*, pp. 74–75.

77 Waterland, *Christianity Vindicated Against Infidelity* (London, 1732), pp. 1–4.
78 Ibid., pp. 28–29.
79 W. Law, *The Case of Reason, or Natural Religion, Fairly and Fully Stated. In Answer to a Book, Entitul'd, Christianity as Old as the Creation* (London, 1731), p. 125.
80 Anon., *The Religious, Rational, and Moral Conduct of Matthew Tindal, L.L.D. Late Fellow of All Souls College in Oxford. In a Letter to a Friend. By a Member of the Same College* (London, 1735), pp. 19–20.
81 See the title page of his *A Succinct History of Priesthood, Ancient and Modern* (London, 1737).
82 Venturi, *Utopia and Reform*, p. 67. See also Jacob, *Radical Enlightenment*, pp. 172–81; Israel, *Radical Enlightenment*, pp. 68–69, 267–73; Thomson, *Bodies of Thought*, pp. 161–64; T. Cavallo, ' "Atheists or Deists, More Charitable Than Superstitious Zealots"': Alberto Radicati's Intellectual Parabola', in Hudson, Lucci, and Wigelsworth (eds), *Atheism and Deism Revalued*, pp. 173–90.
83 G. Berkeley, *The Theory of Vision, or Visual Language, Shewing the Immediate Presence and Providence of a Deity, Vindicated and Explained* (London, 1733), p. 8.
84 A. Radicati, *Twelve Discourses Concerning Religion and Government* (London, 1734), p. 3.
85 Ibid., pp. 10–11.
86 Ibid., p. 11.
87 Ibid., pp. 11–12.
88 Radicati, *Succinct History of Priesthood*, pp. 57–58.
89 G. Berkeley, *Alciphron: Or, the Minute Philosopher. In Seven Dialogues. Containing an Apology for the Christian Religion, Against Those Who Are Called Free-Thinkers*, 2 vols (London, 1732), vol. 1, p. 244.
90 Radicati, *Succinct History of Priesthood*, pp. 58–59.
91 Ibid., pp. 61–62.
92 J. van den Berg, *A Forgotten Christian Deist: Thomas Morgan* (New York, 2021) is an important exception. Morgan is also discussed in the historiography of deism, although significantly less than the better-known deists; see for example Hudson, *Enlightenment and Modernity*, pp. 74–85; Wigelsworth, *Deism in Enlightenment England*, pp. 152–61, 190–94.
93 P. Harrison, 'Morgan, Thomas (1671/2?–1743), Theological and Medical Writer', *ODNB* (2004), available at: www.oxforddnb.com/view/10.1093/ref:odnb/9780198614128.001.0001/odnb-9780198614128-e-19239 (accessed 21 July 2023).
94 Ibid.; D. L. Wykes, 'Subscribers and Non-Subscribers at the Salters' Hall Debate (Act. 1719)', *ODNB* (2009), available at: www.oxforddnb.com/view/10.1093/ref:odnb/9780198614128.001.0001/odnb-9780198614128-e-95681 (accessed 21 July 2023); van den Berg, *Forgotten Christian Deist*, pp. 21–59.
95 [T. Reynolds, B. Robinson, J. Smith, and W. Tong], *The Doctrine of the Blessed Trinity Stated & Defended by Some London Ministers* (London, 1719), p. 46.
96 Ibid.

97　T. Morgan, *A Collection of Tracts, Relating to the Right of Private Judgment* (London, 1726), p. 31.

98　T. Bradbury, *The Necessity of Contending for Revealed Religion* (London, 1720), p. xii.

99　Morgan, *Collection of Tracts*, pp. 50–51.

100　Ibid., p. 51.

101　Ibid.

102　Ibid., p. 59.

103　R. Blackmore, *Modern Arians Unmasked* (London, 1721). Blackmore, *Creation: A Philosophical Poem* (London, 1712), pp. xxxix–xlv, attacked the deists: ''Tis true indeed, that most of the Deists maintain a particular Friendship with the Atheists', and ''tis observable that the present Deists have not drawn and publish'd any Scheme of Religion, or Catalogue of the Duties they are oblig'd to perform'. The poem attacked Hobbes as well: 'here I would address my self to the Irreligious Gentleman of the Age ... Will they confide in Mr *Hobbs*? Has that Philosopher said any thing new? Does he bring any stronger Forces into the Field, than the *Epicureans* did before him?'

104　Morgan, *Collection of Tracts*, p. 304.

105　Ibid., p. 303.

106　Ibid., p. 311.

107　Ibid., pp. 449–50.

108　P. Nisbett, *Comprehension Confusion: Mr. Nisbett's Second Letter to Mr. Morgan* (London, 1724), p. 45.

109　Morgan, *Collection of Tracts*, p, 481.

110　Hobbes, *Behemoth, or the Long Parliament*, ed. P. Seaward (Oxford, 2009), p. 183. Cf. Nisbett, *Comprehension Confusion*, p. 45.

111　Morgan, *Collection of Tracts*, p. 482.

112　Harrison, 'Morgan, Thomas'.

113　Morgan, *Collection of Tracts*, p. 482.

114　See for example Morgan, *A Letter to Mr. Thomas Chubb* (London, 1727), pp. 29–30. See also J. R. Wigelsworth, 'The Disputed Root of Salvation in Eighteenth-Century English Deism: Thomas Chubb and Thomas Morgan Debate the Impact of the Fall', *Intellectual History Review*, 19:1 (2009), pp. 29–43, esp. p. 42.

115　Morgan, *The Moral Philosopher* (London, 1737), p. 392.

116　Ibid.

117　Ibid., p. 393.

118　Ibid., p. 394.

119　Ibid.

120　van den Berg, *Forgotten Christian Deist*, p. 87, alludes to this connection, suggesting that Morgan 'was influenced to some extent by the tradition of critical views of Hobbes and Collins'.

121　Morgan, *Moral Philosopher*, pp. 81–82.

122　Ibid., also p. 98.

123　Cf. Lev 32, p. 580.

124 Morgan, *Moral Philosopher*, p. 94.

125 Ibid., p. 95.

126 Ibid., p. 99.

127 Ibid., p. 71, Morgan similarly described Paul, who was the model for his Christian deism, as 'the great Free-thinker of his Age, the bold and brave Defender of Reason against Authority, in Opposition to those who had set up a wretched Scheme of Superstition, Blindness and Slavery'.

128 Morgan, *The Moral Philosopher. Vol II. Being a Farther Vindication of Moral Truth and Reason* (London, 1739), p. 31.

129 See also Morgan, *The Moral Philosopher. Vol III. Superstition and Tyranny Inconsistent with Theocracy* (London, 1740), pp. 163–67; J. R. Wigelsworth, ' "God Always Acts Suitable to his Character, as a Wise and Good Being": Thomas Chubb and Thomas Morgan on Miracles and Providence', in Hudson, Lucci, and Wigelsworth (eds), *Atheism and Deism Revalued*, pp. 157–72, esp. pp. 169–71.

130 Cf. Lev 37, p. 684.

131 Morgan, *Moral Philosopher. Vol II*, pp. 32–33.

132 Ibid., p. 68. See also *Moral Philosopher. Vol III*, p. 226.

133 See for example *Moral Philosopher. Vol II*, pp. 70–74.

134 Ibid., p. 68.

135 Ibid., p. 69.

136 Lev 33, pp. 590, 594; Hobbes concluded that 'the Books of *Samuel* were also written after his own time'.

137 Morgan, *Moral Philosopher. Vol II*, p. 69. See Malcolm, 'Hobbes, Ezra, and the Bible'; van den Berg, *Forgotten Christian Deist*, pp. 127–30.

138 E. Chambers (ed.), *The History of the Works of the Learned … II* (London, 1737), p. 24; J. Hildrop, *An Essay for the Better Regulation and Improvement of Free-thinking* (London, 1739), p. 30; quoted also in van den Berg, *Forgotten Christian Deist*, pp. 85–86, 114.

139 J. Westby-Gibson and M. J. Mercer, 'Chapman, John (bap. 1705, d. 1784), Theologian and Classical Scholar', *ODNB* (2004), available at: www.oxforddnb.com/view/10.1093/ref:odnb/9780198614128.001.0001/odnb-9780198614128-e-5121 (accessed 21 July 2023).

140 J. Chapman, *Eusebius: Or the True Christian's Defense Against a Late Book Entitul'd the Moral Philosopher* (Cambridge, 1739), e.g., pp. 78, 416.

141 Ibid., p. 415.

142 Ibid., p. 417.

143 Ibid., p. 468. Cf. Morgan, *Moral Philosopher*, pp. 16, 403.

144 Chapman, *Eusebius*, p. 478.

145 W. Warburton, *A Critical and Philosophical Enquiry into the Causes of Prodigies and Miracles, as Related by Historians*, 2 vols (London, 1727), vol. 1, pp. 26–27.

146 Ibid., pp. 29–30.

147 Warburton, *The Alliance between Church and State, or, the Necessity and Equity of an Established Religion and a Test-Law Demonstrated* (London, 1736), p. 49.

148 Ibid., p. 51.

149 Ibid., pp. 73–74.

150 Ibid., p. 83. See B. W. Young, 'Warburton, William (1698–1779), Bishop of Gloucester and Religious Controversialist', *ODNB* (2004), available at: www.oxforddnb.com/view/10.1093/ref:odnb/9780198614128.001.0001/odnb-9780198614128-e-28680 (accessed 21 July 2023); Ingram, *Reformation without End*, pp. 265–343, esp. pp. 275–76, 284–303; S. W. Brown, 'Enlightened Hobbism: Aspects of the Eighteenth-Century Reception of Hobbes in Britain' (Unpublished PhD thesis, Kingston, 2020), pp. 281–321.

151 Young, *Religion and Enlightenment*, pp. 167–212, on pp. 179–80.

152 Warburton, *The Divine Legation of Moses Demonstrated, on the Principles of a Religious Deist, from the Omission of the Doctrine of a Future State of Reward and Punishment in the Jewish Dispensation*, 2 vols (London, 1738–1741), vol. 1, p. ii.

153 Ibid., pp. xix–xxi.

154 Ibid., pp. xxii–xxiii. Warburton seems to have referred to an instance in the correspondence between Collins and Clarke where Collins used Locke to imply that it was impossible to prove 'that Matter is not a self-existent Being', that is, that it was created by God: 'to get an Idea of Creation, or a Conception how Matter might begin to exist, *we must* (as the incomparable Mr. *Locke* with great Modesty expresses himself) *emancipate ourselves from vulgar Notions*', however, Locke 'thought that *this would lead him too far from the Notions, on which the Philosophy now in the World is built, and that it would not be pardonable to deviate so far from them*'. Therefore, Collins concluded, 'the small Compass of this Treatise … must make it more pardonable in me (who own my self to be infinitely below him in Abilities) if I omit for the present so useful a Design, or should leave it entirely to some of those Gentlemen that are appointed annually to preach at the Lecture founded by the Honourable *Robert Boyle*'. Clarke, *Works*, vol. 3, p. 884.

155 Warburton, *Divine Legation*, vol. 1, p. xxv.

156 Bulman, 'Secular Sacerdotalism', esp. pp. 214–15.

157 Lev 23, p. 378.

158 Warburton, *Divine Legation*, vol. 1, p. 49.

159 Ibid., vol. 2, p. ix.

160 For example, Ibid., pp. 343–62, 446–68. Warburton presented an early summary of this thesis in his *Alliance between Church and State*, pp. 168–73. See also Young, *Religion and Enlightenment*, pp. 174–79; Pocock, *Barbarism and Religion. Volume 5*, pp. 230–37.

161 Warburton, *Divine Legation*, vol. 2, p. xx, mentioned Morgan while addressing the Jews as 'a late Writer: who, by the peculiar Felicity of a good Choice, having learnt his *Morality* of our *Tyndal*, and his *Philosophy* of your *Spinoza*, calls himself, by the Courtesy of *England*, a MORAL PHILOSOPHER'.

162 Morgan, *A Brief Examination of the Rev. Mr. Warburton's Divine Legation of Moses* (London, 1742), pp. iii–vi.

163 Ibid., pp. vi–xi.

164 Ibid., pp. xi, xiii.

165 Ibid., p. xlix.
166 Ibid.
167 Ibid., p. 1.
168 Ibid., p. 16.
169 Ibid., e.g., pp. 8–10, 15–17. See Young, *Religion and Enlightenment*, pp. 188–89.
170 Morgan, *Brief Examination*, pp. iii, 141.
171 Ibid., p. 143.
172 Warburton, *A Critical and Philosophical Commentary on Mr. Pope's Essay on Man* (London, 1742), p. xix. John Tillard was the author of *Future Rewards and Punishments Believed by the Ancients; Particularly the Philosophers* (1740).
173 J. Nichols, *Illustrations of the Literary History of the Eighteenth Century*, 8 vols (Cambridge, 2014), vol. 2, pp. 129, 817; several years earlier, Warburton expressed a similar sentiment in another correspondence: 'As for that blasphemous fellow Morgan, he is, I think, below my notice, any farther than to shew my great contempt of him occasionally'. See van den Berg, *Forgotten Christian Deist*, pp. 38, 114.
174 Warburton and R. Hurd, *Remarks on Mr. David Hume's Essay on the Natural History of Religion* (London, 1757), p. 76; quoted also in Young, *Religion and Enlightenment*, p. 211. Bolingbroke, *The Philosophical Works*, 5 vols (London, 1754), vol. 3, pp. 207–208, for example, sympathised with Hobbes's anticlericalism: 'I am not a disciple of Hobbes, but I embrace truth wherever I find it, or whoever shews it to me: and he shews it to me, I think, when he maintains that the present church of Christ … is not the kingdom of Christ. This opinion, however, that it is so … will be supported as long as that order of men can support it, who have assumed, under pretence of being appointed to govern and administer in it, an establishment distinct from the civil, and a most unreasonable and unequal share of wealth and power in almost every christian state'. On Bolingbroke and Warburton, see also Walsh, *Civil Religion*, pp. 80–107.

Conclusion

The anticlerical writers studied in this book exposed and fulfilled Hobbes's most radical potential. They relied on him consciously and consistently and often took positions that were distinctively Hobbesian. Time and again they acknowledged their debts to the philosopher who excelled at the art of pulling down the churches and whose reputation was even worse than theirs.

The 'Radical Enlightenment', according to Jonathan Israel, 'whether on an atheistic or deistic basis, rejected all compromise with the past and sought to sweep away existing structures entirely'.[1] However, Hobbes and his anticlerical successors engaged heavily with the past as well as with the sacred: the inquiry into the authorship and authority of the bible and the analysis of religious history in terms of human interests are good examples. They thought that their accounts would do justice to the pure, original, and simple spirit of Christianity and hence conform to the essence of true religion. Whatever their personal beliefs, they aimed to disprove any *story about* religion that could benefit only the storyteller. Hobbes denied the linguistically absurd idea of incorporeal substances and the deists objected to mysteries in religion because such notions had been brought into religion by the schoolmen, together with elements of paganism and demonology, and advanced by the clerics who corrupted Christianity. It was this position that led some of them to characterise the work of God as consistent and thus in accordance with the laws of nature. The point was not necessarily to destroy the notion of God but the idea that God commands just for commanding-sake, in Tindal's words, because this idea was only beneficial to those who usurped the means to interpret God's commands.

This is not to say that these writers, who certainly were enemies of large parts of the orthodoxy, should be considered part of an English conservative Enlightenment either.[2] They belonged, more accurately, to an *anticlerical*

Enlightenment. Most importantly, they belonged to an Enlightenment which was a joint project of people with different views who offered different ways to achieve the same goal, namely, civil stability, as William Bulman suggests.[3] In this sense, the Anglican Enlightenment that Bulman has identified and the anticlerical Enlightenment that emerges from the present study are two sides of the same coin. On this view, Warburton, for example, and his freethinking enemies, including Hobbes, Morgan, and others, formed an Enlightenment *together*—and the conflict between them took place *within* this Enlightenment. Furthermore, precisely because Anglicans and freethinkers were in conversation with one another as to how to achieve civil peace, writers such as Warburton started to justify religion on pragmatic, even secular grounds, emphasising its social utility. As Bulman notes, even Anglican 'refutations of freethinking were primarily crafted to reach and convince an increasingly large group of lay readers who took very seriously the assumptions and conclusions of the church's enemies'.[4] This reading also helps explain how writers such as Collins and Tindal, who are best-known as advocates of toleration, could at the same time use Hobbesian arguments for the strengthening of the civil authority. Indeed, English anticlericalism often led the freethinkers to support the establishment, not to aim to sweep it away.[5] Even within the anticlerical Enlightenment there was room for a variety of views, but its members—from Hobbes to Morgan—shared the primary goal of eliminating the independent political power of the church, preventing any more sectarianism and religious wars, and ensuring lasting peace and stability.

Future legacies

The 1740s witnessed the decline of deism. It is almost a truism now that 'Deists had ceased to be' by the middle of the century, although at least one figure, Peter Annet, was still active.[6] In 1790, Edmund Burke wondered '[w]ho, born within the last forty years, has read one word of Collins, and Toland, and Tindal, and Chubb, and Morgan, and that whole race who called themselves Freethinkers', adding sarcastically: 'Ask the booksellers of London what is become of all these lights of the world'. Burke went on to dismiss these infamous freethinkers as 'wholly unconnected individuals' who 'never acted in corps, nor were known as a faction in the state, nor presumed to influence ... on any of our public concerns'.[7] This judgment is often accepted in the scholarship. Collins's biographer, for example, agreed that '[i]n England he was almost forgotten'.[8] The reason for the decline, some explain, is that the deists simply lost the battle that they were fighting. They were 'outmanned and outgunned', as Robert Ingram puts it.[9] At the same time, as we have seen, the critics often helped unintentionally to keep deism and freethinking in the public eye even when they were fading, and Burke's attack, too, might well have put the spotlight back on his long-forgotten enemies.[10] In any case, some of Burke's opponents among the radicals of the 1790s were quite well-read in the freethinking literature that he so strongly discredited.

The afterlife of English deism and freethinking is therefore more intriguing than has often been realised, not least because it took different shapes in different places, such as Scotland, France, Germany, and colonial America. The American case is especially interesting as it shows how deist ideas continued to develop—and to be coupled with Hobbes—into the nineteenth century. The founding fathers, amongst others, were very familiar with the English deists, who, like them, were deeply concerned about the problem of religion and civil order. Thomas Jefferson, himself sometimes considered a deist, had many of their titles in his library, classified as 'Moral Philosophy', including works by Blount, Tindal, Shaftesbury, Chubb, and Annet.[11] Benjamin Franklin read Collins and Shaftesbury, which made him 'a real doubter in many points of our religious doctrine', and he famously reported that he had a deistic phase early in his life, apparently in the 1720s: 'Some books against Deism fell into my hands … It happened that they wrought an effect on me quite contrary to what was intended by them; for the arguments of the Deists, which were quoted to be refuted, appeared to me much stronger than the refutations; in short, I soon became a thorough Deist'.[12] This statement is perhaps the ultimate demonstration of the complex way in which deism received meanings and gained momentum over time, often in relation to the 'other', namely, the orthodoxy, while the critiques—in this case it was the Boyle Lectures—helped to perpetuate what they meant to destroy. In the 1750s, John Adams encountered some deistic ideas in Worcester, Massachusetts, where he 'found Morgans Moral Phylosopher, which I was informed had circulated, with some freedom, in that Town and that the Principles of Deism had made a considerable progress among several Persons, in that and other Towns in the County'.[13] Some decades later, Adams wrote to the geographer and minister Jedidiah Morse disapprovingly: 'There is, my dear Doctor, at present existing in the World a Church phylosophic, as Subtle as learned, as hypocritical, as the holy roman, Catholic, Apostolic and Œcumenical Church. This philosophical Church was originally English. Voltaire learned it from Lord Herbert, Hobbes Morgan Collin Shaftsbury Bolingbroke &c &c &c'.[14]

Despite Burke's wishful verdict on the fate of these writers, it appears that they—and their legacies—continued to enjoy their mixed reputation on the other side of the Atlantic. Furthermore, deism continued to be associated with Hobbes in the same manner that it had been in Britain. One churchman from New England wrote in 1783 that 'the established creed of deists', which was first modelled on Herbert of Cherbury, 'underwent some considerable alterations by the labors of the noted Mr. Hobbes of Malmsbury ... in him the boasted succession of deistical writers was begun, which has been continued through many hands, and under various shapes until now'. Among the names this writer mentioned were Blount, Toland, Collins, Tindal, Morgan, and Hume, 'None of these writers passed unanswered, nor unconfuted'.[15] There were of course new representatives of this succession, also in America. Most notably, the names of Thomas Paine and Elihu Palmer would be added to this list in the 1790s and the 1800s, especially with the publication of Paine's *Age of Reason* (1794–1795) and Palmer's *Principles of Nature* (1801). To be sure, there was not necessarily a close connection between them and the previous English deists, but there were some undeniable structural similarities in their ways of thinking, especially in the rejection of miracles and revelation, the radical anticlericalism and biblical criticism, the endorsement of the religion of nature, and the defence of freedom of thought and religion.[16] At times, these authors went further than their British predecessors; Paine, as is well-known, went so far as to claim that 'My own mind is my own church'.[17] Both the *Age of Reason* and the *Principles of Nature* were open defences of deism.[18] Paine stated explicitly: 'The only religion that has not been invented, and that has in it every evidence of divine originality, is pure and simple Deism. It must have been the first, and will probably be the last, that man believes'. All other kinds of religions, he argued, were full of inventions made to serve 'despotic governments' and 'the avarice of priests'.[19] This was evident, Paine argued, as these inventions included horrors such as 'the obscene stories, the voluptuous debaucheries, the cruel and torturous executions, the unrelenting vindictiveness, with which more than half the Bible is filled'.[20] The logical conclusion, then, was clear: 'Is it not more safe that we stop ourselves at the plain, pure and unmixed belief of one God, which is Deism, than that we commit ourselves on an ocean of improbable, irrational, indecent and contradictory tales?'[21] Paine's deistic view remained consistent, and strikingly, the very last paragraph he ever published told the story of Franklin's conversion to deism through the Boyle Lectures. He concluded: 'All America, and more than all America, knows Franklin. His life was devoted to the good and improvement of man. Let, then, those who profess a different creed, imitate his virtues, and excel him if they can'.[22]

Unsurprisingly, the critics frequently pointed to the connections between Paine and the earlier deists, including Hobbes, and vilified them as heretics. One critic argued that 'Hobbes, Spinoza, Bayle, Voltaire, Toland, Tindal, Collins, Morgan, Mandeville, Chubb, have, in their several ways, anticipated every thing to be found in the "Age of Reason"'.[23] Richard Watson, bishop of Llandaff, compared Paine's 'attack on the authority of the five books of Moses' with Hobbes who 'contends that the books of Moses are so called, not from their having been written by Moses, but from their containing an account of Moses', concluding in an answer to Paine: 'You see that this fancy has had some patrons before you'.[24] Another writer denounced 'the cant of every infidel, from the cowardly Hobbes down to the blackguard Paine' and added figuratively that 'the deists ... whine; and so does the Crocodile to seduce its prey'.[25]

In this version of American deism, which had some considerable French connections, Hobbes's authority was still invoked positively from time to time, albeit to a lesser degree than before. What is more, this happened not only in strictly intellectual discussions but also in popular publications such as newspapers. For example, a letter published in the *Religious Inquirer* in 1831 described the path of its author from Presbyterianism to Universalism through deism: 'Between the age of 18 and 20, I had access to the writings of Bollingbroke, Tindall, Collins, Hobbes, Voltaire, &c. and came very near being a Deist'. The author, however, was not fully convinced, because 'The God of the Deist appeared to be a Noble Being yet he was too distant, and not affectionate enough for me'.[26] Another case was the *Temple of Reason*, a weekly newspaper that ran from 1800 to 1803, first in New York and then in Philadelphia. It was edited by Irishman Denis Driscol, a friend of Palmer, with the support of the Deistical Society of New York. The newspaper was expressly deistic, having stated upon its launching that it was 'chiefly intended to combat the enemies of Deism' and that its claims were 'supported from the best Deistical authors, both living and dead', especially Paine. In 1801–1802, the newspaper published a series of articles entitled 'Natural Ideas Opposed to Supernatural', a translation of *Le Bon Sens* by Baron d'Holbach (1772). One piece attacked theology as 'a science, that has for its object only things incomprehensible ... Hobbes calls it the Kingdom of Darkness'. The text described this pretended science along the same lines of Hobbes's kingdom of darkness: 'In this marvelous region, light is only darkness; evidence is doubtful or false; impossibilities are credible; reason is a deceitful guide; and good sense becomes madness'. To sum up, all this was little short of 'a continual insult to the reason of man'.[27]

These views clearly found a supportive audience. The passage from d'Holbach, for example, was reprinted in the *Boston Investigator*, one of the most important freethinking newspapers of the nineteenth century. Interestingly, the first editor of the *Boston Investigator*, Abner Kneeland, was famously jailed for blasphemy; the prosecution emphasised that he was responsible for unprecedented circulation and popularisation of infidelity among both the learned and the unlearned.[28] Subsequently, the *Boston Investigator* praised Hobbes as a 'distinguished Freethinker' in 1857, and as late as 1876 denounced 'the evils of religion or superstition', adding: 'we make no more distinction between them than did the Freethinking and matter-of-fact HOBBES, who thought they meant the same thing'.[29]

Going back to England, a very similar dynamic can be traced there around the same time. The *Oracle of Reason*—almost an identical title to Blount's famous publication—was also an outstandingly aggressive and provocative atheistic weekly published between 1841 and 1843.[30] It declared that it provided the first 'honest' attack of 'supernaturalism', and its target was the same old 'monster': 'Priestcraft poisons all—nothing escapes its polluting—its withering touch'.[31] The resemblance to case of the *Boston Investigator* is striking. Most editors of the *Oracle*, including Charles Southwell and George Jacob Holyoake, were imprisoned on different occasions for blasphemy, in some cases following high-profile trials. Additionally, there were numerous references to Hobbes and the deists in this weekly. The first paragraph of the first issue stated that 'all your mysterious, or *hidden some-things*, belonging, as Hobbes well observed, *to the kingdom of darkness*'.[32] Precisely as did the *Boston Investigator*, the *Oracle* referred elsewhere to Hobbes who 'rightly called theology, "the kingdom of darkness," for dark enough, in all conscience, it must be to the believer, who reflects *ever so little* on the absurd and contradictory *evidences* and *doctrines* of this so-called *science*'.[33] The first editor, Southwell, also paid respect to previous freethinkers in his *Confessions of a Free-Thinker* (1850). Telling the story of establishing the *Oracle*, he was proud that its founders' 'library was an admirable one,—perhaps the best Freethinkers' library ever known in this country. It contained amongst other scarce works (scarce because dangerous to clerical supremacy), those of Chubb, Tindal, Morgan, Blount, and a host of other Free-thinking thinkers, whose profound thoughts, and quaint, but apt expressions, I hope some day or other to familiarize the public with'.[34] Indeed, the *Oracle* introduced these thinkers frequently, albeit ambivalently at times. The deists were praised for their religious doubts—but criticised for not going far enough in their conclusions: 'It is hard to say what such philosophers as Blount, Shaftesbury, Bolingbroke, Collins, Morgan, Chubb, and Tindal *would have written* had they *dared*'.[35] Those who had been considered shockingly daring at their time were now deemed not bold enough. Yet the *Oracle* was forgiving: 'The inconsistencies and absurdities which disfigure the pages of ... all *reputed Deists*, were, I am persuaded, not so much a consequence of their errors in philosophy, as fear of fanatical intolerance'.[36] Finally, the *Oracle* published 'the Unbeliever's Creed' which stated: 'I believe in any *sound* philosophy, first or last—I believe in Chubb, Collins, Toland, Tindal, Morgan, Mandeville, Hobbes, Shaftesbury, ... Paine, and all other men, Saint Paul of course included—*with weight and measure*'.[37]

By that point, then, there had been a freethinking Hobbesian legacy that turned, however gradually, from deistic to atheistic, and in this sense confirmed what the critics suspected all along. There were, to conclude, different legacies for different readers, and there is much room for historians to investigate these avenues further. If there is one lesson to be learned from these later American and English examples, it is that the so-called forgotten deists had in fact long-lasting legacies that could be carried forward in multiple ways, more or less compatible with their original views—indeed, precisely as the deists read and used Hobbes in different ways for their own purposes.

This is, therefore, a story of a plurality of legacies that often differed in their attitudes to religion as a whole or indeed in their political visions; atheistic, republican, or democratic paths were optional but certainly not necessary. What these legacies shared was a common analysis of the political uses and abuses of religion and the forces that drove them. Their primary contribution to modern political thought lay in their deep understanding of the dangers that the politics of religion posed to society—and, crucially, also in their appreciation of the potential of reforming it in ways that would secure peace, stability, and happiness once and for all.

Notes

1 Israel, *Radical Enlightenment*, p. 11.
2 For the Enlightenment in England as a conservative Enlightenment 'within piety', see J. G. A. Pocock, 'Post-Puritan England and the Problem of the Enlightenment', in P. Zagorin (ed.), *Culture and Politics from Puritanism to the Enlightenment* (Berkeley, 1980), pp. 91–111; R. Porter, 'The Enlightenment in England', in R. Porter and M. Teich (eds), *The Enlightenment in National Context* (Cambridge, 1981), pp. 1–18; Pocock, 'Enthusiasm: The Antiself of Enlightenment', *Huntington Library Quarterly*, 60:1–2 (1997), pp. 7–28, esp. pp. 11–12; Young, *Religion and Enlightenment*.
3 Bulman, *Anglican Enlightenment*, esp. pp. 1–13; Bulman, 'Secular Sacerdotalism'.
4 Bulman, 'Secular Sacerdotalism', p. 207. See also W. J. Bulman and R. G. Ingram, 'Religion, Enlightenment and the Paradox of Innovation, c. 1650–1760', in D. A. Yerxa (ed.), *Religion and Innovation: Antagonists or Partners?* (London, 2016), pp. 100–12.
5 Bulman, 'Secular Sacerdotalism', p. 221. Bulman, 'Enlightenment for the Culture Wars', in Bulman and Ingram (eds), *God in the Enlightenment*, pp. 1–41, on pp. 18–19, 22, suggests similarly that we 'think of Enlightenment not in terms of specific propositions or political programs but in terms of the articulation, defense, dissemination, and implementation of ideas under a specific set of guiding historical conditions', and that '[i]t was Hobbes, who

perhaps more than any other single figure makes clear the necessity of dating the Enlightenment to the middle of the seventeenth century once one rejects an ideologically loaded understanding of it'. See also Bulman, 'Hobbes's Publisher'; Champion, 'Godless Politics'.

6 M. Pattison, 'Tendencies of Religious Thought in England, 1688–1750', in *Essays and Reviews* (London, 1860), pp. 254–329, on p. 261; quoted also in Ingram, *Reformation without End*, p. 76. Pattison, 'Tendencies', p. 267 also stated: 'To talk Deism had ceased to be fashionable as soon as it ceased to attract attention'.

7 E. Burke, *Reflections on the Revolution in France*, 2nd edn (London, 1790), p. 133.

8 O'Higgins, *Anthony Collins*, p. 221. For a modified account, see Hudson, *Enlightenment and Modernity*, pp. 144–49.

9 Ingram, *Reformation without End*, p. 76.

10 Clark, *English Society*, p. 396, argues that Burke's attack on the freethinkers 'was true; but his dismissal of politicised Deism was premature. It reawoke with Paine'.

11 For example, Jefferson owned Blount's *Miscellaneous Works* and *The Two First Books of Philostratus*, Tindal's *Christianity as Old as the Creation*, and Chubb's *A Collection of Tracts* (1743). Among the critiques of deism, Jefferson owned works by Clarke, Warburton, Leslie, and many more, classified as 'Religion'. Among Hobbes's works, he owned *De cive* and the translation of Thucydides's *Eight Bookes of the Peloponnesian Warre* (1629), classified as 'Politics' and 'Antient History' respectively. In Jefferson's copy of Blount's *Miscellaneous Works*, a line which mistakenly appears twice has been crossed out in the text 'Concerning the World's Age, Beginning and End' in the *Oracles of Reason* (p. 227). Assuming that it was Jefferson himself who made the correction, this gives us an indication of how closely he read some of the deists' writings, even the lesser known. This copy is found in the Jefferson Collection, Rare Book and Special Collections Division of the Library of Congress, Washington, DC; Jefferson's library is displayed at the Library of Congress. See E. M. Sowerby, *Catalogue of the Library of Thomas Jefferson*, 5 vols (Washington, DC, 1952–1959), e.g., vol. 1, pp. 8–9, vol. 2, pp. 13, 21–23, 43, 149–50, 182, vol. 3, p. 35. See also R. G. Ingram, 'The Reformation in the Age of Jefferson', in P. Griffin and F. D. Cogliano (eds), *Ireland and America: Empire, Revolution and Sovereignty* (Charlottesville, 2021), pp. 178–97, esp. pp. 179–80.

12 B. Franklin, *The Works of Benjamin Franklin*, ed. J. Bigelow, 12 vols (New York, 1904), vol. 1, pp. 53, 149.

13 J. Adams, *Diary and Autobiography of John Adams*, ed. L. H. Butterfield, 4 vols (Cambridge, MA, 1961), vol. 3, p. 263.

14 John Adams to Jedidiah Morse, 15 May 1815, Gates W. McGarrah Autograph Collection, Library of Congress.

15 J. Murray, *Bath-Kol. A Voice from the Wilderness* (Boston, 1783), p. 97.

16 As Mark Philp claims, Paine's 'arguments follow the pattern of criticism developed in the deist controversy in England in the first quarter of the eighteenth century'. Philp, 'Paine, Thomas (1737–1809), Author and Revolutionary',

ODNB (2004), available at: www.oxforddnb.com/view/10.1093/ref:odnb/ 9780198614128.001.0001/odnb-9780198614128-e-21133 (accessed 21 July 2023). J. C. D. Clark, *Thomas Paine: Britain, America, and France in the Age of Enlightenment and Revolution* (Oxford, 2018), pp. 331–55, on pp. 336, 342, suggests that 'Paine's religious opinions were probably formed as a child in England' and that he 'was evidently a lifelong Deist'. K. Fischer, *American Freethinker: Elihu Palmer and the Struggle for Religious Freedom in the New Nation* (Philadelphia, 2021), recovers different aspects of Palmer's thought and life, including his deism. Palmer refereed to Tindal, for example, and recommended *Christianity as Old as the Creation* to 'Whoever wishes to be more fully convinced, that scripture prophecies are destitute of all certitude'. K. S. Walters, *Elihu Palmer's 'Principles of Nature': Text and Commentary* (Wolfeboro, 1990), pp. 147–49.

17 T. Paine, *The Complete Writings of Thomas Paine*, ed. P. S. Foner, 2 vols (New York, 1945), vol. 1, p. 464.

18 See for example Walters, *Palmer's 'Principles of Nature'*, pp. 261–62.

19 Paine, *Complete Writings*, vol. 1, p. 600.

20 Ibid., p. 474.

21 Ibid., p. 572.

22 Ibid., vol. 2, p. 897.

23 W. Jackson, *Observations in Answer to Mr. Thomas Paine's "Age of Reason"* (Dublin, 1795), p. 64.

24 R. Watson, *An Apology for the Bible, in a Series of Letters, Addressed to Thomas Paine*, 6th edn (London, 1796), pp. 41–43. Watson referred to a passage where Paine stated that the books of Moses were 'no other than an attempted history of the life of Moses … written by some very ignorant and stupid pretenders to authorship several hundred years after the death of Moses'. Paine, *Complete Writings*, vol. 1, p. 521.

25 'Second Letter to Dr. Thomas Ewell', *National Messenger* (Georgetown, DC) I, no. 9 (14 November 1817), [p. 2], *Readex: America's Historical Newspapers*.

26 'Extract of a Letter to the Editor, from an Esteemed Correspondent in Pennsylvania', *Religious Inquirer* (Hartford, CT) IX, no. 49 (22 January 1831), p. 385, *Readex: America's Historical Newspapers*.

27 D. Driscol, *The Temple of Reason*, 2 vols (New York and Philadelphia, 1800–1803), vol. 1, pp. 403–404; the passage appears again in vol. 2, p. 1. See also Fischer, *American Freethinker*, pp. 190–205; K. S. Walter, *The American Deists: Voices of Reason and Dissent in the Early Republic* (Lawrence, 1992), pp. 306–31.

28 *Boston Investigator* (Boston, MA) XI, no. 43 (2 March 1842), p. 1, *Readex: America's Historical Newspapers*. See also C. Grasso, *Skepticism and American Faith: From the Revolution to the Civil War* (Oxford, 2018), pp. 333–46.

29 *Boston Investigator* (Boston, MA) XXVII, no. 8 (17 June 1857), p. 4 and XLVI, no. 9 (21 June 1876), p. 4, *Readex: America's Historical Newspapers*.

30 E. Royle, *Victorian Infidels: The Origins of the British Secularist Movement, 1791–1866* (Manchester, 1974), esp. pp. 71–88.

31 C. Southwell, G. J. Holyoake, T. Paterson, and W. Chilton, *The Oracle of Reason: Or, Philosophy Vindicated*, 2 vols (London, 1842–1843), vol. 1, pp. ii–iii.
32 Ibid., p. 1.
33 Ibid., vol. 2, p. 235.
34 Southwell, *The Confessions of a Free-Thinker* (London, 1850), pp. 65–66.
35 Southwell *et al.*, *Oracle of Reason*, vol. 1, p. 393.
36 Ibid., p. 394.
37 Ibid., vol. 2, p. 208. The 'Creed' had been previously published in the *Investigator*, another periodical edited by Southwell. It appeared in the form of a comparison between the Christians' and the atheists' versions. Above is the phrasing of the atheists' version, while the Christians' version of the 'Creed' stated: 'I believe not in the First Philosophy—I believe in Chubb, Collins, Toland … I believe not in St. Paul'. A paraphrase of this version was cited later by the Presbyterian minister John Cumming to attack infidelity, and again by George Eliot, who criticised Cumming's 'misconception as to the character of free-thinking in the present day'. J. Cumming, *Is Christianity from God?* (London, 1847), p. 140; G. Eliot, 'Evangelical Teaching: Dr. Cumming', *Westminster Review*, 64 (1855), pp. 436–62, on pp. 445–46.

Bibliography

Primary works

(Place of publication is London unless otherwise stated)

A., T., *Religio Clerici* (1681).

Adams, J., *Diary and Autobiography of John Adams*, ed. L. H. Butterfield, 4 vols (Cambridge, MA, 1961).

Addison, L., *A Modest Plea for the Clergy* (1677).

Anderson, A., *The Treatise of the Three Impostors and the Problem of Enlightenment: A New Translation of the Traité des Trois Imposteurs (1777 Edition)* (Lanham, 1997).

Anon., *The Character of a Coffee-House, with the Symptoms of a Town-Wit* (1673).

Anon., *The Entertainer: Containing Remarks upon Men, Manners, Religion and Policy* (1720).

Anon., *The Last Sayings, or, Dying Legacy of Mr. Thomas Hobbs of Malmesbury Who Departed This Life on Thursday, Decemb. 4, 1679* (1680).

Anon., *Memorable Sayings of Mr. Hobbes in His Books and at the Table* (1680).

Anon., *The Religious, Rational, and Moral Conduct of Matthew Tindal, L.L.D. Late Fellow of All Souls College in Oxford. In a Letter to a Friend. By a Member of the Same College* (1735).

Anon., *Visits from the Shades* (1704).

Assheton, W., *An Admonition to a Deist* (1685).

Atterbury, F., *Fourteen Sermons Preach'd on Several Occasions* (1708).

Aubrey, J., *Brief Lives, Chiefly of Contemporaries*, ed. A. Clark, 2 vols (Oxford, 1898).

Bayle, P., *The Dictionary Historical and Critical of Mr Peter Bayle*, 2nd edn, 5 vols (1734–1738).

Bentley, R., *The Folly and Unreasonableness of Atheism Demonstrated*, 4th edn (1699).

Bentley, R., *Remarks upon a Late Discourse of Free-Thinking* (1713).

Berkeley, G., *Alciphron: Or, the Minute Philosopher. In Seven Dialogues. Containing an Apology for the Christian Religion, Against Those Who Are Called Free-Thinkers*, 2 vols (1732).

Berkeley, G., *The Theory of Vision, or Visual Language, Shewing the Immediate Presence and Providence of a Deity, Vindicated and Explained* (1733).

Birchley, W. [J. Austin], *The Christian Moderator* (1651).

Birchley, W. [J. Austin], *The Christian Moderator. Third Part* (1653).

Blackmore, R., *Creation: A Philosophical Poem* (1712).

Blackmore, R., *Modern Arians Unmasked* (1721).

Blount, C., *Anima Mundi, or, an Historical Narration of the Opinions of the Ancients Concerning Man's Soul after This Life* (1679).

Blount, C., *An Appeal from the Country to the City, for the Preservation of His Majesties Person, Liberty, Property, and the Protestant Religion* (1679).

Blount, C., *Great Is Diana of the Ephesians, or, the Original of Idolatry Together with the Politick Institution of the Gentiles Sacrifices* (1680).

Blount, C., *A Just Vindication of Learning, or, an Humble Address to the High Court of Parliament in behalf of the Liberty of the Press by Philopatris* (1679).

Blount, C., *King William and Queen Mary, Conquerors, or, a Discourse Endeavouring to Prove That Their Majesties Have on Their Side, Against the Late King, the Principal Reasons That Make Conquest a Good Title* (1693).

Blount, C., *Miracles, No Violations of the Laws of Nature* (1683).

Blount, C., *The Miscellaneous Works of Charles Blount, Esq.* (1695).

Blount, C., *The Oracles of Reason … In Several Letters to Mr. Hobbs and Other Persons of Eminent Quality, and Learning* (1693).

Blount, C., *Reasons Humbly Offered for the Liberty of Unlicens'd Printing* (1693).

Blount, C., *Religio Laici Written in a Letter to John Dryden, Esq.* (1683).

Blount, C., *The Two First Books of Philostratus, Concerning the Life of Apollonius Tyaneus: Written Originally in Greek, and Now Published in English: Together with Philological Notes upon Each Chapter* (1680).

Bolingbroke, H. S. J., *The Philosophical Works*, 5 vols (1754).

Boyer, A., *The Political State of Great Britain, Vol. XXIII* (1722).

Bradbury, T., *The Necessity of Contending for Revealed Religion* (1720).

Burke, E., *Reflections on the Revolution in France*, 2nd edn (1790).

Burnet, G., *The History of the Reformation of the Church of England. The First Part, of the Progress Made in It During the Reign of K. Henry the VIII* (1679).

Burton, R., *The Anatomy of Melancholy. Volume 3: Text*, ed. T. C. Faulkner, N. K. Kiessling, and R. L. Blair (Oxford, 1994).

Butler. J., *The Analogy of Religion, Natural and Revealed, to the Constitution and Course of Nature* (1736).

Carroll, W., *Spinoza Reviv'd* (1709).

Casaubon, M., *A Letter of Meric Casaubon D.D. &c. to Peter du Moulin* (Cambridge, 1669).

Cavendish, W., *Reasons for His Majesties Passing the Bill of Exclusion in a Letter to a Friend* (1681).

Chambers, E. (ed.), *The History of the Works of the Learned … II* (1737).

Chandler, E., *A Defence of Christianity from the Prophecies of the Old Testament* (1725).

Chandler, S., *A Vindication of the Christian Religion* (1725).

Chapman, J., *Eusebius: Or the True Christian's Defense Against a Late Book Entitul'd the Moral Philosopher* (Cambridge, 1739).

Chubb, T., *The Comparative Excellence and Obligation of Moral and Positive Duties, Fully Stated and Considered* (1730).

Chubb, T., *A Discourse Concerning Reason, with Regard to Religion and Divine Revelation* (1731).

Chubb, T., *An Enquiry Concerning Redemption* (1743).

Chubb, T., *Some Short Reflections on the Grounds and Extent of Authority and Liberty* (1728).

Clarke, S., *Remarks upon a Book, Entituled, a Philosophical Enquiry Concerning Human Liberty* (1717).

Clarke, S., *The Works of Samuel Clarke*, 4 vols (1738).

Clarke, S., and A. Collins, *The Correspondence of Samuel Clarke and Anthony Collins, 1707–08*, ed. W. L. Uzgalis (Peterborough, 2011).

Clifford, M., *A Treatise of Humane Reason* (1674).

Collins, A., *The Correspondence of Anthony Collins (1676–1729), Freethinker*, ed. J. Dybikowski (Paris, 2011).

Collins, A., *A Discourse Concerning Ridicule and Irony in Writing* (1729).

Collins, A., *A Discourse of Free-Thinking, Occasion'd by the Rise and Growth of a Sect Call'd Free-Thinkers* (1713).

Collins, A., *A Discourse of the Grounds and Reasons of the Christian Religion* (1724).

Collins, A., *An Essay Concerning the Use of Reason in Propositions, the Evidence Whereof Depends upon Human Testimony* (1707).

Collins, A., *A Letter to the Reverend Dr. Rogers* (1727).

Collins, A., *A Philosophical Inquiry Concerning Human Liberty* (1717).

Collins, A., *A Philosophical Inquiry Concerning Human Liberty. Republished with a Preface by Joseph Priestley* (Birmingham, 1790).

Collins, A., *Priestcraft in Perfection* (1710).

Collins, A., *The Scheme of Literal Prophecy Considered*, 2 vols (1726).

Collins, A., *A Vindication of the Divine Attributes* (1710).

Cooper, A. A., third earl of Shaftesbury, *Characteristicks of Men, Manners, Opinions, Times*, ed. D. Den Uyl, 3 vols (Indianapolis, 2001).

Cooper, A. A., third earl of Shaftesbury, *The Life, Unpublished Letters, and Philosophical Regimen of Anthony, Earl of Shaftesbury*, ed. B. Rand (1900).

Cooper, A. A., third earl of Shaftesbury, *Several Letters Written by a Noble Lord to a Young Man at the University* (1716).

Craig, M., *A Satyr Against Atheistical Deism with the Genuine Character of a Deist* (Edinburgh, 1696).

Cumming, J., *Is Christianity from God?* (1847).

Davenant, C., *The Political and Commercial Works of That Celebrated Writer*, ed. C. Whitworth, 5 vols (1771).

Dodwell, H., *An Epistolary Discourse Proving, from the Scriptures and the First Fathers, That the Soul Is a Principle Naturally Mortal* (1706).

Driscol, D., *The Temple of Reason*, 2 vols (New York and Philadelphia, 1803).

Dryden, J., *Religio Laici: Or, a Layman's Faith. A Poem* (1682).

Eachard, J., *Mr. Hobbs's State of Nature Considered in a Dialogue between Philautus and Timothy* (1672).

Eachard, J., *Some Opinions of Mr. Hobbs Considered in a Second Dialogue between Philautus and Timothy by the Same Author* (1673).

Eliot, G., 'Evangelical Teaching: Dr. Cumming', *Westminster Review*, 64 (1855), pp. 436–62.

[Finch, A.,] *Free-Thinkers. A Poem in Dialogue* (1711).

Franklin, B., *The Works of Benjamin Franklin*, ed. J. Bigelow, 12 vols (New York, 1904).

Gastrell, F., *The Certainty and Necessity of Religion in General, or, the First Grounds & Principles of Humane Duty Establish'd* (1697).

Gildon, C., *The Deist's Manual: Or, a Rational Enquiry into the Christian Religion* (1705).

Gildon, C., *Miscellany Poems upon Several Occasions Consisting of Original Poems* (1692).

Gordon, T., *An Examination of the Facts and Reasonings in the Lord Bishop of Chichester's Sermon* (1732).

Grey, A., *Debates of the House of Commons from the Year 1667 to the Year 1694*, 10 vols (1763).

Harrington, J., *The Oceana of James Harrington and His Other Works*, ed. J. Toland (1700).

Harrington, J., *The Political Works of James Harrington*, ed. J. G. A. Pocock (Cambridge, 1977).

Harris, J., *The Atheist's Objections, Against the Immaterial Nature of God, and Incorporeal Substances, Refuted* (1698).

Harris, J., *Immorality and Pride, the Great Causes of Atheism* (1698).

Harris, J., *The Notion of a God, Neither from Fear nor Policy* (1698).

Harris, J., *A Refutation of the Objections Against Moral Good and Evil* (1698).

Herbert, E., *De causis errorum: una cum tractatu de religione laici, et appendice ad sacerdotes* (1645).

Herbert, E., *De veritate*, trans. M. H. Carré (Bristol, 1937).

Hickes, G., *A Letter to the Author of a Late Paper, Entituled, a Vindication of the Divines of the Church of England, &c.* (1689).

Hickes, G., *Some Discourses upon Dr. Burnet and Dr. Tillotson* (1695).

Hickes, G., *Three Short Treatises* (1709).

Hickes, G., *Two Treatises, One of the Christian Priesthood, the Other of the Dignity of the Episcopal Order* (1707).

Hildrop, J., *An Essay for the Better Regulation and Improvement of Free-thinking* (1739).

Hildrop, J., *Reflections upon Reason* (1722).

Hobbes, T., *Behemoth, or the Long Parliament*, ed. P. Seaward (Oxford, 2009).

Hobbes, T., *The Correspondence of Thomas Hobbes*, ed. N. Malcolm, 2 vols (Oxford, 1994).

Hobbes, T., *The Elements of Law: Natural and Politic*, ed. F. Tönnies (Cambridge, 1928).

Hobbes, T., *The English Works of Thomas Hobbes of Malmesbury*, ed. W. Molesworth, 11 vols (1839–1845).

Hobbes, T., *Leviathan: The English and Latin Texts*, ed. N. Malcolm (Oxford, 2012).

Hobbes, T., *On the Citizen*, ed. and trans. R. Tuck and M. Silverthorne (Cambridge, 1998).

Hobbes, T., *Thomae Hobbes malmesburiensis opera philosophica quae latine scripsit omnia*, ed. W. Molesworth, 5 vols (1839–1845).

Hobbes, T., *A True Ecclesiastical History*, trans. J. Rooke (1722).

Hobbes, T., *Writings on Common Law and Hereditary Right*, ed. A. Cromartie and Q. Skinner (Oxford, 2005).

Howard, R., *The History of Religion* (1694).

Howard, R., *A Twofold Vindication of the Late Arch-Bishop of Canterbury, and of the Author of the History of Religion* (1696).

[Howell], W., *The Spirit of Prophecy* (1679).

Hyde, E., earl of Clarendon, *A Brief View and Survey of the Dangerous and Pernicious Errors to Church and State, in Mr. Hobbes's Book, Entitled Leviathan* (Oxford, 1676).

Jackson, W., *Observations in Answer to Mr. Thomas Paine's "Age of Reason"* (Dublin, 1795).

Jones, J., *A New and Full Method of Settling the Canonical Authority of the New Testament*, 3 vols (Oxford, 1798).

Jones, J., *A Vindication of the Former Part of St. Matthew's Gospel* (1719).

King, J., *Mr. Blount's Oracles of Reason, Examined and Answered* (1698).

King, W., *An Essay on the Origin of Evil*, trans. with notes E. Law, 2nd edn, 2 vols (1732).

Law, W., *The Case of Reason, or Natural Religion, Fairly and Fully Stated. In Answer to a Book, Entitul'd, Christianity as Old as the Creation* (1731).

Leland, J., *A View of the Principal Deistical Writers that Have Appeared in England in the Last and Present Century* (1754).

Leslie, C., *The Charge of Socinianism Against Dr. Tillotson Considered* (Edinburgh, 1695).

Leslie, C., *The Second Part of the Wolf Stript of His Shepherds Cloathing* (1707).

Leslie, C., *A Short and Easie Method with the Deists* (1698).

Locke, J., *The Correspondence of John Locke*, ed. E. S. De Beer, 8 vols (Oxford, 1976–1989).

Locke, J., *An Essay Concerning Humane Understanding* (1690).

Locke, J., *A Letter Concerning Toleration and Other Writings*, ed. M. Goldie (Indianapolis, 2010).

Locke, J., *Mr. Locke's Reply to the Right Reverend the Lord Bishop of Worcester's Answer to His Second Letter* (1699).

Locke, J., *The Reasonableness of Christianity, as Delivered in the Scriptures* (1695).

Locke, J., *Second Treatise of Government*, ed. M. Goldie (Oxford, 2016).

Locke, J., *A Second Vindication of the Reasonableness of Christianity* (1697).

Locke, J. et al., *Some Familiar Letters between Mr. Locke, and Several of His Friends* (1708).

Lowth, W., *A Vindication of the Divine Authority and Inspiration of the Writings of the Old and New Testament* (Oxford, 1692).

M., A., *Plain-Dealing, or, a Full and Particular Examination of a Late Treatise, Entituled, Humane Reason* (1675).

Macaulay, T. B., *The History of England from the Accession of James II*, ed. H. Trevelyan, 5 vols (Cambridge, 2011).

Manning, G., 'The Deist: A Satyr on the Parsons', *The Seventeenth Century*, 8:1 (1993), pp. 149–160.

Marvell, A., *The Prose Works*, eds M. Dzelzainis and A. M. Patterson, 2 vols (New Haven, 2003).

Matar, N. (ed.), *Henry Stubbe and the Beginnings of Islam: The Originall & Progress of Mahometanism* (New York, 2013).

Milton, J., *Areopagitica* (1644).

Morgan, T., *A Brief Examination of the Rev. Mr. Warburton's Divine Legation of Moses* (1742).

Morgan, T., *A Collection of Tracts, Relating to the Right of Private Judgment* (1726).

Morgan, T., *A Letter to Mr. Thomas Chubb* (1727).

Morgan, T., *The Moral Philosopher* (1737).

Morgan, T., *The Moral Philosopher. Volume II: Being a Farther Vindication of Moral Truth and Reason* (1739).

Morgan, T., *The Moral Philosopher. Volume III: Superstition and Tyranny Inconsistent with Theocracy* (1740).

Murray, J., *Bath-Kol. A Voice from the Wilderness* (Boston, 1783).

Newton, I., *Philosophical Writings*, ed. A. Janiak (Cambridge, 2004).

Nicholls, W., *A Conference with a Theist* (1696).

Nichols, J., *Illustrations of the Literary History of the Eighteenth Century*, 8 vols (Cambridge, 2014).

Nichols, J., *An Order of Houshold Instruction* (1595).

Nisbett, P., *Comprehension Confusion: Mr. Nisbett's Second Letter to Mr. Morgan* (1724).

Paine, T., *The Complete Writings of Thomas Paine*, ed. P. S. Foner, 2 vols (New York, 1945).

Parker, S., *A Discourse of Ecclesiastical Politie* (1670).

Pierce, T., *A Decad of Caveats to the People of England of General Use in All Times* (1679).

Prideaux, H., *A Letter to the Deists* (1696).

Radicati, A., *A Phliosophical* [sic] *Dissertation upon Death. Composed for the Consolation of the Unhappy. By a Friend to Truth* (1732).

Radicati, A., *A Succinct History of Priesthood, Ancient and Modern* (1737).

Radicati, A., *Twelve Discourses Concerning Religion and Government* (1734).

[Reynolds, T., B. Robinson, J. Smith, and W. Tong], *The Doctrine of the Blessed Trinity Stated & Defended by Some London Ministers* (1719).

Rogers, J., *The Necessity of Divine Revelation, and the Truth of the Christian Revelation Asserted* (1727).

Rogers, J., *A Vindication of the Civil Establishment of Religion* (1728).

Rousseau, J. J., *The Social Contract; and, Discourses*, trans. G. D. H. Cole (1973).

Rust, G., and H. Hallywell, *A Discourse of the Use of Reason in Matters of Religion: Shewing, That Christianity Contains Nothing Repugnant to Right Reason; Against Enthusiasts and Deists* (1683).

Sault, R., *The Second Spira: Being a Fearful Example of an Atheist, Who Had Apostatized from the Christian Religion, and Dyed in Despair at Westminster, Decemb. 8. 1692* (1693).

Seller, A., *The History of Passive Obedience Since the Reformation* (Amsterdam, 1689).

Skelton, P., *Deism Revealed*, 2nd edn, 2 vols (1751).

Southwell, C., *The Confessions of a Free-Thinker* (1850).

Southwell, C., G. J. Holyoake, T. Paterson, and W. Chilton, *The Oracle of Reason: Or, Philosophy Vindicated*, 2 vols (1842–1843).

Spinoza, B. de, *The Collected Works of Spinoza, Volume I*, ed. and trans. E. Curley (Princeton, 1985).

Spinoza, B. de, *Theological-Political Treatise*, ed. and trans. J. Israel and M. Silverthorne (Cambridge, 2007).

Sprat, T., *The History of the Royal-Society of London, for the Improving of Natural Knowledge* (1667).

Steele, R., *The Guardian*, ed. J. Calhoun Stephens (Lexington, 1982).

Stephens, W., *An Account of the Growth of Deism in England* (1696).

Stillingfleet, E., *A Letter to a Deist, in Answer to Several Objections Against the Truth and Authority of the Scriptures* (1677).

Swift, J., *A Letter to a Young Gentleman, Lately Enter'd into Holy Orders* (1721).

Swift, J., *Mr. C–ns's Discourse of Free-Thinking, Put into Plain English, by Way of Abstract, for the Use of the Poor* (1713).

Tillard, J., *Future Rewards and Punishments Believed by the Ancients; Particularly the Philosophers* (1740).

Tillotson, J., *The Works of the Most Reverend Dr. John Tillotson … Containing Fifty Four Sermons and Discourses* (1696).

Tillotson, J., *The Works of the Most Reverend Dr. John Tillotson … Containing Two Hundred Sermons and Discourses*, 2nd edn, 2 vols (1717).

Tindal, M., *Christianity as Old as the Creation: Or, the Gospel, a Republication of the Religion of Nature* (1730).

Tindal, M., *A Defence of the Rights of the Christian Church* (1707).

Tindal, M., *An Essay Concerning the Laws of Nations, and the Rights of Soveraigns* (1694).

Tindal, M., *An Essay Concerning Obedience to the Supreme Powers, and the Duty of Subjects in All Revolutions* (1694).

Tindal, M., *An Essay Concerning the Power of the Magistrate, and the Rights of Mankind in Matters of Religion* (1697).

Tindal, M., *A Letter to a Member of Parliament, Shewing, That a Restraint on the Press Is Inconsistent with the Protestant Religion, and Dangerous to the Liberties of the Nation* (1698).

Tindal, M., *New High-Church Turn'd Old Presbyterian* (1709).

Tindal, M., *The Rights of the Christian Church Asserted, Against the Romish, and All Other Priests Who Claim an Independent Power Over It*, 2nd edn (1706).

Toland, J., *Adeisidaemon* (The Hague, 1709).

Toland, *Amyntor: Or, a Defence of Milton's Life* (1699).

Toland, J., *An Apology for Mr. Toland in a Letter from Himself to a Member of the House of Commons in Ireland* (1697).

Toland, J., *Christianity Not Mysterious*, 2nd edn (1696).

Toland, J., *A Collection of Several Pieces of Mr. John Toland*, ed. P. Desmaizeaux, 2 vols (1726).

Toland, J., *Letters to Serena* (1704).

Toland, J., *Nazarenus*, ed. J. Champion (Oxford, 1999).

Toland, J. *Nazarenus*, 2nd edn (1718).

Toland, J., *Pantheisticon* (1751).

Toland, J., *Reasons for Naturalizing the Jews in Great Britain and Ireland* (1714).

Toland, J., *The Second Part of the State Anatomy* (1717).

Toland, J., *Socinianism Truly Stated* (1705).

Toland, J., *Tetradymus. Containing 1. Hodegus … 2. Clidophorus … 3. Hypatia … 4. Mangoneutes* (1720).

[Toland, J.] L. P., *Two Essays Sent in a Letter from Oxford to a Nobleman in London* (1695).

Trenchard, J., *The Natural History of Superstition* (1709).

Trenchard, J., and T. Gordon, *Cato's Letters: Or, Essays on Liberty, Civil and Religious, and Other Important Subjects*, 6th edn, 4 vols (1755).

Trenchard, J., and T. Gordon, *The Independent Whig: Or, a Defence of Primitive Christianity, and of Our Ecclesiastical Establishment, Against the Exorbitant Claims and Encroachments of Fanatical and Disaffected Clergymen*, 7th edn, 4 vols (1741–1747).

Villiers, G., second duke of Buckingham, *The Second Volume of Miscellaneons* [sic] *Works*, ed. T. Brown (1705).

Walters, K. S., *Elihu Palmer's 'Principles of Nature': Text and Commentary* (Wolfeboro, 1990).

Warburton, W., *The Alliance between Church and State, or, the Necessity and Equity of an Established Religion and a Test-Law Demonstrated* (1736).

Warburton, W., *A Critical and Philosophical Commentary on Mr. Pope's Essay on Man* (1742).

Warburton, W., *A Critical and Philosophical Enquiry into the Causes of Prodigies and Miracles, as Related by Historians*, 2 vols (1727).

Warburton, W., *The Divine Legation of Moses Demonstrated, on the Principles of a Religious Deist, from the Omission of the Doctrine of a Future State of Reward and Punishment in the Jewish Dispensation*, 2 vols (1738–1741).

Warburton, W., and R. Hurd, *Remarks on Mr. David Hume's Essay on the Natural History of Religion* (1757).

Warren, A., *An Apology for the Discourse of Humane Reason* (1680).

Warren, A., *Eight Reasons Categorical: Wherein Is Examined and Proved, That It's Probable, the Law-Common Will Stand* (1653).

Warren, A., *The Royalist Reform'd* (1650).

Waterland, D., *Christianity Vindicated Against Infidelity* (1732).

Waterland, D., *Scripture Vindicated; in Answer to a Book Intituled, Christianity as Old as the Creation. Part I* (1730).

Watson, R., *An Apology for the Bible, in a Series of Letters, Addressed to Thomas Paine*, 6th edn (1796).

Whichcote, B., *Select Sermons of Dr. Whichcot*, ed. A. A. Cooper (1698).

Whiston, W., *An Essay towards Restoring the True Text of the Old Testament* (1722).

Whiston, W., *Reflexions on an Anonymous Pamphlet, Entituled, a Discourse of Free Thinking* (1713).

Willis, R., *Reflexions upon a Pamphlet Intituled, an Account of the Growth of Deism in England Together with Some Considerations about the Christian Religion* (1696).

Witty, J., *The First Principles of Modern Deism Confuted* (1707).

Wolseley, C., *The Reasonableness of Scripture-Belief. A Discourse Giving Some Account of Those Rational Grounds upon Which the Bible Is Received as the Word of God* (1672).

Wood, A., *The Life and Times of Anthony Wood*, ed. A. Clark, 5 vols (Oxford, 1891–1900).

MANUSCRIPTS AND LETTERS

Athenaeum, London: Blount's Miscellanea MS, 100Ab.

British Library: Tracts on Religion, 873.b.3.

Gates W. McGarrah Autograph Collection, Library of Congress: John Adams to Jedidiah Morse, 15 May 1815.

Hertfordshire Archives and Local Studies: Bundle of Small Volumes Presumed to Belong to Dame Sarah Cowper, DE/P/F47.

NEWSPAPERS: READEX: AMERICA'S HISTORICAL NEWSPAPERS

Boston Investigator (Boston, MA) XI, no. 43 (2 March 1842).

Boston Investigator (Boston, MA) XXVII, no. 8 (17 June 1857).

Boston Investigator (Boston, MA) XLVI, no. 9 (21 June 1876).

'Extract of a Letter to the Editor, from an Esteemed Correspondent in Pennsylvania', *Religious Inquirer* (Hartford, CT) IX, no. 49 (22 January 1831).

'Second Letter to Dr. Thomas Ewell', *National Messenger* (Georgetown, DC) I, no. 9 (14 November 1817).

Secondary works

Abizadeh, A., 'Hobbes's Conventionalist Theology, the Trinity, and God as an Artificial Person by Fiction', *The Historical Journal*, 60:4 (2017), pp. 915–41.

Abizadeh, A., 'Publicity, Privacy and Religious Toleration in Hobbes's *Leviathan*', *Modern Intellectual History*, 10:2 (2013), pp. 261–91.

Agnesina, J., *The Philosophy of Anthony Collins: Free-Thought and Atheism* (Paris, 2018).

Aldridge, A. O., 'Shaftesbury and the Deist Manifesto', *Transactions of the American Philosophical Society*, 41:2 (1951), pp. 297–382.

Baldin, G., *Hobbes and Galileo: Method, Matter and the Science of Motion* (Cham, 2020).

Barber, A., '"Why Don't Those Lazy Priests Answer the Book?" Matthew Tindal, Censorship, Freedom of the Press and Religious Debate in Early Eighteenth-Century England', *History*, 98 (2013), pp. 680–707.

Barnett, S. J., *The Enlightenment and Religion: The Myths of Modernity* (Manchester, 2003).

Barnouw, J., 'The Separation of Reason and Faith in Bacon and Hobbes, and Leibniz's *Theodicy*', *Journal of the History of Ideas*, 42:4 (1981), pp. 607–28.

Beiner, R., *Civil Religion: A Dialogue in the History of Political Philosophy* (Cambridge, 2011).

Beiser, F. C., *The Sovereignty of Reason: The Defense of Rationality in the Early English Enlightenment* (Princeton, 1996).

Bejan, T. M., 'Difference without Disagreement: Rethinking Hobbes on "Independency" and Toleration', *The Review of Politics*, 78:1 (2016), pp. 1–25.

Berman, D., 'Anthony Collins' Essays in the *Independent Whig*', *Journal of the History of Philosophy*, 13:4 (1975), pp. 463–69.

Berman, D., 'Deism, Immortality and the Art of Theological Lying', in J. A. L. Lemay (ed.), *Deism, Masonry, and the Enlightenment* (Newark, 1987), pp. 61–78.

Berman, D., 'Disclaimers as Offence Mechanisms in Charles Blount and John Toland', in M. Hunter and D. Wootton (eds), *Atheism from the Reformation to the Enlightenment* (Oxford, 1992), pp. 255–72.

Berman, D., 'A Disputed Deistic Classic', *The Library*, s6–vii:1 (1985), pp. 58–59.

Berman, D., *A History of Atheism in Britain: From Hobbes to Russell* (London, 1988).

Berman, D., and S. Lalor, 'The Suppression of *Christianity as Old as the Creation*, Vol. II', *Notes and Queries*, 31:1 (1984), pp. 3–6.

Betts, C. J., *Early Deism in France* (The Hague, 1984).

Biddle, J. C., 'Locke's Critique of Innate Principles and Toland's Deism', *Journal of the History of Ideas*, 37:3 (1976), pp. 411–22.

Brown, K. C., 'Hobbes's Grounds for Belief in a Deity', *Philosophy*, 37:142 (1962), pp. 336–44.

Brown, S. W., 'Enlightened Hobbism: Aspects of the Eighteenth-Century Reception of Hobbes in Britain' (PhD diss., Queen's University, Kingston, 2020).

Bulman, W. J., *Anglican Enlightenment: Orientalism, Religion and Politics in England and its Empire, 1648–1715* (Cambridge, 2015).

Bulman, W. J., 'Enlightenment for the Culture Wars', in W. J. Bulman and R. G. Ingram (eds), *God in the Enlightenment* (Oxford, 2016), pp. 1–41.

Bulman, W. J., 'Hobbes's Publisher and the Political Business of Enlightenment', *The Historical Journal*, 59:2 (2016), pp. 339–64.

Bulman, W. J., 'Secular Sacerdotalism in the Anglican Enlightenment, 1660–1740', in A. M. Matytsin and D. Edelstein (eds), *Let There Be Enlightenment: The Religious and Mystical Sources of Rationalism* (Baltimore, 2018), pp. 205–26.

Bulman, W. J., and R. G. Ingram, 'Religion, Enlightenment and the Paradox of Innovation, c. 1650–1760', in D. A. Yerxa (ed.), *Religion and Innovation: Antagonists or Partners?* (London, 2016), pp. 100–12.

Carmel, E., 'Anthony Collins on Toleration, Liberty, and Authority', *History of European Ideas* 48:7 (2022): 892–908.

Carmel, E., 'A Commonwealth for Galileo: Imagining a Hobbesian Utopia', *Hobbes Studies* 35:2 (2022): 176–99.

Carmel, E., 'The History and Philosophy of English Freethinking', in A. Tomaszewska and H. Hämäläinen (eds), *The Sources of Secularism: Enlightenment and Beyond* (Cham, 2017), pp. 121–37.

Carmel, E., '"I Will Speake of That Subject No More": The Whig Legacy of Thomas Hobbes', *Intellectual History Review*, 29:2 (2019), pp. 243–64.

Carmel, E., '"Philosophy, Therefore, Is within Yourself": The Rational Potential in Hobbes's Theory', *Hobbes Studies*, 31:2 (2018), pp. 166–87.

Carroll, R., *Uncivil Mirth: Ridicule in Enlightenment Britain* (Princeton, 2021).

Champion, J., 'Deism', in R. H. Popkin (ed.), *The Columbia History of Western Philosophy* (New York, 1999), pp. 437–45.

Champion, J., 'Godless Politics: Hobbes and Public Religion', in W. J. Bulman and R. G. Ingram (eds), *God in the Enlightenment* (Oxford, 2016), pp. 42–62.

Champion, J., 'An Historical Narration Concerning Heresie: Thomas Hobbes, Thomas Barlow, and the Restoration Debate over "Heresy"', in D. Loewenstein and J. Marshall (eds), *Heresy, Literature and Politics in Early Modern English Culture* (Cambridge, 2006), pp. 221–53.

Champion, J., 'John Toland: The Politics of Pantheism', *Revue de synthese*, 116:2–3 (1995), pp. 259–80.

Champion, J., '"The Kingdom of Darkness": Hobbes and Heterodoxy', in S. Mortimer and J. Robertson (eds), *The Intellectual Consequences of Religious Heterodoxy 1600–1750* (Leiden, 2012).

Champion, J., 'Legislators, Impostors, and the Politic Origins of Religion: English Theories of "Imposture" from Stubbe to Toland', in S. Berti, F. Charles-Daubert, and R. H. Popkin (eds), *Heterodoxy, Spinozism, and Free-Thought in Early-Eighteenth-Century Europe: Studies on the Traité des Trois Imposteurs* (Dordrecht, 1996), pp. 333–56.

Champion, J., '"My Kingdom Is Not of This World": The Politics of Religion after the Restoration', in N. Tyacke (ed.), *The English Revolution c. 1590–1720: Politics, Religion and Communities* (Manchester, 2007), pp. 185–202.

Champion, J., *The Pillars of Priestcraft Shaken: The Church of England and Its Enemies 1660–1730*, 2nd edn (Cambridge, 2014).

Champion, J., '"Private Is in Secret Free": Hobbes and Locke on the Limits of Toleration, Atheism and Heterodoxy', in C. Y. Zarka, F. Lessay, and J. Rogers (eds), *Les fondements philosophiques de la tolerance* (Paris, 2002), pp. 221–53.

Champion, J., *Republican Learning: John Toland and the Crisis of Christian Culture, 1696–1722* (Manchester, 2003).

Champion, J., ' "Syllables Governe the World": Biblical Criticism, Erudition, Heterodoxy and Thomas Hobbes', in R. Armstrong and T. Ó hAnnracháin (eds), *The English Bible in the Early Modern World* (Leiden, 2018), pp. 183–212.

Clark, J. C. D., *English Society, 1660–1832: Religion, Ideology and Politics during the Ancien Regime*, 2nd edn (Cambridge, 2000).

Clark, J. C. D., *Thomas Paine: Britain, America, and France in the Age of Enlightenment and Revolution* (Oxford, 2018).

Colie, R., 'Spinoza and the Early English Deists', *Journal of the History of Ideas*, 20:1 (1959), pp. 23–46.

Collins, J. R., *The Allegiance of Thomas Hobbes* (Oxford, 2005).

Collins, J. R., *In the Shadow of Leviathan: John Locke and the Politics of Conscience* (Cambridge, 2020).

Collins, J. R., 'Thomas Hobbes's Ecclesiastical History', in A. P. Martinich and K. Hoekstra (eds), *The Oxford Handbook of Hobbes* (New York, 2016), pp. 520–44.

Como, D. R., *Radical Parliamentarians and the English Civil War* (Oxford, 2018).

Cromartie, A., 'The God of Thomas Hobbes', *The Historical Journal*, 51:4 (2008), pp. 857–79.

Curley, E., 'Hobbes and the Cause of Religious Toleration', in P. Springborg (ed.), *The Cambridge Companion to Hobbes's Leviathan* (Cambridge, 2007), pp. 309–34.

Curley, E., ' "I Durst Not Write So Boldly" or, How to Read Hobbes' Theological-Political Treatise', in D. Bostrenghi (ed.), *Hobbes and Spinoza: Science and Politics* (Naples, 1992), pp. 497–593.

Daniel, S. H., *John Toland: His Methods, Manners, and Mind* (Kingston, 1984).

Day, A. K., 'Hobbes's Changing Ecclesiology', *The Historical Journal*, 62:4 (2019), pp. 899–919.

Douglass, R., *Rousseau and Hobbes: Nature, Free Will, and the Passions* (Oxford, 2015).

Duncan, S., 'Toland, Leibniz, and Active Matter', in D. Garber and D. Rutherford (eds), *Oxford Studies in Early Modern Philosophy, VI* (Oxford, 2012), pp. 249–78.

Dybikowski, J., 'Anthony Collins' Defense of Freethinking', in G. Paganini, M. Benítez, and J. Dybikowski (eds), *Scepticisme, clandestinité et libre pensée— Scepticism, Clandestinity and Free-Thinking* (Paris, 2002), pp. 299–326.

Dzelzainis, M., 'Albertus Warren on Milton and Toleration: An Unnoticed Allusion', *Notes and Queries*, 46:3 (1999), pp. 335–36.

East, K. A., *The Radicalization of Cicero: John Toland and Strategic Editing in the Early Enlightenment* (Cham, 2017).

Ellenzweig, S., *The Fringes of Belief: English Literature, Ancient Heresy, and the Politics of Freethinking, 1660–1760* (Stanford, 2008).

Evrigenis, I. D., *Images of Anarchy: The Rhetoric and Science in Hobbes's State of Nature* (Cambridge, 2014).

Ferguson, J. P., *The Philosophy of Dr. Samuel Clarke and Its Critics* (New York, 1974).

Figgis, J. N., 'Erastus and Erastianism', *Journal of Theological Studies*, 2 (1900), pp. 66–101.

Fischer, K., *American Freethinker: Elihu Palmer and the Struggle for Religious Freedom in the New Nation* (Philadelphia, 2021).

Gay, P., *Deism: An Anthology* (Princeton, 1968).

Gay, P., *The Enlightenment: An Interpretation. The Rise of Modern Paganism* (New York, 1966).

Glover, W. B., 'God and Thomas Hobbes', in K. C. Brown (ed.), *Hobbes Studies* (Oxford, 1965), pp. 141–68.

Goldie, M., 'Charles Blount's Intention in Writing "King William and Queen Mary Conquerors" (1693)', *Notes and Queries* 223 (1978), pp. 527–32.

Goldie, M., 'John Locke and Anglican Royalism', *Political Studies*, 31:1 (1983), pp. 61–85.

Goldie, M., 'John Locke, the Early Lockeans, and Priestcraft', *Intellectual History Review*, 28:1 (2018), pp. 125–44.

Goldie, M., 'Priestcraft and the Birth of Whiggism', in N. Phillipson and Q. Skinner (eds), *Political Discourses in Early Modern Britain* (Cambridge, 1993), pp. 209–31.

Goldie, M., 'The Reception of Hobbes', in J. H. Burns with M. Goldie (eds), *The Cambridge History of Political Thought 1450–1700* (Cambridge, 1991), pp. 589–615.

Goldie, M., and R. Popkin, 'Scepticism, Priestcraft, and Toleration', in M. Goldie and R. Wokler (eds), *The Cambridge History of Eighteenth-Century Political Thought* (Cambridge, 2006), pp. 79–109.

Gorham, G., 'The Theological Foundation of Hobbesian Physics: A Defence of Corporeal God', *British Journal for the History of Philosophy*, 21:2 (2013), pp. 240–61.

Grasso, C., *Skepticism and American Faith: From the Revolution to the Civil War* (Oxford, 2018).

Hanley, R. P., *The Political Philosophy of Fénelon* (New York, 2020).

Harris, J. A., *Of Liberty and Necessity: The Free Will Debate in Eighteenth-Century British Philosophy* (Oxford, 2005).

Harrison, P., *'Religion' and the Religions in the English Enlightenment* (Cambridge, 1990).

Harth, P., *Contexts of Dryden's Thought* (Chicago, 1968).

Herrick, J. A., *The Radical Rhetoric of the English Deists: The Discourse of Skepticism, 1680–1750* (Columbia, SC, 1997).

Higgins, I., 'Remarks on *Cato's Letters*', in D. Womersley, P. Bullard, and A. Williams (eds), *Cultures of Whiggism: New Essays on English Literature and Culture in the Long Eighteenth Century* (Newark, 2005), pp. 127–46.

Hill, C., *The World Turned Upside Down: Radical Ideas During the English Revolution* (London, 1972).

Hoekstra, K., 'The de facto Turn in Hobbes's Political Philosophy', in T. Sorell and L. Foisneau (eds), *Leviathan after 350 Years* (Oxford, 2004), pp. 33–73.

Hoekstra, K., 'Disarming the Prophets: Thomas Hobbes and Predictive Power', *Rivista di storia della filosofia*, 59:1 (2004), pp. 97–153.

Hoekstra, K., 'The End of Philosophy (The Case of Hobbes)', *Proceedings of the Aristotelian Society*, 106:1 (2006), pp. 25–62.

Hood, F. C., *The Divine Politics of Thomas Hobbes* (Oxford, 1964).

Hudson, W., *The English Deists: Studies in Early Enlightenment* (London, 2009).

Hudson, W., *Enlightenment and Modernity: The English Deists and Reform* (London, 2009).

Hudson, W., D. Lucci, and J. R. Wigelsworth (eds), *Atheism and Deism Revalued: Heterodox Religious Identities in Britain, 1650–1800* (Farnham, 2014).

Hunter, M., *The Decline of Magic: Britain in the Enlightenment* (New Haven, 2020).

Hutton, S., 'Liberty of Mind: Women Philosophers and the Freedom to Philosophize', in J. Broad and K. Detlefsen (eds), *Women and Liberty, 1600–1800: Philosophical Essays* (Oxford, 2017), pp. 123–38.

Ingram, R. G., 'The Reformation in the Age of Jefferson', in P. Griffin and F. D. Cogliano (eds), *Ireland and America: Empire, Revolution and Sovereignty* (Charlottesville, 2021), pp. 178–97.

Ingram, R. G., *Reformation without End: Religion, Politics and the Past in Post-Revolutionary England* (Manchester, 2018).

Israel, J. I., *Radical Enlightenment: Philosophy and the Making of Modernity 1650–1750* (Oxford, 2001).

Jacob, J. R., *Henry Stubbe: Radical Protestantism and the Early Enlightenment* (Cambridge, 1983).

Jacob, M. C., *The Newtonians and the English Revolution, 1689–1720* (Ithaca, NY, 1976).

Jacob, M. C., *The Radical Enlightenment: Pantheists, Freemasons and Republicans* (London, 1981).

Jesseph, D. M., 'Hobbes's Atheism', *Midwest Studies in Philosophy*, 26 (2002), pp. 140–66.

Jesseph, D. M., *Squaring the Circle: The War Between Hobbes and Wallis* (Chicago, 1999).

Johnston, D., *The Rhetoric of Leviathan: Thomas Hobbes and the Politics of Cultural Transformation* (Princeton, 1986).

Keene, N., '"A Two-Edged Sword": Biblical Criticism and the New Testament Canon in Early Modern England', in A. Hessayon and N. Keene (eds), *Scripture and Scholarship in Early Modern England* (Aldershot, 2006), pp. 94–115.

Keith, J., and C. T. Kairoff (eds), *The Cambridge Edition of the Works of Anne Finch, Countess of Winchilsea. Volume 1: Early Manuscript Books* (Cambridge, 2019).

Kewes, P., '"The Idol of State Innovators and Republicans": Robert Persons's *A Conference About the Next Succession* (1594/5) in Stuart England', in P. Kewes and A. McRae (eds), *Stuart Succession Literature: Moments and Transformations* (Oxford, 2018), pp. 149–85.

Klein, L. E., *Shaftesbury and the Culture of Politeness: Moral Discourse and Cultural Politics in Early Eighteenth-Century England* (Cambridge, 1994).

Knights, M., *The Devil in Disguise: Deception, Delusion, and Fanaticism in the Early English Enlightenment* (Oxford, 2011).

Knights, M., 'The "Highest Roade to Happiness": The "Active Philosophy" of James Boevey (1622–1696)', in M. J. Braddick and J. Innes (eds), *Suffering and Happiness in England 1550–1850: Narratives and Representations* (Oxford, 2017), pp. 173–89.

Lærke, M., *Spinoza and the Freedom of Philosophizing* (Oxford, 2021).

Lake, P., 'Anti-Popery: The Structure of a Prejudice', in R. Cust and A. Hughes (eds), *Conflict in Early Stuart England: Studies in Religion and Politics, 1603–1642* (London, 1989), pp. 72–106.

Lake, P., 'Anti-Puritanism: The Structure of a Prejudice', in K. Fincham and P. Lake (eds), *Religious Politics in Post-Reformation England: Essays in Honour of Nicholas Tyacke* (Woodbridge, 2006), pp. 80–97.

Lake, P., 'Defining Puritanism–Again?', in F. J. Bremer (ed.), *Puritanism: Transatlantic Perspectives on a Seventeenth-Century Anglo-American Faith* (Boston, 1993), pp. 3–29.

Lake, P., 'The Historiography of Puritanism', in J. Coffey and P. C. H. Lim (eds), *The Cambridge Companion to Puritanism* (Cambridge, 2008), pp. 346–71.

Lalor, S., *Matthew Tindal, Freethinker* (London, 2006).

Lamprecht, S. P., 'Hobbes and Hobbism', *The American Political Science Review*, 34:1 (1940), pp. 31–53.

Lancaster, J. A. T., 'From Matters of Faith to Matters of Fact: The Problem of Priestcraft in Early Modern England', *Intellectual History Review*, 28:1 (2018), pp. 145–65.

Lancaster, J. A. T., and A. McKenzie-McHarg, 'Priestcraft. Anatomizing the Anti-Clericalism of Early Modern Europe', *Intellectual History Review*, 28:1 (2018), pp. 7–22.

Levitin, D., 'From Sacred History to the History of Religion: Paganism, Judaism, and Christianity in European Historiography from Reformation to "Enlightenment"', *The Historical Journal*, 55:4 (2012), pp. 1117–60.

Levitin, D., 'Matthew Tindal's *Rights of the Christian Church* (1706) and the Church-State Relationship', *The Historical Journal*, 54:3 (2011), pp. 717–40.

Lloyd, S. A., *Ideals as Interests in Hobbes's Leviathan: The Power of Mind over Matter* (Cambridge, 1992).

Love, H., *Scribal Publication in Seventeenth-Century England* (Oxford, 1993).

Lucci, D., 'Deism, Freethinking and Toleration in Enlightenment England', *History of European Ideas*, 43:4 (2017), pp. 345–58.

Lucci, D., *John Locke's Christianity* (Cambridge, 2020).

Lucci, D., *Scripture and Deism: The Biblical Criticism of the Eighteenth-Century British Deists* (Bern, 2008).

Lund, R. D., *Ridicule, Religion and the Politics of Wit in Augustan England* (Farnham, 2012).

Lupoli, A., 'Power (Conatus-Endeavour) in the "Kinetic Actualism" and in the "Inertial" Psychology of Thomas Hobbes', *Hobbes Studies*, 14 (2001), pp. 83–103.

Malcolm, N., *Aspects of Hobbes* (Oxford, 2002).

Malcolm, N., *Leviathan: Editorial Introduction* (Oxford, 2012).

Marshall, J., 'The Ecclesiology of the Latitude-Men 1660–1689: Stillingfleet, Tillotson and "Hobbism"', *The Journal of Ecclesiastical History*, 36:3 (1985), pp. 407–27.

Marshall, J., *John Locke: Resistance, Religion and Responsibility* (Cambridge, 1994).

Martinich, A. P., *Hobbes's Political Philosophy: Interpretation and Interpretations* (Oxford, 2021).

Martinich, A. P., *The Two Gods of Leviathan: Thomas Hobbes on Religion and Politics* (Cambridge, 1992).

McDowell, G. L., 'The Language of Law and the Foundations of American Constitutionalism', *The William and Mary Quarterly*, 55:3 (1998), pp. 375–98.

McMahon, M. P., *The Radical Whigs, John Trenchard and Thomas Gordon: Libertarian Loyalists to the New House of Hanover* (Lanham, 1990).

McQueen, A., 'Absolving God's Laws: Thomas Hobbes's Scriptural Strategies', *Political Theory*, 50:5 (2022), pp. 754–79.

Miller, P. N., '"Freethinking" and "Freedom of Thought" in Eighteenth-Century Britain', *The Historical Journal*, 36:3 (1993), pp. 599–617.

Milton, P., 'Hobbes, Heresy, and Lord Arlington', *History of Political Thought*, 14:4 (1993), pp. 501–46.

Mintz, S. I., *The Hunting of Leviathan: Seventeenth-Century Reactions to the Materialism and Moral Philosophy of Thomas Hobbes* (Cambridge, 1962).

Mortimer, S., 'Christianity and Civil Religion in Hobbes's *Leviathan*', in A. P. Martinich and K. Hoekstra (eds), *The Oxford Handbook of Hobbes* (New York, 2016), pp. 501–19.

Mossner, E., *The Life of David Hume*, 2nd edn (Oxford, 2001).

O'Higgins, J., *Anthony Collins: The Man and His Works* (The Hague, 1970).

Overhoff, J., *Hobbes's Theory of the Will: Ideological Reasons and Historical Circumstances* (Lanham, 2000).

Pacchi, A., 'Hobbes and the Problem of God', in G. A. J. Rogers and A. Ryan (eds), *Perspectives on Thomas Hobbes* (Oxford, 1988), pp. 171–87.

Parkin, J., 'Baiting the Bear: The Anglican Attack on Hobbes in the Later 1660s', *History of Political Thought*, 34:3 (2013), pp. 421–58.

Parkin, J., 'Hobbes and Paradox', in A. P. Martinich and K. Hoekstra (eds), *The Oxford Handbook of Hobbes* (New York, 2016), pp. 624–42.

Parkin, J., 'Hobbes and the Reception of "Leviathan"', *Journal of the History of Ideas*, 76:2 (2015), pp. 289–300.

Parkin, J., 'Liberty Transpros'd: Andrew Marvell and Samuel Parker', in W. Chernaik and M. Dzelzainis (eds), *Marvell and Liberty* (Basingstoke, 1999), pp. 269–99.

Parkin, J., *Science, Religion and Politics in Restoration England: Richard Cumberland's De Legibus Naturae* (Woodbridge, 1999).

Parkin, J., *Taming the Leviathan: The Reception of the Political and Religious Ideas of Thomas Hobbes in England, 1640–1700* (Cambridge, 2007).

Pattison, M., 'Tendencies of Religious Thought in England, 1688–1750', in *Essays and Reviews* (London, 1860), pp. 254–329.

Peacey, J. T., 'Nibbling at "Leviathan": Politics and Theory in England in the 1650s', *Huntington Library Quarterly*, 61:2 (1998), pp. 241–57.

Peacey, J., R. G. Ingram, and A. W. Barber, 'Freedom of Speech in England and the Anglophone World, 1500–1850', in R. G. Ingram, J. Peacey, and A. W. Barber (eds), *Freedom of speech, 1500–1850* (Manchester, 2020), pp. 1–27.

Pocock, J. G. A., *Barbarism and Religion. Volume 1: The Enlightenments of Edward Gibbon, 1737–1764* (Cambridge, 1999).

Pocock, J. G. A., *Barbarism and Religion. Volume 5: Religion: The First Triumph* (Cambridge, 2010).

Pocock, J. G. A., 'Enthusiasm: The Antiself of Enlightenment', *Huntington Library Quarterly* 60:1–2 (1997), pp. 7–28.

Pocock, J. G. A., *The Machiavellian Moment: Florentine Political Thought and the Atlantic Republican Tradition*, 3rd edn (Princeton, 2016).

Pocock, J. G. A., *Politics, Language and Time: Essays on Political Thought and History*, 2nd edn (Chicago, 1989).

Pocock, J. G. A., 'Post-Puritan England and the Problem of the Enlightenment', in P. Zagorin (ed.), *Culture and Politics from Puritanism to the Enlightenment* (Berkeley, 1980), pp. 91–111.

Pocock, J. G. A., 'Within the Margins: The Definitions of Orthodoxy', in R. D. Lund (ed.), *The Margins of Orthodoxy: Heterodox Writing and Cultural Response, 1660–1750* (Cambridge, 1995), pp. 33–53.

Popkin, R. H., 'The Deist Challenge', in O. P. Grell, J. I. Israel, and N. Tyacke (eds), *From Persecution to Toleration: The Glorious Revolution and Religion in England* (Oxford, 1991), pp. 195–215.

Porter, R., 'The Enlightenment in England', in R. Porter and M. Teich (eds), *The Enlightenment in National Context* (Cambridge, 1981), pp. 1–18.

Prince, M. B., '*Religio Laici* v. *Religio Laici*: Dryden, Blount, and the Origin of English Deism', *Modern Language Quarterly*, 74:1 (2013), pp. 29–66.

Rappaport, R., 'Questions of Evidence: An Anonymous Tract Attributed to John Toland', *Journal of the History of Ideas*, 58:2 (1997), pp. 339–48.

Redwood, J. A., 'Charles Blount, Deism, and English Free Thought', *Journal of the History of Ideas*, 35:3 (1974), pp. 490–98.

Reventlow, H. G., *The Authority of the Bible and the Rise of the Modern World*, trans. J. Bowden (Philadelphia, 1985).

Rivers, I., *Reason, Grace, and Sentiment: A Study of the Language of Religion and Ethics in England, 1660–1780. Volume 2: Shaftesbury to Hume* (Cambridge, 2000).

Robbins, C., *The Eighteenth-Century Commonwealthman* (Cambridge, MA, 1959).

Robertson, J., *The Enlightenment: A Very Short Introduction* (Oxford, 2015).

Rose, J., *Godly Kingship in Restoration England: The Politics of the Royal Supremacy, 1660–1688* (Cambridge, 2011).

Ross, G. M., *Starting with Hobbes* (London, 2009).

Royle, E., *Victorian Infidels: The Origins of the British Secularist Movement, 1791–1866* (Manchester, 1974).

Russell, P., *The Riddle of Hume's Treatise: Skepticism, Naturalism, and Irreligion* (Oxford, 2008).

Ryan, A., 'Hobbes, Toleration and the Inner Life', in D. Miller and L. Siedentop (eds), *The Nature of Political Theory* (Oxford, 1983), pp. 197–218.

Ryan, A., 'A More Tolerant Hobbes?', in S. Mendus (ed.), *Justifying Toleration: Conceptual and Historical Perspectives* (Cambridge, 1988), pp. 37–59.

Sagar, P., *The Opinion of Mankind: Sociability and Theories of the State from Hobbes to Smith* (Princeton, 2018).

Schwartz, L., *Infidel Feminism: Secularism, Religion and Women's Emancipation, England 1830–1914* (Manchester, 2013).

Serjeantson, R. W., 'Herbert of Cherbury before Deism: The Early Reception of the *De veritate*', *The Seventeenth Century*, 16:2 (2001), pp. 217–38.

Shapin, S., and S. Schaffer, *Leviathan and the Air-Pump: Hobbes, Boyle, and the Experimental Life* (Princeton, 1985).

Sheehan, J., *The Enlightenment Bible: Translation, Scholarship, Culture* (Princeton, 2005).

Sheppard, K., *Anti-Atheism in Early Modern England 1580–1720* (Leiden, 2015).

Skinner, Q., *Liberty Before Liberalism* (Cambridge, 1998).

Skinner, Q., *Visions of Politics*, 3 vols (Cambridge, 2002).

Snobelen, S., 'The Argument over Prophecy: An Eighteenth-Century Debate between William Whiston and Anthony Collins', *Lumen*, 15 (1996), pp. 195–213.

Sommerville, J. P., *Thomas Hobbes: Political Ideas in Historical Context* (Basingstoke, 1992).

Sowerby, E. M., *Catalogue of the Library of Thomas Jefferson*, 5 vols (Washington, DC, 1952–1959).

Springborg, P., 'Hobbes, Heresy, and the *Historia Ecclesiastica*', *Journal of the History of Ideas*, 55:4 (1994), pp. 553–71.

Springborg, P. 'Hobbes on Religion', in T. Sorell (ed.), *The Cambridge Companion to Hobbes* (Cambridge, 1996), pp. 346–80.

Springborg, P., 'Hobbes the Atheist and his Deist Reception', in M. Geuna and G. Gori (eds), *I filosofi e la società senza religione* (Bologna, 2011), pp. 145–63.

Springborg, P., 'Hobbes's Challenge to Descartes, Bramhall and Boyle: A Corporeal God', *British Journal for the History of Philosophy*, 20:5 (2012), pp. 903–34.

Spurr, J., '"Latitudinarianism" and the Restoration Church', *The Historical Journal*, 31:1 (1988), pp. 61–82.

State, S., *Thomas Hobbes and the Debate over Natural Law and Religion* (New York, 1991).

Stauffer, D., *Hobbes's Kingdom of Light: A Study of the Foundations of Modern Political Philosophy* (Chicago, 2018).

Stuart-Buttle, T., *From Moral Theology to Moral Philosophy: Cicero and Visions of Humanity from Locke to Hume* (Oxford, 2019).

Sullivan, R. E., *John Toland and the Deist Controversy: A Study in Adaptions* (Cambridge, MA, 1982).

Sullivan, V. B., *Machiavelli, Hobbes, and the Formation of a Liberal Republicanism in England* (Cambridge, 2004).

Tarantino, G., 'The Books and Times of Anthony Collins (1676–1729)', in A. Hessayon and D. Finnegan (eds), *Varieties of Seventeenth- and Early Eighteenth-Century English Radicalism in Context* (Farnham, 2011), pp. 221–40.

Tarantino, G., 'Martin Clifford and His *Treatise of Humane Reason* (1674): A Europe-Wide Debate', in R. Savage (ed.), *Philosophy and Religion in Enlightenment Britain: New Case Studies* (Oxford, 2012), pp. 9–28.

Tarantino, G., *Republicanism, Sinophilia, and Historical Writing: Thomas Gordon (c. 1691–1750) and His 'History of England'* (Turnhout, 2012).

Taylor, A. E., 'The Ethical Doctrine of Hobbes', *Philosophy*, 13:52 (1938), pp. 406–24.

Thomson, A., *Bodies of Thought: Science, Religion, and the Soul in the Early Enlightenment* (Oxford, 2008).

Torrey, N., *Voltaire and the English Deists* (New Haven, 1930).

Treadwell, M., 'The Stationers and the Printing Acts at the End of the Seventeenth Century', in J. Barnard and D. F. McKenzie with M. Bell (eds), *The Cambridge History of the Book in Britain. Volume 4: 1557–1695* (Cambridge, 2002), pp. 755–76.

Tuck, R., 'The "Christian Atheism" of Thomas Hobbes', in M. Hunter and D. Wootton (eds), *Atheism from the Reformation to the Enlightenment* (Oxford, 1992), pp. 111–30.

Tuck, R., 'The Civil Religion of Thomas Hobbes', in N. Phillipson and Q. Skinner (eds), *Political Discourses in Early Modern Britain* (Cambridge, 1993), pp. 120–38.

Tuck, R., *Hobbes: A Very Short Introduction* (Oxford, 2002).

Tuck, R., 'Hobbes and Locke on Toleration', in M. G. Dietz (ed.), *Thomas Hobbes and Political Theory* (Lawrence, 1990), pp. 153–71.

Tuck, R., *Philosophy and Government 1572–1651* (Cambridge, 1993).

Tuck, R., 'The Utopianism of Leviathan', in T. Sorell and L. Foisneau (eds), *Leviathan after 350 Years* (Oxford, 2004), pp. 125–38.

Van Apeldoorn, L., and R. Douglass (eds), *Hobbes on Politics and Religion* (Oxford, 2018).

Van den Berg, J., *A Forgotten Christian Deist: Thomas Morgan* (New York, 2021).

Venturi, F., *Utopia and Reform in the Enlightenment* (Cambridge, 1971).

Waldmann, F., 'John Locke as a Reader of Thomas Hobbes's *Leviathan*: A New Manuscript', *The Journal of Modern History*, 93:2 (2021), pp. 245–82.

Waldron, J., 'Hobbes and the Principle of Publicity', *Pacific Philosophical Quarterly*, 82:3–4 (2001), pp. 447–74.

Walsh, A., *Civil Religion and the Enlightenment in England, 1707–1800* (Woodbridge, 2020).

Walter, K. S., *The American Deists: Voices of Reason and Dissent in the Early Republic* (Lawrence, 1992).

Warrender, H., *The Political Philosophy of Hobbes: His Theory of Obligation* (Oxford, 1957).

Wigelsworth, J. R., *Deism in Enlightenment England: Theology, Politics, and Newtonian Public Science* (Manchester, 2009).

Wigelsworth, J. R., 'The Disputed Root of Salvation in Eighteenth-Century English Deism: Thomas Chubb and Thomas Morgan Debate the Impact of the Fall', *Intellectual History Review*, 19:1 (2009), pp. 29–43.

Wilson, D., 'Reading Restoration Freethought: Charles Blount's Impious Learning' (PhD diss., Royal Holloway, University of London, 2003).

Worden, B., *The Rump Parliament 1648–53* (Cambridge, 1974).

Wright, G., *Religion, Politics and Thomas Hobbes* (Dordrecht, 2006).

Yolton, J. W., *Thinking Matter: Materialism in Eighteenth-Century Britain* (Minneapolis, 1983).

Young, B. W., *Religion and Enlightenment in Eighteenth-Century England: Theological Debate from Locke to Burke* (Oxford, 1998).

Oxford Dictionary of National Biography (accessed 31 August 2022)

Daniel, S. H., 'Toland, John (1670–1722), Freethinker and Philosopher' (2004), available at: www.oxforddnb.com/view/10.1093/ref:odnb/9780198614128.001. 0001/odnb-9780198614128-e-27497.

Dybikowski, J., 'Collins, Anthony (1676–1729), Philosopher and Freethinker' (2008), available at: www.oxforddnb.com/view/10.1093/ref:odnb/9780198614128.001. 0001/odnb-9780198614128-e-5933.

Garnham, N., 'Skelton, Philip (1707–1787), Church of Ireland Clergyman and Religious Controversialist' (2004), available at: www.oxforddnb.com/view/ 10.1093/ref:odnb/9780198614128.001.0001/odnb-9780198614128-e-25664.

Harrison, P., 'Morgan, Thomas (1671/2?–1743), Theological and Medical Writer' (2004), available at: www.oxforddnb.com/view/10.1093/ref:odnb/9780198614128. 001.0001/odnb-9780198614128-e-19239.

Pfanner, D., 'Blount, Charles (1654–1693), Freethinker and Author' (2004), available at: www.oxforddnb.com/view/10.1093/ref:odnb/9780198614128.001.0001/ odnb-9780198614128-e-2684.

Philp, M., 'Paine, Thomas (1737–1809), Author and Revolutionary' (2004), available at: www.oxforddnb.com/view/10.1093/ref:odnb/9780198614128.001.0001/ odnb-9780198614128-e-21133.

Porter, M. H., 'Boevey, James (1622–1696), Merchant and Philosopher' (2006), available at: www.oxforddnb.com/view/10.1093/ref:odnb/9780198614128.001. 0001/odnb-9780198614128-e-70859.

Sambrook, J., 'Gildon, Charles (c. 1665–1724), Writer' (2008), available at: www.oxforddnb.com/view/10.1093/ref:odnb/9780198614128.001.0001/odnb-9780198614128-e-10720.

Tarantino, G., 'Clifford, Martin (c. 1624–1677), Headmaster and Author' (2004), available at: www.oxforddnb.com/view/10.1093/ref:odnb/9780198614128.001. 0001/odnb-9780198614128-e-5656/version/0.

Westby-Gibson, J., and M. J. Mercer, 'Chapman, John (bap. 1705, d. 1784), Theologian and Classical Scholar' (2004), available at: www.oxforddnb.com/ view/10.1093/ref:odnb/9780198614128.001.0001/odnb-9780198614128- e-5121.

Wykes, D. L., 'Subscribers and Non-Subscribers at the Salters' Hall Debate (Act. 1719)' (2009), available at: www.oxforddnb.com/view/10.1093/ref:odnb/ 9780198614128.001.0001/odnb-9780198614128-e-95681.

Young, B. W., 'Law, Edmund (1703–1787), Bishop of Carlisle and Theologian' (2004), available at: www.oxforddnb.com/view/10.1093/ref:odnb/9780198614128. 001.0001/odnb-9780198614128-e-16141.

Young, B. W., 'Tindal, Matthew (bap. 1657, d. 1733), Freethinker and Religious Controversialist' (2004), available at: www.oxforddnb.com/view/10.1093/ ref:odnb/9780198614128.001.0001/odnb-9780198614128-e-27462.

Young, B. W., 'Warburton, William (1698–1779), Bishop of Gloucester and Religious Controversialist' (2004), available at: www.oxforddnb.com/view/ 10.1093/ref:odnb/9780198614128.001.0001/odnb-9780198614128-e-28680.

Index